Global Steel
in the 1990s

Global Steel
in the 1990s

Growth or
Decline

by

William T. Hogan, S.J.
Fordham University

Lexington Books
D.C. Heath and Company/Lexington, Massachusetts/Toronto

HD
9510.5
H568
1991

Library of Congress Cataloging-in-Publication Data

Hogan, William Thomas, 1919–
    Global steel in the 1990s: growth or decline / by William T. Hogan.
        p. cm.
    Includes index.
    ISBN 0-669-20489-7
    1. Steel industry and trade—Forecasting. 2. Steel industry and trade—United States—
Forecasting. I. Title.
HD9510.5.H568   1991
338.4'7669142—dc20   90-48637
                                                                          CIP

Published simultaneously in Canada.
Printed in the United States of America.
International Standard Book Number: 0–669–20489–7
Library of Congress Catalog Card Number: 90–48637

The paper used in this publication meets the minimum requirements of American National
Standard for Information Sciences—Permanence of Paper for Printed Library Materials, ANSI
Z39.48-1984. ∞™

91 92 93 94 95 8 7 6 5 4 3

Contents

Preface

The steel industry worldwide suffered a severe depression in the 1980s. As a consequence, capacity was cut significantly in the industrialized countries. In the Third World, on the contrary, capacity was increased appreciably in spite of the depression that gripped the industry between 1982 and 1986. The increase in capacity in the Third World slowed down considerably at the end of the decade. However, a number of countries in the Third World have ambitious plans for increasing their steel potential during the 1990s. The integrated companies in the industrialized world, having suffered cuts in production, have no intention of increasing their steelmaking potential during the decade of the 1990s. The emphasis is being placed on investments that reduce costs, increase productivity, and improve quality.

This work was undertaken to attempt to determine what would likely happen to the steel industry in the 1990s. The analysis is by no means confined to the potential for growth or decline, although that constitutes a significant part of the work. In addition, a study was made of other aspects of the industry, namely, raw-material availability; technological improvements that will take place; the market for steel; joint ventures (both domestic and international), which have become popular since the middle 1980s; and the future of international trade.

In respect to sources, most of the material for the study was obtained from conversations with steel executives on a worldwide basis. In addition, valuable data were obtained from the International Iron and Steel Institute, American Iron and Steel Institute, Association of Iron and Steel Engineers, Japan Iron and Steel Federation, *American Metal Market, Metal Bulletin, Steel Times International,* as well as the Bureau of Mines, U.S. Department of the Interior. Other sources are noted throughout the work. One excellent source on India and China is the book entitled *Asian Crucible: The Steel Industry in China and India,* by Jacques Astier, Hari Bhushan, and Dai Zhong.

In discussing statistics, particularly in relation to production and shipments, both metric tonnes and net tons are used, the spelling of which differs according to the unit. Most of the statistics used were the latest available at the time of publication.

Global Steel
in the 1990s

1
Introduction

In the post–World War II period, the global steel industry has undergone a number of radical changes. Perhaps the most basic has been its growth, moving up from 192 million tonnes of raw-steel production in 1950 to 783 million in 1989. Other developments, both corporate and technological, that took place in that forty-five year period set the stage for what is to come in the 1990s.

In 1947, some 57 percent of the world's raw steel was produced in the United States. This was a consequence of the increase in capacity during World War II, as well as the fact that the industry was unscathed. During the 1950s, the war-torn countries began gradually to rebuild their steel industries. At first, this was a slow process, but it accelerated significantly in the 1960s. For example, in 1950, the Japanese produced about 5 million tonnes of raw steel. By 1960, this had grown to 23 million tonnes. Between 1960 and 1970, the growth was rapid and extensive, reaching 93 million tonnes. Japan's record year for producing raw steel was 1973: 119 million tonnes.

The European Community, which in the 1950s included the original six countries, followed the same trend. In 1950, its output was about 32 million tonnes. By 1960, it had increased to 72 million tonnes, and in 1974, at which time the United Kingdom was a member, it hit its peak: 156 million tonnes. As an individual country, the United States, except for one year, continued to lead the world in raw-steel production through 1973, when its output reached 136 million tonnes.

The Soviet Union, whose steel industry was severely damaged during World War II, recovered to a point where it produced some 27 million tonnes in 1950. It moved ahead to lead the rest of the world in 1974.

The Third World had a very small steel output up to 1950; its leading producer in 1950 was India with 1.5 million tonnes. It was followed by Brazil with 750,000 tonnes, and in the same year, Mexico with 210,000, a drop from 340,000 tonnes in 1949. Other countries with significant production in the Third World during the 1980s had such small amounts of production in 1950 that it is difficult to find statistics. China, for example, had less than 200,000 tonnes.

The early to mid-1970s, particularly 1973 and 1974, witnessed the culmination of steel growth in the industrialized world. Japan, the United States, and the European Economic Community (EEC) reached a high point, which has not since been surpassed. Other producers, such as Canada, accounted for some 14 million tons in 1973, about a fivefold growth from its immediate postwar output.

The mid-1970s, beginning in 1975, saw the first significant reversal of steel industry output in the postwar period. This was caused, in part, by the increase in the price of oil, engineered by the Organization of Petroleum Exporting Countries (OPEC), raising it from $3 a barrel to $12 in a matter of two years. Steel production in 1975 fell 14 percent in Japan, 19 percent in the European Community, and 20 percent in the United States. Subsequent to that year, the output of the industrialized countries fluctuated considerably. There was a significant recovery in 1979; however, 1982 witnessed a deep depression that hit the steel industries in the industrialized countries and persisted through 1986.

Table 1–1 indicates fluctuations in steel output in the United States, Japan, and the European Community between 1973 and 1988. In terms of the European Community, it includes retroactively the twelve current members.

Table 1–1
Raw Steel Output in the United States, Japan, and the EEC; 1973–1989
(millions of tonnes)

	United States	Japan	EEC[a]
1973	136.8	119.3	162.0
1974	132.8	117.1	168.1
1975	105.8	102.3	137.8
1976	116.1	107.4	146.1
1977	113.7	102.4	138.4
1978	124.3	102.1	145.3
1979	123.7	111.7	154.0
1980	101.5	111.4	142.0
1981	109.6	101.7	139.9
1982	67.7	99.5	125.1
1983	76.8	97.2	123.2
1984	83.9	105.6	134.4
1985	80.1	105.3	135.7
1986	74.0	98.3	125.9
1987	80.9	98.5	126.5
1988	90.7	105.7	137.7
1989	88.4	107.9	140.0

Source: International Iron and Steel Institute.

a Includes production of current twelve member countries for all years.

In contrast, during this depressed period for the industrialized world, the Third World countries, experienced a remarkable growth. Brazil rose from 7.5 million tonnes in 1974 to 25 million tonnes in 1989. During the same period, South Korea rose from 1.9 million tonnes to 21.9 million, China increased its output from 22 million tonnes to 61 million, and Taiwan rose from .6 million to 8.6 million, while Mexico advanced from 5.1 million tonnes to 7.8 million. New steel capacity appeared in countries such as Saudi Arabia, which in 1989 had a 1.5-million-tonne potential, and in Nigeria, where new installations have a capacity of approximately 1 million tonnes. In Indonesia, current capacity is over 2 million tonnes, as compared to 80,000 tonnes in the mid-1970s.

In 1987, the deep depression that hung over the steel industry in the industrialized countries lifted, and most of the companies in these areas returned to profitability. Stronger markets improved the situation, and some companies had record profits. In that year, there was considerable concern about the duration of the recovery, expressed in virtually all the industrialized countries. The five-year depression between 1982 and 1986 had left scars that brought caution.

During the decade 1977–1987, the industrialized world reduced capacity dramatically. Some 45 million tonnes were eliminated in the United States and 35 million in the European Community, and between 25 and 30 million tonnes were decommissioned in Japan. This process in Japan does not necessarily mean that facilities are abandoned. Some are taken out of operation but not dismantled.

Another aspect of the steel industry that has changed drastically in the postwar period is international trade in steel. This trade was quite limited before World War II and immediately after. However, with the growth of the steel industry outside the United States, industrialized countries sought markets abroad. Prior to World War II, trade was usually carried on between those countries that produced steel and those that did not. A substantial change took place beginning in the late 1950s insofar as trade developed among countries that produced steel, such as Japan, the United States, and those of Western Europe.

In 1950, some 10 percent of world steel products was traded, amounting to approximately 15 million tonnes. In 1985, 165 million tonnes were traded, or almost 28 percent of the steel products produced. The total in 1988 was 169 million tonnes, or 26 percent of world output. This trade caused problems within the industrialized world and in a number of countries led to restrictive measures.

In considering the future of the steel industry on a global basis, a number of items must be taken into account:

1. Will more capacity be added and, if so, where?
2. Is there an adequate supply of raw materials for the future?
3. What changes are to be expected in the market for steel, particularly in reference to substitute materials?
4. What developments can be expected in international trade?
5. Can essential changes be expected in technology?
6. Will there be further restructuring of individual companies to form merged units or joint ventures?
7. What are the future prospects for labor in the steel industry?
8. What will the magnitude of capital investment be?

A review of the outstanding developments in the postwar period covering these areas will help set the stage for projections of the future.

2
Steel Capacities in Industrialized Countries

F or 30 years following World War II, the rapid growth in steel demand required the continual installation of new steelmaking capacity. In 1974, a year of peak production, 703 million tonnes of raw steel were made from a capacity of approximately 750 million tonnes. This put the operating rate at better than 90 percent for the entire world and brought ideas of further expansion to the steel industry.

At a meeting of the International Iron and Steel Institute (IISI) in Munich in October 1974, plans were revealed to add 240 million tonnes of steelmaking capacity on a worldwide basis, increasing production potential by approximately one-third. The installations were to be spread over a number of countries, in both the industrialized countries and the Third World (table 2–1).

The projected increase in capacity was in response to forecasts made in the early 1970s that raw-steel output by 1980 would reach 900 million to 1 billion tonnes. Logan Johnson, chairman of the IISI and of Armco Steel Corporation, in his address to the IISI in 1970, quoted Edwin Gott, chairman of United States Steel Corporation, on the subject of future steel production: "World production of steel is expected to exceed 600 million metric tons this year [1970] and to grow to about 720 million metric tons by 1975 . . . and

Table 2–1
Additional Steel Capacity by Regions, 1974–1985
(millions of tonnes)

EEC (9 members)	41.3
Other Western Europe	26.7
North America	28.5
Latin America	37.2
Africa	12.3
Middle East	23.8
Far East	67.9
Oceania	2.3
Total	240.0

Source: IISI, *Report of Proceedings*

the steel companies of the world will be approaching one billion short tons of steel by 1980 . . . or 900 million metric tons."[1]

Unfortunately, there was a world recession in 1975, and steel output dropped sharply: by 14 percent in Japan, 19 percent in the European Community, and 20 percent in the United States. As a consequence, much of the planned increase in capacity, particularly in the industrialized countries, was put on hold. There were a few exceptions, such as the Ogishima plant of NKK, Inc. in Japan, which was built in 1975 and 1976, adding some 6 million tonnes to NKK's steelmaking potential.

With demand falling, the capacity to produce steel became excessive. During the late 1970s and early 1980s, world overcapacity was estimated at 200 million tons. However, in spite of this large excess, the Third World countries proceeded with the installation of capacity after 1975. In a number of cases, the installations were sizable, as in the People's Republic of China, Brazil, South Korea, and, to a lesser extent, Taiwan. Additions were also made in Mexico, India, Saudi Arabia, Indonesia, and Nigeria.

The Third World steel industry increase was countered by a reduction in capacity in the industrialized countries, as the United States, Japan, and Western Europe abandoned or decommissioned an extensive number of facilities.

The situation in regard to capacity in 1990 is somewhat fluid. Its current estimated size worldwide bears analysis, as do plans for this decade in both the industrialized and Third World countries. Any discussion of the growth or decline in capacity must be made on an individual country basis and should be preceded by an analysis of the concept of capacity.

Capacity Measurement

The capacity for steel production is perhaps the most significant statistic in any analysis of the industry's growth or decline. Capacity figures apply to every facility, beginning with coke ovens and sinter plants and extending through blast furnaces, steelmaking operations, and finishing equipment.

In the United States, the figure is determined by the amount of raw-steelmaking ability of the industry. In Western Europe, capacity calculation emphasizes finishing facilities. In Japan, the steel industry is heavily dependent on blast furnace capability, a significant factor, since the Japanese basic-oxygen converters, which constitute 70 percent of steel output, are fed by at least 90 percent hot metal from the blast furnace.

In terms of raw-steel output, the availability of materials such as blast furnace iron and scrap is crucial. If either or both of these is limited, the capacity of the industry to produce iron and raw steel will also be limited.

For a number of years, the American Iron and Steel Institute (AISI) has included the availability of raw materials in its calculation of capacity in the

United States. Thus, the situation in which a number of blast furnaces would be shut down for relining at the same time or where coke was in short supply would have an effect on steel capacity.

Generally all units throughout the industry are measured by nameplate capacity. This is usually conservative since most facilities are expected to exceed it. For example, oxygen converters are estimated to produce varying tonnages depending on their size, which varies from less than 100 tonnes per heat to 300 tonnes. Obviously capacity is stated on the basis of the size of the converter; however, a certain amount of downtime is allowed for repair and maintenance. Further, units that are old and obsolete are often included, but they should be downgraded since they can no longer produce up to the original rated tonnage potential.

Another element entering into measurement of capacity is the application of auxiliary technology. In the electric furnace operation, the installation of water-cooled side panels has done a great deal to increase the output of the furnace. The same can be said for the ladle furnace, which is installed to refine the steel melted in the electric furnace.

The installation of high-top pressure at the blast furnace in the 1950s and early 1960s was also a factor in improving output. More important for increased blast furnace production, however, was the beneficiation of raw materials. In the immediate postwar period, the charge in most of the American furnaces was raw iron ore direct from the mine. Later in the 1960s and through the 1980s, raw iron ore was converted into sinter or pellets. Charging this improved material increased output of some blast furnaces by 50 percent.

In terms of finishing facilities, the annual rating depends on the number of turns per week they are operated as well as their size and the power applied. Obviously a facility operated at eighteen turns will differ markedly in capacity from one operating at twenty turns.

Political Implications

Capacity has entered the political arena. During the 1960 presidential campaign in the United States, the steel industry was operating at 68 percent, a relatively low rate of capacity. Candidate John F. Kennedy said in campaign speeches that it was necessary to get the country's economy moving, pointing out that the steel industry was operating at little more than half its capacity. This irked the steel industry executives to a point where, capacity figures were not published for a number of years after 1960. The reasons given were that the concept was complex and not fully understood, and the publication of a single number was often misleading. Further, a number of units that were relatively high cost and obsolete were included in the industry's capacity because they had not yet been removed from the productive rolls.

In Europe, capacity has figured significantly in the production quotas established by the European High Commission. Consequently, it was to the advantage of individual companies to have the highest possible figure for capacity. In the 1980s, figures published for the various countries in the European Community by the Organization for Economic Cooperation and Development (OECD) were somewhat inflated. For example, in 1974 when the industry in the European Economic Community (EEC) was operating at almost full capacity, production stood at 156 million tonnes. In the early 1980s, an OECD publication placed the figure at 198 million tons, despite the fact that relatively little had been added in the intervening years.[2]

Excess Capacity

The question of steel capacity, particularly overcapacity, has been widely discussed by steel producers in the industrialized, as well as the Third World. During the late 1970s and early to mid-1980s, there was considerable concern voiced by the representatives of the industrialized world about the increase in capacity taking place in the Third World. The addition of capacity was considered detrimental to the steel industry on a global basis since it would provide much more supply than was needed and consequently would affect steel trade and the price structure. The steel companies in the industrialized world were in favor of limiting new capacity at home and in the Third World.

In regard to this position, the steel mill equipment manufacturers in the industrialized world voiced strong opposition. These companies were literally starving for business, since there was very little investment in new facilities either made or planned by the integrated companies of the industrialized countries. In the mid- to late 1970s, as well as in the early 1980s, most orders for new equipment were coming from the Third World.

A case in point was the Kwangyang integrated mill built by Pohang Iron and Steel Company of South Korea in the mid-1980s. When the mill was announced, there was concern on the part of steel producers; however, it was welcome news to the mill equipment suppliers, who came from all over the industrialized world with low prices to secure orders, which were financed by the various import-export banks. The principal suppliers were Europeans, although the Japanese built the hot-strip mill.

Current Capacity Estimates

The capacities of the various steel-producing countries have fluctuated significantly in the past ten years. As of 1989, the United States had approximately 100 million metric tons; the European Community, consisting of twelve members since the admission of Spain and Portugal, had approximately 175 million; and Japan's potential was approximately 125 million.

The Japanese figure is the most difficult to estimate since part of Japan's capacity has been decommissioned but not abandoned and is capable of restoration to activity on relatively short notice. In the United States and the European Community, a great deal of the capacity that has been eliminated has been dismantled. Capacity in other countries, such as Canada, amounted to some 18 million tonnes, while that of South Africa and Australia was in the range of 7 million tonnes to 10 million tonnes.

In contrast, the steel industry in the Third World has grown substantially in the last ten years as individual countries have added steelmaking facilities. This trend will continue. Currently China has about 65 million tonnes of steelmaking potential, South Korea has approximately 23 million tonnes, Brazil about 27 million, and India some 17 million. These Third World countries have every intention of increasing their capacities.

In addition to the major Third World nations, there are others with smaller potential, such as Mexico with 9 million tonnes, Taiwan with 8 million, Venezuela with 5 million, and Argentina with approximately 6 million. Smaller capacities exist in Indonesia with somewhat in excess of 2 million tonnes, and Saudi Arabia has 1.5 million. It is necessary to look at countries individually to determine capacity with a relative degree of accuracy. One must also examine future plans of companies so that either growth or decline can be projected.

United States

The steel industry in the United States can be divided into two segments:

1. The integrated companies, which operate blast furnaces, as well as steelmaking and finishing facilities.
2. The electric furnace segment, which consists of companies of varying sizes that produce steel from scrap in electric furnaces. In this division, there are some thirty minimill companies, in addition to larger producers, as well as specialty steel companies.

The integrated segment consists of fifteen companies, including those considered majors, such as United States Steel, LTV Steel, Bethlehem, Inland, Armco, and National, and a number of smaller companies also operating on an integrated basis—Wheeling-Pittsburgh, Weirton, McLouth, Rouge, Sharon, Acme, Gulf States, Geneva, and Warren. The last three have been recently organized as a result of spin-offs and sales of segments of United States Steel and LTV. In the past few years, two companies, Lone

Star and CF&I, have dropped from the integrated ranks and are now producing steel in electric furnaces.

A survey of the integrated companies indicates that they have virtually no intention of adding new capacity in terms of more or larger furnaces. The investment programs of these companies in the 1980s were directed at improving quality and reducing costs. For example, in the past ten years, there has been feverish activity in the installation of continuous-casting units, increasing the production of continuously cast steel from 20 percent of total output in 1980 to 65 percent in 1989.

Current and future programs for capital investment up to 1995 are concentrated, as they have been in the past decade, on improving quality and productivity, as well as reducing costs, so that the steel produced will be competitive not only with that made in other countries but also with substitute materials. A sizable segment of the capital investment will be devoted to the replacement of current equipment, which in some cases will be in kind and in others with improved facilities. New technology, such as a revolutionary direct method of steel production, a joint venture between the AISI and the Department of Energy, is in the development stage and awaiting the completion of a pilot plant.

Continuous casting will continue to be added, and rolling facilities, particularly strip mills, will be upgraded. During the next ten years, there will probably be ten or twelve continuous casters brought on stream at the integrated mills. Most of these will be slab casters. By the year 2000, the steel industry in the United States will be casting over 80 percent of its steel.

Coating facilities such as galvanizing lines will be increased in number. Since 1980, six coating lines to produce electrolytic galvanized sheets have been installed, five of them on a joint venture basis. These are units now operated by Inland and Bethlehem, United States Steel and Rouge, NKK and National, Sumitomo and LTV, and Wheeling-Pittsburgh and Nisshin. The installations have been so successful that a number of new units are planned. The need for these facilities arose from the desire of the automobile industry to improve its anticorrosion program by using galvanized sheets in exposed parts of the bodies.

The electric furnace segment of the industry, which includes some thirty minimill companies, as well as specialty steel units, such as Quanex, Carpenter, and Allegheny-Ludlum, and those producers larger than mini-mills, such as Lukens, Northwestern Steel and Wire, Lone Star and CF&I, will continue to invest in improving quality and reducing costs. However, in contrast to the integrated segment, some additional capacity has recently been installed; two new mills, constructed by Nucor, have come on stream. Further, some minimills have replaced small electric furnaces with larger units, as was done at the Structural Metals plant in Texas.

Judging from the plans of the electric furnace companies for the coming decade, the total capacity in the United States will be increased by a limited tonnage, since the additions will be somewhat neutralized by a small number of facilities that will be abandoned.

An indication of what may be expected in the way of steelmaking capacity in the mid- to late 1990s can be had from an examination of the recent past actions, as well as the future plans, of the individual companies.

Integrated Companies

United States Steel. United States Steel, a subsidiary of USX, is the largest steel company in the United States; thus, it is not surprising that its restructuring efforts involve more investment than other steel companies. These efforts in the 1980s included joint ventures, diversification, plant closures, and the sale of assets.

Currently the company operates six plants at which steel is made: The Gary Works in Gary, Indiana; the South Works in Chicago; the Lorain Works at Lorain, Ohio; the Edgar Thomson works in the Pittsburgh area; the Fairless Works near Trenton, New Jersey; and the Fairfield Works at Fairfield, Alabama, near Birmingham.

In 1973, the year of peak steel production in the United States, United States Steel produced 35 million net tons of raw steel. At that time, total industry output was 151 million tons, while total capacity was between 155 million and 160 million net tons. The operating rate overall was well above 90 percent, and that of United States Steel, which had a capacity of approximately 36 million to 37 million tons, was about 95 percent.

The capacity figure remained intact until 1977, when the decline in business forced cutbacks. United States Steel gradually eliminated a considerable amount of its capacity, and as of 1990, it had a potential to produce between 18 million and 19 million tons. This reduction, although drastic, still leaves United States Steel as the largest producer in the country.

One of the basic reasons for the reduction in capacity was that, in the late 1970s, the management of United States Steel calculated that it would be virtually impossible, with the funds available, to maintain 37 million tons of steelmaking capacity in competitive condition into the future. As a consequence, reductions were planned that would still allow the corporation to maintain its leading position and operate at a profit.

In the 1980s, plants and parts of plants were closed while sizable sums were invested in modernizing the remaining facilities. Among the major plants closed were Texas Works at Baytown, Texas; the Homestead and Duquesne Works in the Pittsburgh area; and the Geneva Works at Geneva, Utah. After closure the Geneva plant was sold to an investment group in Utah, which put it back into operation.

Parts of plants, such as the rail mill at Gary, Indiana, the blast furnace and oxygen-steelmaking capacity at South Works in Chicago, the rod mills at the Fairless Works and South Works, as well as that at the Cuyahoga plant, were closed and subsequently sold—the Fairless rod mill to China, the South Chicago rod mill to Colombia, and the Cuyahoga plant to a group of investors.

Many of these facilities were high-cost operating units, and their elimination allowed the corporation to improve its operating performance and increase productivity. In contrast to the closures, several billion dollars was invested in new facilities, such as continuous casters and a new seamless pipe mill.

Coke ovens at a number of locations, such as Lorain, the Fairless Works, and the Fairfield Works, were closed, and coke was supplied from the Clairton plant, near Pittsburgh. Clairton also supplied part of the requirement of Gary. Currently United States Steel is considering coal injection into the blast furnaces of up to 400 pounds per ton of iron produced. This would relieve the necessity of rebuilding some coke ovens to supply the full blast furnace requirement. If the plan succeeds, there will be a reduction of some 35 percent in coke required.

A number of nonsteelmaking facilities—such as American Bridge, a construction company, which was one of the original components of the corporation when it was organized in 1901, and United States Steel Supply, a chain of service centers—were sold. Other assets, including chemical companies and transportation units, which involved railroads and barge lines, as well as a cement company, were sold. The disposal of these assets yielded several billion dollars.

In the matter of joint ventures, there has been considerable activity:

1. An agreement with Rouge Steel to operate a 700,000-ton-capacity electrolytic galvanizing line located at the Rouge plant near Detroit.

2. An arrangement with Worthington Corporation to process several hundred thousand tons of sheets for the automobile industry.

3. An international venture with Pohang Iron and Steel Company, entered into in 1986, to build a $400 million modern cold-rolling facility in California. This is to be supplied, in great part, with hot bands from the new integrated steel mill built by Pohang at Kwangyang in South Korea, which has a fully modern hot-strip mill capable of providing excellent feedstock for the California facility.

4. Two agreements with Kobe Steel of Japan, one for a joint fifty-fifty ownership of the Lorain integrated plant, which currently produces bars and pipe. The principal reason for the joint venture is the desire to

develop high-quality bars to be sold to the Japanese automobile plants that have been erected in the United States. The reason for the other is to develop a 600,000-ton galvanizing line with a fifty-fifty ownership located in Ohio to supply sheets to the plants of the Japanese automobile companies in the United States.

Perhaps the most radical change that has taken place since the formation of United States Steel in 1901 is the diversification into nonsteel activities. In 1982, United States Steel acquired Marathon Oil, the seventeenth largest oil company in the United States, for an investment of some $6 billion. In 1984, Texas Oil and Gas was acquired on the basis of a stock transfer. As a consequence, over 50 percent of the corporation's revenue is derived from energy and the rest from steel and other items. The diversification led to a change in name from United States Steel Corporation to USX in 1986, under which the oil companies and the steel company are wholly owned subsidiaries.

In terms of the future, a large capital investment of some $3 billion will be made in the steel segment of USX by 1994. At the Gary plant, a third continuous caster is currently under construction, as well as extensive renovations to the large No. 13 blast furnace. A major project will be injection of powdered coal at all of the blast furnaces, which could reduce the coke rate by one-third. In the Pittsburgh area, a continuous caster will be installed at Edgar Thomson, along with a ladle furnace, while the Irvin Works hot-strip mill will be completely renovated. At Lorain, a joint venture with Kobe Steel, a bloom caster will be installed, and a major blast furnace renovation will be undertaken. At Fairfield, much work has been done in terms of two continuous casters and a seamless-pipe mill. In the future, the six-stand cold mill, one of only three in the United States, will be upgraded so that its capacity will be considerably increased.

The joint venture with Kobe Steel, calling for the construction of a hot-dipped galvanizing line with a 650,000-ton capacity to furnish galvanized sheets to the automobile industry with emphasis on the Japanese transplants, should be in place and operating by 1992.

Downstream facilities, such as continuous annealing and added galvanizing lines, will receive considerable attention. There is, however, no plan to increase capacity for raw-steel production, so that United States Steel will continue to produce steel from its 18-million- to 19-million-ton potential and, with increased continuous casting, will have the ability to ship between 13 million and 14 million tons of product annually. This reduced output produced efficiently on modern equipment will allow the corporation to operate profitably.

In regard to the future, there has been considerable discussion concerning the possibility of other joint ventures or the sale of United States Steel in whole or in part. This could be somewhat involved, since the corporation currently has three major joint ventures. Interest has been expressed by European companies, such as British Steel and Thyssen, in an arrangement that could take the form of a partnership through joint ownership of individual plants, such as the USS/Kobe and the USS/Posco ventures, or possibly joint ventures with the remaining plants not already involved in joint ventures.

Bethlehem. Bethlehem Steel Corporation is the second largest steel company in the United States, although in 1984, it had lost that position to LTV, which was formed by a merger of Jones & Laughlin and Republic Steel. Since then LTV has reduced its capacity so that Bethlehem is again in second place among steel producers.

At its peak, Bethlehem had a capacity to produce 22 million to 23 million tons of raw steel. However, through the closure of plants and parts of plants, this has been reduced to 15 million to 16 million tons. The most drastic reduction came as a result of the closure of the Lackawanna plant near Buffalo, New York which at one time had a capacity of 5 million tons. Several facilities at that location continue to operate, including coke ovens, a relatively new bar mill, and a galvanizing line. Billets for the bar mill are made at Johnstown and coils for the galvanizing line at Sparrows Point.

At Johnstown, which was a fully integrated plant, the blast furnace, coke ovens, and open-hearth steelmaking facilities were closed. In their place, two large electric furnaces have been installed, so the shop now operates on scrap. The Sparrows Point plant, which early in the post–World War II period vied with United States Steel's plant at Gary for the largest in the world, has been reduced in size, as has the plant at Bethlehem, which produces structural beams.

Burns Harbor, Bethlehem's newest plant, is the last fully integrated plant to be built in the United States. It was constructed during the 1960s and now represents state-of-the-art equipment, with output consisting of plates and various types of sheets.

Part of the reduction in the company's capacity was achieved by the closure of a relatively small electric furnace plant in Los Angeles and the sale of a similar-size electric furnace plant in Seattle.

In terms of capital investment and modernization, Bethlehem has invested in a large blast furnace at Sparrows Point, which shares with the Inland furnace in Indiana Harbor the distinction of the largest in the Western Hemisphere. A battery of coke ovens to supplement this facility has also been installed, along with a large-capacity continuous caster, so that the ironmaking and steelmaking facilities at Sparrows Point are world class.

Bethlehem has installed additional continuous casters at Burns Harbor and Steelton. The latter plant, located near Harrisburg, Pennsylvania, operates electric furnaces for the production of steel for rails. Recently some $50 million has been expended on the structural mill at the Bethlehem plant, which was the company's original installation. It has been reduced in size so that it operates one or, at the most, two-blast-furnaces.

In 1989, a rail mill built at the Monessen works of Wheeling-Pittsburgh was repossessed by the government, which had guaranteed the loan that was necessary to build the facility in the early 1980's. Bethlehem purchased the mill and now has two of the three remaining rail mills in the United States.

Perhaps the largest single expenditure on any one facility involves the complete reconstruction of the 68-inch hot-strip mill at Sparrows Point. The result will be practically a new strip mill with a reversing roughing stand and a coil box, as well as much-improved finishing stands. This was necessary since the mill, although it had been updated, dates from the late 1930s. The product from the new mill to be completed by 1991 will be distinctly superior to that formerly produced.

Future expenditures of $2 billion by 1994 contemplate no added steel-making capacity but include the modernization of the cold-reduction mills, as well as the tinplate and the galvanizing lines, and annealing and pickling facilities at Sparrows Point will be upgraded. In the modernization program, a vacuum degassing unit has been installed at Burns Harbor. This plant will also receive attention at its plate mill and hot-strip mill.

Participation in an electrolytic galvanizing line, currently operating as a joint venture involving Inland Steel and Pre-Finish Steel, will be expanded as Bethlehem acquires one-half of Inland's share. Hot-dipped galvanizing facilities will also be augmented with the installation of three new hot-dipped lines—one at Sparrows Point, one at Burns Harbor, and a possible third in the Southwest. In the future, continuous-casting units might be installed at the Johnstown and Bethlehem plants.

One venture that Bethlehem moved into in the mid-1980s was the acquisition of a service center complex owned by Tull Industries. This was rather short-lived; within a year, the company was sold to Inland Steel.

Bethlehem has a very high percentage of continuous casting for its sheet product, which has improved its competitive position in terms of quality and costs. It will continue to concentrate on improvements in productivity, costs, and quality, without any intention of increasing steelmaking capacity. Recently it announced a joint venture with France's Usinor-Sacilor for the production of rolls.

LTV Steel. LTV Steel, a subsidiary of LTV of Texas, which among other things is engaged in aerospace, was formed as a result of the merger of Jones & Laughlin, an LTV subsidiary, and Republic Steel. Although this was initially rejected by the Justice Department, it subsequently was permitted in 1984 when the companies agreed to spin off the Gadsden plant of Republic, as well as its hot-strip stainless steel segment.

Jones & Laughlin in 1977 acquired the Youngstown Sheet and Tube Company, with plants in Youngstown, Ohio, and Indiana Harbor, Indiana. Youngstown Sheet and Tube Company was in serious financial trouble, and although the merger was questioned by the Justice Department, it was allowed by the attorney general on the basis of the failing company doctrine. A short time after the acquisition, the Youngstown plant was abandoned except for the seamless-pipe mill, which was upgraded with an investment of some $70 million.

Jones & Laughlin concentrated its development, as Youngstown Sheet and Tube had before it, on the Indiana Harbor facility, where considerable capital was invested in the blast furnace and the steelmaking segment, as well as in a new 84-inch hot-strip mill.

As a result of the merger in 1984, LTV became the second-largest company in the United States. Unfortunately for the new company, prices collapsed in 1985, the year following its formation, and it incurred substantial losses. In 1986, LTV Steel filed for bankruptcy under Chapter 11 of the bankruptcy code. The collapse of prices in 1985—they fell as much as 30 percent below list—was particularly unfortunate; although LTV had reduced its costs appreciably, these potential savings were wiped out by the price decline.

When formed in 1984, the company had a rated capacity in excess of 20 million tons. With subsequent reductions because of the closure of its Chicago and Aliquippa plants, as well as the sale of the fully integrated Warren plant, an operation with 1.5 million tons of capacity, and other rationalizations, including the sale of its bar division, the rated capacity was reduced to about 10 million tons.

A number of changes on the positive side have been made and are planned for the future. Continuous casters have been installed in the Indiana Harbor and Cleveland plants. Improvements have been made to the hot-strip mill finishing stands, allowing the production of steel sheets with a much more uniform gauge. The center crown has been reduced by some 30 percent. A ladle furnace and a vacuum-degassing unit have been installed in the Indiana Harbor plant.

For the future, an annual investment of approximately $350 million will be necessary to update facilities, including a second continuous caster, continuous annealing blast furnace improvements, and two coke oven batteries with a 1-million-ton capacity, all to be constructed at the Cleveland plant. The coke oven batteries will be much wider than the conventional units in operation throughout the United States. The individual ovens will be 24 inches in width as compared to 18 inches, currently the standard.

The corporate structure of LTV was reorganized into three divisions: one for pipe, one for bars, and a third for flat-rolled products. Subsequent to this revision, the bar division has been sold, so LTV will be predominantly a flat-rolled producer. The pipe will be welded from skelp rolled on the strip mills.

LTV entered into a joint venture with Sumitomo Metals of Japan, which resulted in the construction of a continuous electrolytic galvanizing line. This has been so successful that a second unit is under construction in Columbus, Ohio.

The company as restructured is expected to be profitable with 10 million tons of raw-steel production.

Armco. Armco is unusual as an integrated steel company insofar as it is significantly involved in the production of specialty steels, as well as carbon steel. The company has also been diversified along a number of lines for many years. In the early 1980s, it had less than half of its sales in steel.

The diversification received impetus in 1958 with the purchase of National Supply Company, at the time the leading manufacturer and supplier of pipe and machinery for oil well drilling. Subsequently Armco acquired Oregon Metallurgical Corporation, a titanium producer, and Armco-Booth Corporation, an equipment leasing company. It also purchased Hitco, a producer of nonmetallic composites, which had applications in aerospace technology.

In the mid-1960s, the company launched a program that cost $800 million, directed at installing a basic-oxygen steelmaking shop, 86-inch-wide hot- and cold-strip mills at Middletown, Ohio, and electric furnaces at its Butler, Pennsylvania, works.

In the late 1970s and early 1980s, as the oil business was booming and the number of drilling rigs in operation in late 1981 exceeded 4,500, Armco considered building a new seamless-pipe facility, at a cost of some $700 million, to meet the demand. In 1982, the oil country equipment business declined sharply, as drilling activity plummeted. As a consequence, the plan for the new seamless mill was abandoned. This had an impact on the Ashland plant, which had a newly installed continuous caster to provide blooms for seamless-tube production. Within a very few years, Armco abandoned the oil country tubular business, and the caster at Ashland was converted to a slab caster at a cost of some $60 million.

Because of the losses incurred over 1982–1986, a number of businesses, including Hitco and the insurance company, were sold. Subsequently the Houston plant, which produced plates and structural sections, was shut down, as was half of the Kansas City operation. Ashland has been reduced in capacity and coordinated more closely with the Middletown plant to improve productivity and efficiency. In 1990, the company has a capacity to produce approximately 6 million tons of steel, including specialty steel, which is made at its Butler, Pennsylvania, and Baltimore works.

In 1989, Armco entered into an agreement with Kawasaki Steel of Japan under which it sold 40 percent of its carbon-steel facilities located at Middletown, Ohio, and Ashland, Kentucky, forging a partnership between the two companies for the production of carbon steel.

Armco has also entered into an international joint venture with Acerinox of Spain, a stainless steel producer, to construct two stainless sheet and strip plants, one in the midwestern United States and the other in Spain. The U.S. plant, a green-field rolling mill costing $220 million, will be known as North American Stainless and will be supplied with 60-inch hot bands from Acerinox. In Spain, the joint venture plant will be known as Acerinox–Armco Europa and will be located near Madrid. Its output will be limited to auto-emission grades of stainless to supply European auto manufacturers.

In terms of the future, Armco envisions a massive program costing approximately $1.3 billion. This will include adjustments to the cold-reduction mills in order to improve product gauge. At Middletown, slab furnaces on the hot-strip mill will be converted to walking-beam units, and the finishing stands will be upgraded, as will the pickling line. A new continuous caster will be installed at the Middletown works, as well as additional facilities for both hot-dipped and electrolytic galvanizing. Continuous annealing is also contemplated, as well as paint lines. It is possible that an additional caster for thin slabs may be installed at the Ashland plant, which would require adjustments to the hot-strip mill there. Batch annealing will also be increased at Ashland.

As a result of the steps taken, including the partnerships with Kawasaki and Acerinox, Armco should be able to provide high-grade, low-cost steel for the U.S. market with no planned increase in raw-steel capacity.

Inland. Unlike the other major steel producers, Inland Steel has only one integrated plant, located at Indiana Harbor. Until recently the plant was the largest in the United States, with a capacity to produce some 9 million tons; however, with the closure of the open-hearth shop, capacity has been substantially reduced to approximately 6.5 million tons of raw steel.

The company is predominantly a flat-rolled producer with some 5 million tons of capacity devoted to this product, all of it continuously cast. Bar products are another significant item; they are produced on a modern bar mill tied to an electric furnace with a continuous caster. Inland is also involved in the production of plates and structurals. However, the structural mill is in jeopardy since Nucor installed a 650,000-ton new structural mill in Arkansas. Plates may also be discontinued because the mill is not modern.

In the late 1970s, the company studied the possibility of building a new plate mill with an investment of $400 million. It abandoned this project when the plate market softened and projections indicated that it would remain so for some time.

In recent years, Inland has spent over $2 billion for installations at its Indiana Harbor plant, including coke ovens and one of the two largest blast furnaces in the Western Hemisphere. The other of equal size—10,000 tons per day capacity—is located at Bethlehem's Sparrows Point plant.

In late 1987, Inland entered into a joint venture with Nippon Steel of Japan to build a cold-reduction rolling mill, complete with continuous annealing and pickling. This went into operation in 1990 and constitutes the ultimate in cold-rolling technology. The cold mill is a six-high mill and, along with the facility installed in California by United States Steel and Pohang Iron and Steel of South Korea, will represent the only two six-high mills in the United States. The product from this mill will be second to none and superior to most. The total cost of $400 million was financed $90 million by Inland, $60 million by Nippon, and $250 million by three Japanese trading companies (Mitsubishi, Mitsui, and Nisshio-Iwai). Nippon has the right to take 20 percent of the product and sell it wherever it sees fit. In order to feed coils to the cold-reduction mill, which is located in northern Indiana, the hot-strip mill at Inland's Indiana Harbor plant has been upgraded.

In 1985, Inland formed a joint venture with Bethlehem Steel and Pre-Finish Steel Products to produce 400,000 tons of electrolytic galvanized sheets for the automobile industry. Future planning involves further development of galvanized steel, both hot dipped and electrolytic, to be produced in conjunction with the new continuous cold mill. This will also be a joint venture with Nippon Steel at the cold-reduction mill site in northern Indiana. Total capacity of the two lines will be 900,000 tons, requiring an investment of $450 million. When it is in operation, Inland will sell half of its earlier joint venture to Bethlehem.

In addition to the steel segment of Inland Industries, the company operates the largest steel service center system in the world. It consists of two companies, Ryerson, which has been part of Inland for over fifty years, and Tull, which was recently acquired.

In terms of corporate organization, Nippon Steel has purchased 13 percent of the voting rights of Inland Steel Company for $185 million, which, added to the 1 percent it already owned, gives it a sizable share in the company.

Inland has no plans to increase steelmaking capacity.

National. National Steel had a capacity to produce 12 million tons of raw steel in the mid- to late 1970s. Since that time, its potential has been reduced to approximately 6 million to 7 million tons. A significant part of the reduction was due to the spin-off of Weirton Steel in 1984, when it was sold to the employees and organized in the form of an employee stock ownership plan (ESOP). In addition, the Great Lakes plant, near Detroit, was reduced in capacity by about 3 million tons. Currently steel is produced at the Great Lakes plant, as well as at the Granite City plant near St. Louis. The company operates a modern finishing mill, Midwest Steel, near Chicago.

In 1983, National established a holding company, known as National Intergroup, which reflected the diversification that had taken place beginning in the late 1960s, when the company entered the aluminum business with the acquisition of a participating percentage in Southwire Corporation. In the late 1970s, the company further diversified by acquiring United Financial Corporation of California. In 1981, an additional financial company was acquired. The basis for diversification was stated in the 1979 *Annual Report*: "The overall strategy of our company has included, as a major thrust, diversification in other lines of business which either (a) complements or supports our business, or (b) affords us an opportunity to grow in totally unrelated lines where prospects for profitability are promising. We propose to continue to emphasize that effort."[3]

The decision in 1983 to spin off Weirton was based on the fact that National decided to limit its future capital investment in Weirton in order to direct its capital funds to areas yielding a higher return. In spite of this diversification, National still insisted that "as National Intergroup, we remain strongly committed to our core business—steel. Our steel operations continue to carry the name National Steel Corporation." However, the company at the same time stated that emphasis would be placed on target markets: "National is a market-driven, customer-oriented steel supplier intent on becoming the quality, low-cost producer of sheet steel products."[4]

In 1984, the predominance of steel in National Intergroup faded considerably when the company tried to dispose of its steel facilities by selling them to United States Steel. A press release stated, "Under the agreement, United States Steel would acquire all of the steel-related business of National Steel Corporation including its three plants, iron ore and coal operations."[5] The price for these facilities was $575 million; in addition, United States Steel would acquire some of National's long-term debt. The arrangement was frustrated by the Justice Department, which denied the acquisition. Less than a month after the Justice Department's denial of the merger, National Intergroup announced that it had agreed to sell 50 percent of its interests in its steel facilities to Nippon Kokan of Japan for approximately $300 million. National Intergroup has since sold 20 percent of its remaining 50 percent to NKK with the option to sell 20 percent more.

In 1985, a West Coast pharmaceutical company, Bergen Brunswig Corporation of Los Angeles, agreed to acquire National Intergroup. Stockholders of both companies approved the plan; however, conditions changed, and the merger was abandoned.

From 1984 through 1989, the partnership of National Intergroup and Nippon Kokan of Japan operated the steel facilities. Capital expenditures for the period amounted to some $930 million, spent on such improvements as blast furnace rebuilds, installation of two ladle stations, a continuous caster, and a continuous electrolytic galvanizing line at the Great Lakes plant

A recent development has been a joint venture with Dofasco of Canada to construct a hot-dipped galvanizing line with approximately 350,00 tons of capacity.

There are significant plans for the company's development in the early 1990s. Between 1989 and 1993, the company plans to spend approximately $1 billion on a continuous caster and a pickling line at the Granite City plant and to update the plant's hot-strip mill to improve gauge and shape. Two blast furnaces at that location will be rebuilt.

At Great Lakes, a vacuum degassing station will be installed to improve the quality of the steel sheets, which constitute the only output of that plant. There will also be a considerable amount of work done on the hot-strip mill and the cold-reduction mill, where gauge controls will be installed to produce a more uniform gauge throughout the sheet. Further, the mill will be adjusted to improve the shape of the finished product.

A blast furnace rebuild will be necessary at Great Lakes at a cost of some $90 million, and a decision has been made for a complete rebuild of a coke oven battery, requiring an investment of $60 million to $70 million. This decision was made during 1989 when coke became scarce and the price increased significantly. Two years earlier, the opinion at National had been that coke could be purchased for less than it could be produced, considering the amount of the investment required for the rebuild. At that time, coke was selling for about $86 a ton on the East Coast. However, with the shortage and many of the integrated companies entering the market to purchase coke, the price of imported coke went to $120 a ton. Under these conditions, there was no choice but to rebuild the coke oven battery at Great Lakes.

By 1992 or 1993, when all of these projects have been completed, National will be in a position to improve its efficiency, productivity, and profitability. It should be noted, however, that there is no intention of increasing steelmaking capacity. Capital expenditures will be directed at improving quality, as well as reducing costs.

Wheeling-Pittsburgh. Wheeling-Pittsburgh Steel Corporation was formed in 1968 by the merger of Pittsburgh Steel Corporation and Wheeling Steel Corporation. The new entity had integrated plants in Steubenville, Ohio, as well as Monessen, Pennsylvania. Finishing facilities were located at other plants, such as Yorkville, Ohio, and Allentown, Pennsylvania.

The company modernized considerably in 1982 and 1983 with a major capital investment program that included two continuous-casting units—one at Steubenville for slabs for the hot-strip mill and the other at Monessen for blooms to feed the newly constructed rail mill. The rail mill, one of three in the United States, went into operation in 1983 with a capacity to produce some 400,000 tons of high-quality rails in lengths up to 82 feet.

In 1985, as a result of labor problems and the steel depression, Wheeling-Pittsburgh declared bankruptcy under Chapter 11.

Subsequently Wheeling-Pittsburgh developed ambitious plans for the period 1989–1993. It is upgrading the 80-inch hot-strip mill at Steubenville, Ohio, one of the second-generation hot-strip mills installed in the 1960s. The projected work is designed to improve gauge and shape. It consists of a coil box and the installation of roll bending and side shifting equipment on the finishing stands. Ladle metallurgy is also in the program. At its Allenport, Pennsylvania, plant, a cold-reduction mill is to be upgraded to improve gauge and shape.

In the early 1990s, Wheeling-Pittsburgh will consider a new tinning line, as well as rebuilding the coke ovens, and it will study the possibility of a thin slab caster. It is also contemplated that an additional heavy caster, capable of producing slabs 10 inches thick, will be installed at the hot-strip mill in Steubenville, Ohio. This new caster, plus the improvements on the hot-strip mill, will allow the company to produce a superior sheet product.

Currently Wheeling-Pittsburgh has a capacity to produce 2.8 million tons of raw steel, which was reduced from 4 million tons. No increase in capacity is contemplated since most of the attention will be concentrated on the finishing facilities, ladle furnaces, and casting equipment to raise the proportion of steel cast to 100 percent.

Wheeling intends to remain a flat-rolled producing company and has derived considerable advantage from its joint venture with Nisshin Steel, which provides galvanized sheets as well as aluminum-coated material. The joint venture entered into in 1984 provided for a 10 percent ownership of the Wheeling Steel Company by Nisshin Steel, as well as a two-thirds ownership of the coating line.

Weirton. The steel plant at Weirton, West Virginia, was the original plant of National Steel Corporation and was known up until 1929 as Weirton Steel. Subsequently there was a merger with Great Lakes, and the name was changed to National Steel.

In 1983, National Steel Corporation decided to spin off the Weirton facility rather than invest heavily to improve its operations when it was felt that the investment would not bring a satisfactory return. The facility was sold to the Weirton employees in January 1984, who subsequently organized it as an ESOP. The company has been profitable since its origin. It is a producer of flat-rolled products, among which tinplate stands out as its primary offering.

Currently it is in the throes of a major capital program designed to improve its finishing facilities and bring them up to a competitive position. The revamped continuous caster, which was installed in the late 1960s, will be improved and enlarged so that an additional million tons can be cast, enabling Weirton to cast all of its steel.

The hot-strip mill, which was originally installed in the late 1920s and has been improved considerably since, will be completely revamped through the installation of a reversing rougher, as well as improvements on the finishing stands. Other expenditures will be made on environmental equipment and blast furnace improvements, reducing the number from four to three. The program should be completed by 1991. Beyond that, the company has no precise plans but intends to keep abreast of technology developments in its area.

The current capacity, which will remain into the foreseeable future, is 3 million tons of raw steel.

Rouge Steel. Rouge Steel Company, which has been in operation for more than sixty years, was formerly known as the steel division of Ford Motor Company. In 1982, the name was changed, and Rouge Steel became a wholly owned subsidiary of Ford.

In late 1982, negotiations were undertaken with Nippon Kokan of Japan with the purpose of selling either 75 percent or the entire company to the Japanese. Negotiations were terminated in 1983, and Ford Motor Company was faced with the decision of closing the plant entirely or investing substantial amounts of capital to make it competitive. The company was organized by the United Autoworkers of America, and employment costs were $5 an hour more than steelworker-organized companies.

The plant lacked a continuous caster, and its cold-reduction mill was not adequate to produce high-quality sheets required for the automobile industry's exposed body parts. As a consequence, the amount of Rouge's product sold to the Ford Motor Company dropped from over 65 percent to 35 percent.

A large investment was made in the late 1980s in a number of key facilities. The hot-strip mill was improved with greater computerization, as well as adjustments to the finishing stands, which resulted in better shape and reduced crown. A continuous caster was added that could process most of the steel output. A ladle furnace, as well as a new pickler, were installed, along with vacuum degassing. All of these improvements made it possible for Rouge to regain much of the requirement of the Ford Motor Company that it had lost.

Rouge and United States Steel, a subsidiary of USX, entered into a joint venture in 1985 to build a continuous electrolytic galvanizing line with a 700,000-ton capacity. This currently supplies the automotive industry with sheets that prevent corrosion in exposed parts of the automobile body.

In December 1989, Ford Motor Company sold Rouge Steel for $180 million to a combination of investors, led by Marico Acquisition Corporation, which had been formed in July of that year by Carl Valdiserri. Participating in the acquisition were Worthington Industries, Chase Manhattan Capital Corporation, and Ford Motor Company. Ford Motor Company retained 20 percent interest in the operation. Worthington acquired 20 percent, as did Chase Manhattan Capital Corporation, with Valdiserri taking 40 percent.

In conjunction with the sale, Ford agreed to purchase 40 percent of its flat-rolled requirements from Rouge for a ten-year period, and Worthington agreed to purchase 50 percent of its requirement of this product for seven years, ensuring Rouge of a substantial market for the future.

There is no plan to increase capacity at Rouge, which now stands at approximately 2.9 million tons of raw steel.

Warren Consolidated Industries. Warren Consolidated Industries was formed as a result of the purchase of the Warren steel plant from LTV Steel in late 1988. As part of the arrangement, the blast furnace was relined by LTV before the new owners took over. Since that time, the company has operated profitably on a product mix of flat-rolled items, including terne plate, cold-rolled sheets, hot-rolled sheets, silicon sheets, and galvanized sheets.

In the immediate future, plans call for the installation of a continuous caster and a ladle furnace. The investment in these units will be in the area of $180 million.[6] The ladle furnace will be in operation at the end of 1990, and the continuous caster will function in late 1991. To supplement its raw materials, the company acquired a sinter plant in Youngstown, which formerly belonged to LTV. The total investment is directed, as that of other integrated companies, toward improving quality, cost reduction, and increased productivity. Raw steel capacity of some 1.5 million tons will be maintained but could undergo a minor expansion with the installation of ladle metallurgy. The Warren 56-inch hot-strip mill with a reversing roughing stand, installed in the early 1960s as the first of the second generation hot-strip mills, will be upgraded.

In respect to raw materials, Warren does not have an interest in an iron ore mine or a coal mine. Consequently it must buy its basic raw materials. The iron ore is purchased principally from Cleveland-Cliffs. Coke is purchased from a variety of sources, in both the United States and abroad. It seems that these arrangements will continue for a number of years.

Acme Steel. Acme Steel was formed from the merger of Acme Steel and Interlake Iron in 1954. The name Interlake was adopted. The company functioned well and in the 1970s launched a diversification plan by which it acquired a number of other operations, including a large producer of iron powder. In 1987, Interlake Inc. spun off Acme, and it adopted its original name as an independent unit.

The company has two blast furnaces and usually operates one, with the other on standby. Steel is made in an oxygen converter and rolled down on a narrow hot-strip mill and several cold-reduction mills.

Acme keeps close touch on improving technologies and maintains its facilities, making improvements from time to time. The hot-strip mill has just been upgraded with the installation of a coil box, and automatic gauge control has been added to the cold mills. Consideration will be given to installing a thin-slab caster in the near future.

During the early 1990s, there is no intention of increasing capacity, which will be maintained at about a million tons.

Acme recently acquired Alpha Tube and Tool Company and will be on the lookout for further acquisitions to strengthen its position.

To date, Acme has not installed a continuous caster because of the large number of slab sizes it rolls, varying from 8 inches up to 30 inches in width. It is possible that some accommodations may be worked out with a thin-slab caster, but this must be studied and will not take place until 1992 or 1993.

Geneva Steel. Geneva Steel Corporation was founded in 1987 as a result of the purchase by a Utah investor group of the Geneva steel works, which was formerly owned and operated by the USS division of USX. It remained closed after the six-month strike against USS that lasted from August 1986 to February 1987. Late in 1987, the purchase was made, and Geneva Steel began operations. The company was fortunate insofar as the demand for its products—predominantly plates and hot-rolled bands—was strong at the time, and it was able to sell its entire output at favorable prices.

The plant is one of two integrated plants in the United States completely dependent on the open-hearth process for its steel. Further, it does not have a continuous caster, and the 132-inch-wide strip mill, its major rolling facility, was built as a plate mill during World War II and needs considerable upgrading. Geneva's future plans call for the installation of a number of major facilities. Recently the company has offered stock for purchase and arranged for a loan; the proceeds will be used to finance the improvements.

The first phase includes a coil box on the strip mill, as well as the installation of a Q-Bop to replace the open hearth. This will be installed by Klockner. The two vessels that constitute this facility will be taken from the Republic Steel plant in South Chicago, which has been closed for some time. The heat size is 225 tons and should be capable of producing between 1.8 million and 1.9 million tons a year. A ladle furnace will accompany the installation of the Q-Bop. The second phase will include a continuous caster, which could be either a thin-slab or a conventional-slab unit. After the caster is installed, significant improvements will be made to upgrade the hot-strip mill, including a walking-beam furnace.

In 1988, Geneva exported some 130,000 tons of hot-rolled coils to Japan and, on the domestic scene, sold steel in twenty-nine states.

Gulf States. Gulf States Steel Inc. consists of an integrated plant in Gadsden, Alabama, formerly owned and operated by Republic Steel. In 1984, when Republic merged with Jones & Laughlin to form LTV steel, one of the conditions laid down by the Justice Department was that the Gadsden plant should be spun off. This was done, and within a year the Brenlin Group of Akron, Ohio, purchased the plant and established it as an independent, integrated steel company. The plant has one blast furnace supported by two coke oven batteries, both of which are operating and will continue to do so for a few years. Steel is made in an oxygen converter. Finishing facilities consist of a hot-strip mill, a plate mill, and cold-reduction and galvanizing facilities.

Future plans call for an enlargement of the blast furnace from 2,600 tons a day to 3,000 tons. This will provide additional iron, which will allow the basic-oxygen furnace (BOF) to increase its steel output by some 200,000 tons up to approximately 1.4 million tons. Coal injection will be provided at the blast furnace, reducing coke requirements by about 30 percent. The BOF vessels will be replaced in 1991 and 1994. A continuous caster, purchased from Spain, is under construction and will be started up in late 1990. This will be accompanied by a ladle furnace. The caster has an 800,000-ton capacity, which is adequate to handle all of the sheet products and approximately half of the plate products. The hot-strip mill will be upgraded to improve gauge control. Attention will also be given to annealing, as well as some improvements to the galvanizing line.

The increase in blast furnace capacity will allow the company to be self-sufficient in terms of slabs. Heretofore, some 150,000 tons were purchased annually. The investment involved in the continuous caster, as well as the other improvements over the next five-year period, will be in the area of $150 million to $160 million.

Sharon. Sharon Steel, located in western Pennsylvania, has a capacity to produce approximately 1.5 million tons of raw steel. The plant is composed of electric furnace operations, as well as a basic-oxygen converter. Until recently, the company had to purchase all of its coke for the blast furnace operations; however, in 1988, the Monessen plant of Wheeling-Pittsburgh was purchased to obtain coke ovens, which Sharon now operates, producing most of its needs. The steel output is more in the carbon specialty area than in run-of-the-mill carbon products.

Sharon's electric furnaces have a capacity for about 50,000 tons a month. Production in 1989 was 35,000 tons, 8,000 of which are assigned to bottom-poured ingots for sale and 27,000 for sheets. Of the 27,000, some 8,000 is for alloy sheets, leaving 19,000 for carbon. Consequently the annual production will include about 100,000 tons for bottom-poured ingots, 100,000 tons for alloy sheets, and 220,000 for low-carbon sheets. Residuals are carefully watched in the scrap, so that the sheets made from the electric furnaces have applications for all but the critical exposed parts.

The strip mill will be upgraded with the addition of a coil box, as well as improvements to the finishing stands, and a continuous caster will be installed. It is also probable that a third electric furnace will be added, ensuring the continuance of 1.5 million tons of raw steel.

Sharon is currently in bankruptcy under Chapter 11 of the bankruptcy statutes and in the process of reorganization.

McLouth. McLouth Steel, located at Trenton, Michigan, near Detroit, has two blast furnaces and usually operates one, with the second as a standby. In addition to the blast furnaces, which feed the BOF, there are two electric furnaces. Capacity is approximately 1.5 million tons. Finished products include hot- and cold-rolled sheets.

The company has been through a series of financial crises stretching back to the early 1980s; now it is an ESOP, with the employees owning 87 percent of the stock.

McLouth has instituted a plan, referred to as "business continuity," by which some $100 million will be spent from 1989 to 1993, to rebuild the blast furnaces and the basic-oxygen converters, as well as to upgrade the continuous caster significantly. Other routine tasks, such as rebuilding cranes and rewiring some electric equipment on the hot-strip mill, will also be undertaken. At the conclusion of this plan, the second phase, entitled "business opportunities," will be pursued, with much attention given to upgrading the hot-strip mill and the cold mills but with no intention of increasing capacity.

Lone Star and CF&I. These two companies were fully integrated operations until recently. In 1983, CF&I closed its blast furnaces, coke ovens, and basic-oxygen converters, so that it currently operates as an electric furnace shop with about 600,000 to 700,000 tons of capacity. It continues to produce rails and pipe, as well as a limited tonnage of rods.

In 1986, Lone Star followed the same route by closing its blast furnaces and open-hearth facilities so that it is an electric furnace operation with a capacity of fewer than 500,000 tons. It continues to produce oil country tubular goods, as well as hot-rolled sheets. Much of the production is achieved by rolling purchased slabs. In June 1989, the company was forced into Chapter 11 of the bankruptcy statutes and is in the process of revising its corporate structure.

Electric Furnaces

In addition to the integrated steel mills, some of which operate electric furnaces, as well as oxygen converters, over 30 million tons of steel are produced by electric furnace steel companies. These fall into several categories. One is specialty steel, including alloy and stainless that is produced by such companies as Allegheny-Ludlum, Quanex, and Carpenter Industries. Another is a group of steel producers too large or specialized to be considered minimills, such as Northwestern Steel and Wire and Lukens Steel. The third category is the minimills, of which there are some fifty-two in the United States owned by thirty companies.

Specialty Steel.

Allegheny-Ludlum. Allegheny-Ludlum became an independent specialty steel company in 1980 when it was purchased from the parent company, Allegheny Industries. It remained a private company until 1987 when the company was purchased from George Tippins, the principal owner, and shortly after its stock was sold to the public.

It is the largest producer of specialty and stainless steel in the United States. Other producers include Carpenter Technology, Armco, Slater Steel, Cyclops, Jones and Laughlin Special Steel, Jessup, and Washington Steel. Specialty steel, particularly stainless, is often measured in pounds produced rather than tons. During the past several decades, the production of stainless steel and other specialty steels increased rapidly, so that growth on an annual basis was approximately 4 percent.

During the 1980s when the carbon-steel industry incurred tremendous losses, a number of specialty steel producers, particularly Allegheny-Ludlum, were continually profitable. Recently, to meet increased demand, Allegheny-

Ludlum made commitments to increase its finishing capacity by some 30 percent. The principal item in this regard was the acquisition of the Vandergrift plant of United States Steel, which will be improved substantially by the installation of a 48-inch-wide Zendzimir mill to go into operation in 1990.

Allegheny-Ludlum has two plants currently—one at Brackenridge, Pennsylvania, and the other at Lockport, New York. In terms of tonnage, its 1988 output was 506,000 net tons.

During the next few years, some $150 million will be spent, principally on upgrading the hot-strip mill and other rolling mills, as well as the caster.

A major initiative in technology, pursued for a number of years by Allegheny-Ludlum, is the casting of steel strip. Recently a joint venture has been entered into with Voest-Alpine of Austria, and significant progress has been made. A facility will be constructed by 1992 to produce cast strip. This could be a major breakthrough insofar as it will eliminate the hot-strip mill for certain applications.

Unlike carbon steel, the specialty steel industry looks forward to continued growth in the decade ahead.

Minimills. Minimills are a relatively new development in the steel industry of the United States. They consist of a number of small plants that have sprung up since the early 1960s, operating electric furnaces, continuous casters, and bar mills. The term *minimill* was applied since the capacities were very small compared with the integrated mills, ranging from 60,000 tons of raw steel to over 200,000 tons.

There were small mills in this tonnage range long before the minimill label was coined. In fact, some of these existed at the turn of the century. However, it was in the 1960s that the name was given, and it has remained to the present.

In addition to small tonnages, minimills had a limited number of products, principally concrete reinforcing bar and, in a number of instances, small structurals, such as channels and angles and smooth, round bar. Since the early 1960s, a number of the original minimills have expanded in size, market range, and number of products. Currently several of these mills are capable of producing 500,000 tons or more. One plant, Chaparrel, located in Texas, began as a 400,000-ton unit producing the typical minimill products. The company is now capable of producing 1.5 million tons of raw steel and rolling heavy structural beams up to 15 inches wide. It is adding another beam mill.

Another development in the minimill segment has been the concentration of several plants under one ownership. There are seven companies that operate more than one mill: Florida Steel, Nucor, North Star Steel, Atlantic Steel, Birmingham Steel, Structural Steel, and Newport.

The minimill has found a niche in the American steel picture and constitutes approximately 20 percent to 25 percent of the industry's total capacity. The companies are scrap based with the exception of Georgetown Steel, where a percentage of its electric furnace charge is direct-reduced iron, which it produces.

There is a difference of opinion concerning the inclusion of some companies in the minimill category. This is particularly so when one considers the size of these units, as well as their products. For example, Northwestern Steel and Wire, located in Sterling, Illinois, has been in operation as an electric furnace plant for over fifty years. It operates the largest electric furnace in the world, capable of producing 400 tons per heat and has a capacity in excess of 2 million tons. This plant produces structural members that include wide-flange beams up to 18 inches and for years has never been considered a minimill, particularly since it has a capacity in excess of some of the integrated companies, such as Sharon, McLouth, and Acme.

Recently, in addition to its Sterling plant, it acquired the former Armco Steel plant in Houston, Texas with a rolling mill capable of producing wide-flange beams up to 27 inches at weights of 257 pounds per foot. The plant is rated at 600,000 tons, but could produce 1 million tons. In 1989, the past president and chief executive officer of Northwestern Steel and Wire, Robert Wilthew, presented a paper at a seminar. After announcing the acquisition of the Armco mill in Texas, he stated, "This is our approach to the 1990s. This is our effort to continue the increase of 'mini-mill' capabilities into the ever growing selection of steel products." Thus, the past president of Northwestern Steel and Wire seems to regard this company as a minimill, despite the fact that it has well over 2 million tons of capacity to produce steel and to roll finished products. He stated further that the Sterling mill and the Houston facility will enable his company to serve 80 percent of the U.S. wide-flange beam specifications and nearly 40 percent of world specifications.[7]

The minimill concept has unquestionably been expanded so that it covers a much wider range than originally conceived. Further, Nucor Corporation has constructed a mill in partnership with Yamato of Japan to roll wide-flange beams up to 24 inches with a capacity of 650,000 tons. Nucor has also constructed a mill to produce flat-rolled products, both hot- and cold-rolled sheets. Capacity is 800,000 tons of finished product. North Star Steel, a latecomer to the minimill business, has acquired seven plants, one of which can produce 300,000 tons of seamless pipe for oil country use.

Thus, the minimills have moved into larger tonnages and are producing products heretofore considered the province of the integrated mill. The name *minimill* will unquestionably remain in usage for some time to come; however, the original concept has radically changed, and one wonders whether it would be more appropriate to refer to these plants as electric furnace operations, which all are.

Some of the changes in the minimill concept, as well as corporate structure, present an interesting picture, and it is of interest to discuss a limited number of these companies.

Nucor. Nucor has been in operation since 1967, having started with a single plant in South Carolina. Since that time, it has added five plants in various locations: Texas, Utah, Nebraska, Arkansas, and Indiana. Total capacity is in the 4-million-ton range.

The most significant move undertaken by the company is the entrance into the light, flat-rolled product area, heretofore considered almost the exclusive province of the integrated steel mill. The plant, constructed at Crawfordsville, Indiana, began to produce sheets from thin slabs in mid-1989. In this respect, it not only began the production of a new product for minimills, hot- and cold-rolled sheets, but also constitutes the first plant in the world to employ a thin slab caster on a production basis.

The plant represents an investment of $265 million and has a capacity to produce 1 million tons of raw steel and some 800,000 tons of sheet product divided equally between hot and cold rolled. Since it operates on 100 percent scrap as a furnace feed, there has been some question about its ability to produce a full line of high-quality sheets where clean steel with very few contaminants is required. This situation could change since Nucor has decided to improve the electric furnace charge with the addition of direct-reduced iron, which will have the effect of diluting the residuals in the scrap segment of the charge. Currently the intention of the company is to aim at the lower-quality sheet market, which it will be capable of servicing.

The other new project is the joint venture between Nucor and Yamato of Japan. The investment was approximately $190 million, and with the modern technology it employs, it is competitive with the other producers of wide-flange beams. The electric furnace is no problem since many of the structural producers operate electric furnaces. Recently the company announced a 30 percent increase in the plant's capacity.

Co-Steel. Co-Steel, an unusual minimill operation with headquarters in Canada, has plants in three countries: Lake Ontario Steel in Ontario, Canada; Sheerness Steel in England; and Raritan River Steel in New Jersey. It is an international company, with each of the three plants having a capacity of approximately 800,000 tons, representing a total of 2.4 million tons.

Co-Steel owns 25 percent of Texas Industries, which in turn owns 100% of Chaparrel. This plant has a capacity of 1.5 million tons, bringing the potential output for the entire group close to 4 million tons.

In the future, Co-Steel will be looking for acquisitions to expand its line of products. It has also ensured part of its scrap supply by purchasing Parry Metals, a scrap producer in England with a half-million-ton capacity.

Birmingham Steel. Birmingham Steel, one of the larger minimill complexes, was founded in 1984 through the acquisition of two minimills, one located at Kankakee, Illinois, and the other at Birmingham, Alabama. Since that time, four more mills have been added: Mississippi Steel in Jackson, Mississippi; Intercoastal Steel in Norfolk, Virginia; Northwestern Rolling Mills in Seattle, Washington; and Judson Steel in Emeryville, California. Total melting capacity in 1990 is approximately 1.3 million tons. This will be increased in the years ahead by the addition of a larger furnace at Kankakee and improvements at Mississippi Steel.

In 1989, Birmingham announced plans to construct a mill for the production of flat-rolled products. In this connection, the company indicated its interest in the electric furnaces and continuous casters at the Baytown plant of United States Steel. The plate mill was not involved in the transaction. It hoped to erect a continuous hot-strip mill with a capacity of 1.2 million tons of flat-rolled steel provided by Danieli of Italy. It was a conventional mill with a reversing roughing stand and six finishing stands. The product was to be hot-rolled sheets, with no plan to install a cold-reduction mill. Ownership in the project was to be 50 percent Birmingham, 35 percent Prohler, and 15 percent Danieli. In the spring of 1990, Birmingham announced that it was withdrawing, and the project collapsed.

Subsequently Birmingham announced the construction of a new mill near Phoenix, with a capacity for 500,000 tons of minimill products. This is, in part, a replacement for the mill purchased from Judson Steel at Emeryville, California. At the time of its purchase, Birmingham agreed to close the facility within ten years. The new mill at Phoenix will be within 300 miles of Los Angeles and will serve the southern California market. It will add to Birmingham's capacity, since the Emeryville plant is capable of producing some 200,000 tons.

North Star. North Star Steel Corporation, a subsidiary of Cargill, entered the steel business in 1974. The first plant acquired was North Star Steel Company of Minneapolis, owned jointly by Cargill and Co-Steel Company of Canada. Since that time, Cargill, through North Star, has acquired six additional plants with a total steelmaking capacity of approximately 2.5 million tons.

At North Star's plant in Youngstown, a seamless-pipe mill capable of producing 300,000 tons has been installed. Finishing facilities for this plant have been purchased in Texas.

The company has given serious consideration to entering flat-rolled products production. There is a possibility it may follow Nucor's lead and install a thin-slab caster and rolling mill; however, the entrance will be delayed until the picture at Nucor is clarified. If such a course is followed, the plant will not depend on 100 percent scrap but will use a portion of direct-reduced iron in its electric furnace charge.

In the 1990s, minimills in the United States will add some capacity. Nucor, with its two new plants, has already increased capacity by 1.5 million to 1.6 million tons. Further, it has already placed an order for engineering to build a second sheet mill with a thin-slab caster. This will probably have a capacity for 1.5 million to 2.0 million tons. Some other mills will increase their output by replacing the currently operating electric furnaces with those that are somewhat larger.

There has been considerable speculation on just how many minimills will undertake flat-rolled-product production. The amount of activity in this area will depend on the success of Nucor's operation, as well as the ability of small companies to raise the large amounts of money needed—probably close to $300 million. Further, there is a question as to whether the market needs additional capacity for this type of flat-rolled product.

An announcement has been made by a group of companies to install a 300,000-ton special-quality bar mill in the Johnstown, Pennsylvania, area. The companies involved include North Star Steel and C. Itoh, a Japanese trading company. In addition to producing steel, the company, through two co-generation plants, plans to produce electricity, which will be sold to a utility. The investment is approximately $500 million.

The growth in minimills, much of which has taken place in the 1970s and early 1980s, was based, in part, on the abandonment by the integrated companies of such products as concrete reinforcing bars, small structural members, and later wire rods. There is extensive capacity in some of these areas, and as a consequence, minimills are looking elsewhere to develop business. This accounts, to some extent, for the recent foray into sheets, wide-flange beams, and seamless pipe, all of which involve a considerable investment. Another area that minimills are operating in is that of special-quality bars. This does not involve a large investment, since many of their bar mills are capable of producing the special-quality product.

In the traditional minimill products, there is, at the present time, an overcapacity, and minimills more than ever are faced with competition for these products that is more intensive than it has been for most of their history. Faced with these conditions and the lack of abundant funds, many of the mills, incapable of moving into other product lines, are forced to compete actively with each other. The situation was stated succinctly by

Robert Garvey, President of North Star Steel Company, which operates some seven minimills. He stated, "Minimills today are confronted by the same problem that the integrated mills have faced throughout the 1980s—excess capacity in their basic product lines."[8]

Some minimills will grow during the 1990s, and a limited number will be added. However, for the most part, they must concentrate on reducing costs and improving quality to stay competitive in their product lines.

Canada

The Canadian steel industry has a capacity to produce 18 million tons of raw steel. This was reduced from 21 million tons when Stelco closed its open-hearth shop in the late 1980s. The industry consists of two fully integrated companies and several electric furnace operations, a number of them classified as minimills.

There were three integrated companies until 1988: Stelco, at that time the largest, Dofasco, and Algoma. In 1988, Algoma and Dofasco were merged, leaving two integrated entities. As a result of the merger, Dofasco/Algoma is now the larger of the two, with Stelco maintaining a capacity of somewhat over 5 million tons and the combined Dofasco/Algoma unit with 7.5 million tons. There are two medium-sized companies that are not considered minimills. One is Sydney Steel in Nova Scotia, which was at one time an integrated mill but within the last decade has been transformed into an electric furnace operation with less than 1 million tons, producing rails and billets. The other is Sidbec-Dosco, located near Montreal, producing flat-rolled products from electric furnace steel made from direct-reduced iron rather than scrap. It has a capacity to produce approximately 1.4 million tons.

In the minimill sector of the industry, there are eight companies that produce steel as well as rolled, finished products. These are principally long products, although Ipsco is predominantly a pipe producer and Atlas a specialty steel producer. Lake Ontario Steel, also known as Lasco, has a capacity to produce more than 1 million tons of long products.

The integrated companies are well provided with raw materials since Canada produces substantial amounts of ore and has coal available from mines in the United States in which the companies have an ownership share. In addition, Stelco has a significant ownership share in iron ore mines in the United States.

The Canadian industry has been quite profitable with the exception of one or two years during the postwar period. Dofasco has the enviable record of continual profits without a loss during the steel depression of the late 1970s and early to mid-1980s.

Much has been done to improve the steel facilities in both the integrated sector and a number of minimills. Current plans call for large expenditures, principally to upgrade facilities, which will improve quality, reduce costs, and increase productivity. Little or no consideration is given to expanding capacity.

Stelco

Stelco reduced its capacity to 5 million tons with the closure of its open-hearth shop at the Hilton works in Hamilton, Ontario. The company feels that this is an optimum tonnage that can be marketed profitably under most economic conditions. The integrated plant, constructed during the 1970s at Nanticoke, Ontario, on the north shore of Lake Erie, will represent the last expansion of Stelco for many years to come. The management feels that the facilities now in place are up to date and will permit plants to be competitive on a domestic and international basis for the 1990s.

The company will concentrate on downstream activities where it has invested considerable money in finishing facilities and also in joint ventures with other companies. One example is Jannock Steel, a fabricating company, owned 50 percent by Stelco. In addition, considerable attention is being given to developing products with value-added. Most of these are steel connected, such as Molylop of Canada, which is a joint venture with Armco producing a variety of heat-treated, grinding balls for the mining industry. Another partnership with Armco, ME International, produces high-chrome grinding balls and the consumerable-wear parts for the mineral industry. One venture into nonsteel operations is a connection with Cautex of Canada, a plastic manufacturer, which produces plastic gasoline tanks for automobiles. Stelco shares its ownership equally with Cautex Werke of Bonn, Germany.

The management feels it is necessary to become North American rather than just Canadian, so it will have partners in various joint ventures in the United States and also own some operations 100 percent. Recently Stelco purchased 40 percent of Bliss Laughlin, a producer of bars. The company is also engaged in a joint venture with Mitsubishi of Japan on a 350,000-ton hot-dipped galvanizing line.

Dofasco

Dofasco, which in 1988 was the second largest integrated company in Canada, acquired Algoma, the third largest company, to become the leading producer in Canada, with some 7.5 million tons of raw steel capacity. During the next few years, the company has extensive plans for modernization through the replacement of facilities, as well as the installation of new downstream facilities, particularly galvanizing lines.

One of the major projects is the replacement of the cold-reduction facilities at Hamilton, which will involve a new cold-reduction mill as well as a new pickle line and possibly a continuous annealing line. The facility will be completed in 1992. Considerable investment will be made in upgrading the steelmaking facilities at Algoma, as well as at Hamilton, although the Algoma upgrading will be more extensive.

There are two joint ventures in galvanizing: one with Sidbec-Dosco for a 125,000-ton hot-dipped unit and one with National Steel and NKK for a 350,000-ton unit, which will be located somewhere between Detroit and Hamilton.

In terms of raw materials, Dofasco shut its Adams and Sherman mines in early 1990. These facilities will be replaced with a 50 percent ownership in Quebec-Cartier, which was purchased from United States Steel. Dofasco purchased the entire operation but then sold 50 percent off to Caemi of Brazil and Mitsui of Japan.

There is no intention of increasing the melting capacity of the Dofasco/Algoma complex. The effort is on improving quality and increasing productivity to reduce costs.

Sydney Steel

Sydney Steel in Nova Scotia has been recently restructured and is now an electric furnace operation (in the 1970s and 1980s, it was a blast furnace–open-hearth operation). Current capacity is approximately 350,000 tons which is turned into rails and billets. There is a move underway to privatize the company.

Sidbec-Dosco

Sidbec-Dosco, located near Montreal, is an electric furnace operation based on direct-reduced iron. It has a capacity of 1.4 million net tons and produces flat-rolled products. Its direct-reduced iron unit is one of the most effective in the world.

Other Units

Among the other producing units that are minimills, two stand out: Lake Ontario Steel, or Lasco, part of Co Steel, which is an efficient plant with a million-ton capacity to produce long products, and Ipsco, located in western Canada, with approximately 750,000 tons, most of it converted to large-diameter welded pipe.

Sammi Steel Company of South Korea has recently acquired two special steelmaking facilities in Canada: Atlas Stainless Steel in Quebec and Atlas Specialty Steel in Ontario.

Very little, if any, new capacity will be installed by the Canadian industry, although some minimill capacity might be expanded.

Japan

There is some difficulty in establishing a reasonably accurate figure for Japanese steel capacity because of a number of developments that took place between 1986 and 1989. In 1986, for the first time in three years, Japanese crude-steel production fell below 100 million tonnes. In assessing the situation, there was considerable concern about the future of the industry and what measures should be taken. The problem was stated in the 1987 report of the Japan Iron and Steel Federation:

> The year 1986 was an extremely difficult one for the Japanese steel industry. The sharp appreciation of the yen, triggered by the G-5 meeting in September 1985, brought about significant decreases in both direct and indirect exports of steel. This development, coupled with steel demand stagnation both at home and abroad and increasing steel imports into the Japanese market, accelerated the slump in steel production. Consequently, crude steel output in 1986 dropped by 6.7% from the previous year, to 98.28 million tons, coming in below the 100-million-tonne mark for the first time in three years.
>
> The steel companies thus ran into the red. To cope with their difficult situation, they began to implement several measures, including partially paid leaves for personnel in production and administrative departments, consolidating production facilities, and reorganizing steel mills.
>
> Under these circumstances, the steelmakers are compelled to urgently address a number of issues: practicing thorough rationalization in every area of activity, pushing technological innovation, expanding operations in new fields of business, improving financial bases, and promoting tie-ups with overseas steel companies.[9]

In addition, there was a need "to implement radical new business strategies."[10]

When steel operations declined in 1986 and early 1987, a projection made from a survey of the steel market, both domestic and foreign, concluded that raw-steel output by 1990 would drop to approximately 90 million tonnes. The domestic market in Japan had fallen from a high of 55 million tonnes in 1980 to 49 million in 1986, and it was evident that exports in 1987 were going to decline significantly. In fact, by the year's end, they had dropped to a fourteen-year low of 25.7 million tonnes—appreciably below the 30 million or more that had been exported since the 1970s. The reasons for this decline in exports included the development of the steel industry in the Third World, restrictions put on Japanese imports by a number of other countries in the industrialized world, and the appreciation of the yen.

In 1987, exports to the Third World declined. This was particularly true of China, where they fell from 9.2 million tonnes in 1986 to 5.8 million in 1987. Further, reduced amounts of steel were exported to countries such as the United States, where the figure fell to less than 5 million tonnes in three successive years. In addition, imports increased to 5 million tonnes in 1987. This was in sharp contrast to the 1970s, when they amounted to an average of 200,000 tonnes per year. It is interesting to note that in 1976, when Japan exported a record-high 37 million tonnes, imports amounted to 150,000 tonnes.

In the late 1980s, imports had increased from South Korea, Taiwan, and Brazil, and in the 1990s, they are expected to grow further. However, it should be noted that although Japanese exports have declined while imports have increased, imports were in the lower grades of steel, but exports were among the higher-priced, higher-quality items.

By mid-1987, drastic measures were proposed to cope with the expected drop in steel production to 90 million tonnes. This appeared to be virtually certain when the production figures for 1986 and, particularly, early 1987 were examined.

The decline that took place in late 1986 was accentuated in early 1987. In the first quarter of the year, a total of 23 million tonnes was produced, which would indicate 92 million tonnes that year. However, measures taken by the government in both 1986 and 1987 resulted in a turnaround in the last few months of 1987 and brought steel production for that year up to 98.5 million tonnes. These measures, the first of which was instituted in September 1986, committed the government to an economic package involving the expenditure of 3,630 billion yen, the largest in Japanese history. The plan was announced on May 29, 1987, to be considered in the context of an emergency economic package for fiscal year 1987. This was expanded in July with the supplemental budget for fiscal year 1987 adopted by the national Diet.

The emergency economic package was created to help Japan to break out of its existing pattern of export-oriented growth and to accelerate domestic growth. It was made up to two components: 1.5 trillion yen for tax reduction and 4.5 trillion yen for various public-works expenditures. This began to have its effect in late 1987 and continued into 1988, when it reversed the decline in raw-steel output.

In 1988, raw-steel production rose to 105.7 million tonnes. In 1989, the upward trend continued, reaching 108 million tonnes. All of this created an atmosphere of optimism, and many of the plans that were made in 1987 to reduce capacity and employment in the major steel companies were put on hold. In some cases, it was stated that the increase in raw-steel output in 1988 and 1989 was a temporary phenomenon and the drop to 90 million tonnes would occur by 1992 or 1993; thus, the plans for retrenchment were not completely abandoned but postponed. It is interesting to examine these plans, since many feel that they will shape the structure of the Japanese steel companies for most of the 1990s.

The current capacity that exists in Japan and was needed to allow the production of 108 million tonnes has been estimated at between 120 million and 125 million tonnes. The forecast for the reduced output in the early 1990s, which still persists in some quarters, calls for a drastic cut in work force: approximately one-third of the personnel in the integrated companies. It is expected now that this may be achieved by 1992 or, at the latest, 1993. Some of the proposed cuts, which were to take place by 1990, have been delayed since manpower was necessary to produce the 108 million tonnes.

Many of the closures and decommissionings scheduled for 1990 have been postponed and will not be put into effect until the early 1990s.

The boom in steel was caused in part by very heavy active domestic demand, which consumed almost 60 million tonnes in 1988 and over 60 million in 1989. Prices at home and abroad were increased, which was particularly true of exports in the last half of 1988. For example, the price of rails shipped to the United States was increased by $110 per tonne. Plate shipments to the Soviet Union were increased by $40 per tonne, the price of plates to Iran was upgraded by $20 a tonne, and there was a $30 a tonne markup on cold-rolled sheets to Southeast Asia. A number of products were sold for prices in excess of $600 a tonne. Total exports in 1988 fell below the 1987 figure to 23.65 million tonnes; however, the value increased to $16 billion. Thus, in spite of the drop in volume of exports, the value increased by almost $3 billion. The average price per tonne for exports rose to $680, exceeding the 1987 figure by $169.

In 1989, exports fell to 20.2 million tonnes, while imports increased considerably, with the principal suppliers being South Korea, Brazil, and Taiwan. These three sources accounted for 3.8 million tonnes.

As for the future of the Japanese steel industry, a review of the plans drawn up by the integrated companies indicates the position that each expects to occupy during the coming decade, as well as the degree of emphasis to be placed on the diversity of operations. As a consequence, a significant portion of each company's income will be represented by nonsteel operations, for it is interesting to note that all of the major integrated companies are expected to diversify to a point where steel will represent approximately 50 percent of their income. Further, each of the six major integrated companies has entered into significant joint ventures with steel companies in other countries. In addition, aggregate investment for the major producers will range between $4 billion and $5 billion a year for the early 1990s.

Nippon Steel

Nippon Steel, the largest producer in the world, has eight ironmaking and steelmaking plants. By 1991, according to the rationalization plan, the conventional iron and steelmaking facilities of four of these plants will be abandoned, but the finishing facilities will be kept in operation. Production will continue at the other four, and semifinished steel will be provided to those where facilities have been closed. At two of the plants slated for closure, Muroran and Hirohata, the oxygen facilities will be used to melt scrap so that steel production on a limited basis will continue. At Muroran, production will range between 800,000 and 900,000 tonnes a year, and at Hirohata, it will be approximately 500,000 tonnes. The plant at Muroran will, in great part, be devoted to the production of alloy specialty steel bars. It will be augmented by a joint venture with Mitsubishi for the production of specialty steel.

When the blast furnace at Hirohata is closed, in addition to its limited steelmaking capacity, some 800,000 tonnes of slabs or hot bands will be received from Oita, so that the hot-strip mill and the cold-reduction mill will continue to operate, producing between 1.2 million and 1.4 million tonnes.[11]

With the boom in steel demand in 1988 and 1989, these plans were altered somewhat. The blast furnace at Muroran will be kept in operation until the end of 1990, when it is scheduled for closure. And the blast furnace at Hirohata, scheduled for closure in June 1989, has been given a reprieve and will operate at least until the end of 1990.

Another blast furnace at Sakai was to be shut down in March 1989. Its life was extended to the second quarter of 1990, since the output of Nippon in 1989 was almost 20 percent higher than originally expected, thus leading to the temporary postponement in closing facilities.

When the furnace is shut down, the plant will produce structural shapes with blooms obtained from Oita. The blast furnace at the Kamaishi Works has been shut down. This plant now produces wire rods with billets from Kimitsu.

When the rationalization plans are ultimately carried out, Nippon will reduce its steelmaking capacity to 26 million to 27 million tonnes of raw steel. In any year when more than that is needed, it will be obtained by adding more scrap to the basic-oxygen steelmaking furnace charge. Currently scrap is limited to 7 or 8 percent of the charge, and it is felt that by increasing the percentage of scrap in each heat, the hot metal can be spread over more heats and will result in a larger raw-steel output. The 26 million to 27 million tonnes of steelmaking potential Nippon will have in the 1990s is commensurate with its output of 27.2 million tonnes for the fiscal year ending March 1988. In 1989, the strong demand pushed Nippon's output to 28.3 million tonnes, which is higher than the contemplated capacity under the reorganization plan. Nippon's planned reduction in capacity is dramatic when one considers that in the mid-1970s, after the construction of the Oita works, the company had a steelmaking potential of over 45 million tonnes.

In the future Nippon will rely heavily on the research in iron smelting currently being conducted through a joint effort of the five integrated steel producers. If it is successful, the new process will replace a number of coke ovens and blast furnaces that would have to be renewed within the next ten years. It is hoped that by that time the new smelting process can be applied, and very little reconstruction of coke ovens will be needed. The 1987 Nippon Annual Report states the objective for the 1990s:

> With a time of fundamental change in Japan's industrial structure, in world markets and in technology, Nippon Steel has made multiple-business management the centerpiece of its corporate strategy. Key aspects of this approach are already moving toward fulfillment: streamlining of the company's steelmaking operations as well as business expansion into other promising fields in which its R&D capabilities, human resources and expertise can make Nippon Steel a dynamic competitor.
>
> Steelmaking is now and will remain the company's core, maintaining cutting-edge technologies and competitive operations. As the world's leading steelmaker, Nippon Steel is a full-range supplier of quality steel products and of chemical products. On the way to becoming a full-range supplier of key industrial materials, the company now offers titanium products as well and has entered full-scale business in new materials fields.
>
> Fitting well into Nippon Steel's multiple-business management strategy is its recognized strength in engineering. The company is a world-ranking firm in plant and machinery supply and technical cooperation, civil engineering and marine construction, building construction and urban development.
>
> To gain the additional flexibility that is needed in today's business environment, Nippon Steel's entry into the dynamic fields of electronic equipment, information and communication systems, and telecommunications is backed by a long history of computer applications and software development to meet the company's own needs. And now Nippon Steel is becoming active in a range of businesses in the fast-expanding services sector and in biotechnology fields.[12]

By the mid-1990s, Nippon expects to have only 50 percent of its revenues from steel.

A plan is in operation to reduce the number of employees at the steel mills by 19,000, many of whom will be placed with other companies controlled by Nippon that are not in the steel business. This placement may not initially result in the most efficient operation, but Nippon considers itself responsible to provide employment for many of the displaced workers and considers this cost a legitimate social one. In terms of additional facilities, Nippon will add two galvanizing lines, both hot dipped, and will install continuous annealing as well as pickling at Kimitsu.

In terms of new product development, work is being done on composites of steel and plastics, such as sandwich sheets with a plastic sandwiched between two sheets of steel. Currently, 10 percent of Nippon's income is from chemicals, 10 percent from engineering, and 10 percent from computer and electronic operations. In 1989, capital investment was $1.1 billion in steel and $250 million in other items, as well as $125 million in development. These investments will continue at this rate for a few years. At Kimitsu, as well as at Nagoya and Hirohata, there is a six-high, cold-reduction mill. These facilities put the company on the cutting edge of technology and allow it to produce a superior sheet.

Nippon has engaged in foreign joint ventures, two of them in the United States formed with Inland Steel. The first involved the construction of a six-high, cold-reduction mill, complete with cleaning, continuous annealing, and temper-rolling facilities, for a total investment of somewhat over $400 million, with Nippon contributing $60 million, Inland $90 million, and three Japanese trading companies $250 million. Nippon has the right to purchase 20 percent of the output.

A second joint venture with Inland Steel involves the construction of two galvanizing lines, one hot dipped and one electrolytic, with a total capacity of 900,000 tonnes. This required an investment of over $450 million, with Nippon and Inland contributing $60 million each and the remainder furnished in the form of a loan from the Industrial Bank of Japan. As a consequence of these ventures, Nippon purchased 13 percent of the voting rights in Inland Steel for $185 million. This added to the previous 1 percent gives Nippon a substantial share in Inland Steel Company.[13]

NKK, Inc.

NKK, Inc. has two integrated steel plants, one at Fukuyama and the other at Ogishima. At its peak, the company had a total capacity of some 22 million tonnes of raw steel, 16 million of which were at Fukuyama, the largest pant in the world in the late 1970s. Ogishima is the newest plant in Japan; it was built in 1975 with a rated capacity of 6 million tonnes. With the downward revision made in Japan's steel capacity, both plants have been reduced in size, so that the total is 12 million tonnes.

Future investments by NKK in steel facilities will be designed to reduce the costs of producing carbon steel and increase the production of high-quality steel.

In June 1988, NKK issued a release outlining its future plans. Of significance was the fact that its corporate name is now NKK, Inc. rather than Nippon Kokan. Its new goal was cited, which would carry the company into the twenty-first century. The business structure in the late 1990s will be 50 percent steelmaking, 25 percent engineering, 12.5 percent integrated community development, and 12.5 percent for advanced materials, electronics, and biotechnology. It is stated emphatically that the main business will be steelmaking; however, the company will continue to explore new business opportunities and expand into fundamental technology areas, such as electronics, advanced materials, and biotechnology.

NKK has developed a process of continuous annealing, which, although expensive, is an in-line operation for which many advantages are claimed over the batch annealing process:

1. All five of the steps required by the conventional annealing process are incorporated in a single line, reducing both construction costs and installation space.

2. Production time is greatly reduced from the ten days required by the conventional process to less than ten minutes.

3. Substantial labor savings can be achieved during processing.

4. Both overaging and the overall length of the line are reduced through the adoption of a rapid water cooling system.

5. Coil handling is minimized, and so are scrap losses. This results in improved product yield.

6. It is possible to produce economically various types of grades of high-quality cold-rolled sheets and strip ranging from drawing quality to high-strength steel.[14]

The technology has been installed at a number of plants throughout the world, including Usinor in France and Bethlehem Steel, Inland Steel, and LTV Steel in the United States.

In the early 1990s, the company is considering installing three galvanizing lines. Both hot-dipped and electrolytic units are planned, since the automobile companies in Japan have different preferences. Toyota leans toward hot dipped, while Nissan prefers electrolytic. Further, the No. 1 hot-strip mill at Fukuyama, as well as the cold-reduction mill, will be rebuilt and upgraded.

In terms of steel production, NKK's current 12-million-tonne capacity will remain intact, since it is estimated by some that, by the year 2000, Japanese annual crude steel output will be 85 million to 90 million tonnes. Of the tonnes projected, NKK expects to produce 9 million to 10 million tonnes. There is no thought of increasing capacity.

In keeping with the reduction in capacity, NKK plans to cut back its work force by 6,000 employees, or one-third, from a high of 19,000 at the end of 1986 to 13,000.

Kawasaki Steel Corporation

Kawasaki operates two integrated plants for the production of raw steel and its products: Chiba in the Tokyo area and Mizushima. In the mid-1980s, the capacity to produce raw steel at Mizushima was 12 million tonnes, and that of Chiba was 8.5 million. The recent decline in the steel market has necessitated a reduction in the steelmaking capacity of each of these plants. Chiba has been reduced to 4 million tonnes, and Mizushima, the most recent installation of Kawasaki, has an estimated capacity of some 11 million tonnes. If production falls in the 1990s, the plant will produce some 7 million tonnes, all of which will be continuously cast.

Kawasaki has diversified its operations, so that by the late 1990s, 40 percent of its revenue will come from nonsteel functions. The company has reduced its work force from 19,000 to 14,000.

Kawasaki has made considerable investments in other countries. It owns 5.5 percent of the Tubarao plant in Brazil, which produces 3 million tons of semifinished slabs annually. It also owns 50 percent of California Steel, located at Fontana, California. This company operates on purchased slabs, some 600,000 of which come from the Tubarao plant. In 1989, Kawasaki purchased 40 percent of Armco's carbon steel operation, thus increasing its presence in the United States significantly. In July 1990, its participation was increased to 45 percent.

At Mizushima, an electrolytic galvanizing line will be added, as well as another caster. At Chiba, a hot-dipped galvanizing line will be added, and three cold-reduction mills will be reduced to two with the same capacity. Chiba will modernize the hot-strip mill installed in 1957, as well as steelmaking and casting. Its production will be pretty much confined to sheets, whereas Mizushima will be 70 percent sheets, 10 percent pipe, 10 percent shapes, and 6–7 percent plates, as well as some rods.

Kawasaki's sales currently come 10 percent from engineering construction, 5 percent from chemicals, 1 percent from electronics, and 84 percent from steel. In the recent past, 45 percent of output came from the Chiba mill, with 55 percent from Mizushima. By the year 2000, this will be changed so that 30 percent will come from Chiba and 70 percent from Mizushima.

Sumitomo

Sumitomo has three integrated plants, producing raw steel and finished products: Wakayama, Kashima, and Kokura. Kashima is the largest, with a capacity to produce 10.2 million tonnes of raw steel, although it is expected that production at this plant will decline to between 5.5 million and 6.0 million tonnes in the early 1990s. Ninety-seven percent of the steel will be continuously cast.

Wakayama has five blast furnaces: one has been abandoned, two are in operation, and two are in standby condition. In the steelmaking division, there are three LD shops: No. 1, with 4.5 million tonnes of capacity has been shut down; No. 2, with 4.6 million tonnes, is operating; and No. 3 is held in standby.

Kokura is the smallest plant; in the early 1980s, it had a nominal capacity of approximately 2 million tonnes of raw steel. In 1987, Sumitomo considered closing the ironmaking and steelmaking facilities at the Kokura plant, but this possibility has been dropped, at least for the near future.

Sumitomo has no plans for a drastic cut in capacity. The overall plan is to emphasize quality and more value-added so that exported products can bring as much as $600 per tonne.

Sumitomo had a capital structure with 90 percent debt and 10 percent equity. Consequently it had a high interest cost, which it reduced; now the company's debt is 74 percent and equity is 26 percent. Income from nonsteel operations is approximately 8 percent, with an immediate target of 20–25 percent, which will include electronics, computer systems, plant engineering, construction engineering, and medical operations. As is the case with the other integrated steel companies, Sumitomo plans to obtain 40–50 percent of its income in the coming decade from nonsteel activities.

If total Japanese output of raw steel is reduced to 90 million tonnes, Sumitomo expects its share of 10 million tonnes to be profitable. In keeping with the reduction in steel output, the personnel at Sumitomo in its steel operations have been reduced from 25,000 to 19,000.

In terms of new facilities, a hot-dipped galvanizing line will be added with a 360,000-tonne capacity. In order to provide more cold-reduced sheets for an expanding galvanized operation, Sumitomo plans to install a tandem cold-reduction mill with a 1.2-million-tonne per year capacity, located at its Kashima works. There are two new galvanizing lines, one of which will be installed at Kashima with 350,000 tonnes of capacity to go into operation in 1992. The new cold-rolled mill should be in operation at approximately that time.[15]

In the United States, another electrolytic galvanizing line will be added to one already installed in conjunction with LTV Steel.

In 1989 Sumitomo's capital budget was about $1 billion. In 1990, it will be approximately $800 million, which will be spent for galvanizing lines, modernizing the cold mill, rebuilding blast furnaces, and modernizing a bar mill. In the very recent past, the hot-strip mill has been improved so that the crown in the center of the sheet has been considerably reduced. The company will also install continuous annealing and increased coal injection at the blast furnace.

Kobe Steel

Kobe Steel's total production in the early 1990s, should the entire steel market in Japan decline, will be in the area of 6 million tons. Currently 50 percent of the company's revenues are from nonsteel areas, and it is planned that this will be increased to 60 percent in the early 1990s.

The company is interested in developing its downstream facilities, such as coating and electrolytic galvanizing lines, as well as hot-dipped galvanizing facilities. Its integrated steel plants feature ladle furnaces, which improve the quality of the steel. At present, there is coal injection at the blast furnaces, consisting of about 50 kilograms per tonne of iron produced. This is necessitated by a coke shortage. Coal injection at the blast furnaces at both plants will be increased to 100 kilograms (200 pounds).

In terms of future investment, a continuous caster will have to be replaced, and if additional steel should be required in any particular year, its production will be achieved by adding more scrap to the LD charge.

The Amagasaki works has been closed down completely, eliminating the blast furnace and steelmaking capacity in accordance with the plan for restructuring the steel industry. At Kobe works, there are two blast furnaces—one in operation and the second idle. The main operations in this plant are the rod mill and bar mill. At Kakogawa, there are two blast furnaces in operation; a third is out. Total steelmaking capacity for the two plants is 8.9 million tonnes.

At Kakogawa, a new continuous-slab caster for slabs for plates, as well as sheets, will replace an existing one. The hot-strip mill will have its capacity increased by adding two roughing stands and improving the heating furnace. One hot-dipped galvanizing line under construction at Kakogawa will be added to two electrolytic lines and one hot-dipped line.

Kobe Steel is reasonably in line with environmental regulations so that no large amount of investment is needed.

Kobe is very much interested in the production of aluminum sheets, which are used for beer cans and, to some extent, in the automotive industry. It is also the largest producer of titanium in Japan.

Capital investment is placed in three categories: that which will take place in the next three years; that which will take place by 1995, which is referred to as the target; and that, referred to as the vision, which includes investment to the year 2000. Fifty percent of the capital investment will be in steel, and the total investment will be in excess of depreciation. Capital expenditures from March 1989 to April 1990 were $670 million, of which $430 million were for steel facilities. In the succeeding year—April 1990 to

March 1991—total expenditures will be $940 million, of which $740 million will be for steel facilities.

In keeping with the reduction in steelmaking capacity, the company will cut its work force in the next two years to 22,000 employees from the 28,000 level of 1988.

In 1989, Kobe entered into a joint venture with United States Steel, whereby the Lorain, Ohio, integrated steel plant of United States Steel was set aside as a new company with 50 percent ownership by Kobe and 50 percent by United States Steel. The object is to make high-quality bars for the transplanted Japanese automobile plants in the United States.

A second joint venture will consist of a hot-dipped galvanizing line with a 600,000-tonne capacity. Again, it is designed to serve the Japanese transplants and will be located in Ohio.

Nisshin

Nisshin Steel, the sixth largest integrated steel company in Japan, was formed in 1959 through the merger of Nichia Steel and Nihonteppan. It became an integrated steel company in 1962 when a blast furnace was installed at the Kure Works. Subsequently, another blast furnace was added, and the ironmaking and steelmaking capacity increased. Iron production for 1988 stood at 3.041 million tonnes, raw-steel production was 3.448 million, and finished products shipped amounted to 3.150 million tonnes, showing an exceptionally high yield.

Nisshin is rightfully called a specialty steel company, particularly when one considers the makeup of its production. In 1988, coated-steel products amounted to 40 percent, stainless steel 29 percent, special steel 10 percent, and ordinary hot- and cold-rolled steel 22 percent. Nisshin is over-whelmingly a flat-rolled producer in all of these categories. In 1988, in terms of yen sales, ordinary hot- and cold-rolled steel constituted 19 percent, as opposed to 81 percent for the other three categories; the largest was coated steel at 45 percent.

Nisshin has two plants at which steel is made: the Kure Works, a fully integrated plant with two blast furnaces and three oxygen converters, as well as two continuous-casting machines and a hot-strip mill, and Shunan Works, an electric steelmaking plant with seven furnaces of varying sizes, ranging from 6.5 tonnes per heat to 40 tonnes. It produces electric furnace steel, which is continuously cast, and its final product is cold-rolled sheets of various types. There are four other plants, which are strictly finishing mills with a number of coating lines including zinc, aluminum, and copper.

Nisshin has invested many millions of dollars in capital improvements aimed principally at upgrading quality and productivity and reducing costs. The 1988 *Annual Report* states, "In fiscal 1988, the company began con-

Table 2–2
Percentage of Total Exports to Various Countries,
1986 and 1988

Southeast Asia	44.0	56.8
China	14.5	11.2
Middle East	12.7	6.9
Europe	4.3	5.3
North America	13.1	12.5
Latin America	2.9	1.9
Australia	2.8	1.9
All other	5.7	3.5

Source: Misshim Steel Annual Report, 1988, p.10.

centrating on the implementation of investments related to cost reductions, energy conservation, and other rationalization measures. Therefore, capital investment for the period was on a relatively small scale, totaling Y12.2 billion ($96.9 million)."[16] For the next few years, the capital investment of Nisshin Steel will continue along the same lines. Attention will be given to reducing energy costs, thus far carried out by the injection of pulverized coal into the blast furnace.

Exports of Nisshin Steel are worldwide, although the percentage shifted somewhat in 1988 as prices in Southeastern Asia improved (table 2–2).

Nisshin Steel intends to reduce its work force during the next few years but maintain its capacity at about the current level, which varies between 3.5 million and 4.0 million tonnes.

Nisshin has modernized its hot-strip mill by putting in two six-high stands in the finishing train. This places it among the very few mills in the world so equipped.

In terms of overseas activity, Nisshin has a joint venture with Wheeling-Pittsburgh Steel Company in the United States. This consists of a coating line in which Nisshin has a two-thirds interest. The company has also purchased a 10 percent interest in the Wheeling-Pittsburgh Steel Company.

There are two other integrated steel plants in Japan, Nayama Steel and Godo Steel. Both are quite small, with raw steel capacities of less than 2 million tonnes.

Electric Furnaces

The electric furnace segment of the Japanese steel industry consists of over fifty companies, many of them small with an average of 350,000 tonnes of capacity. Some ten companies have less than 200,000 tonnes, and three have capacities in excess of 1 million tonnes.

Tokyo Steel is the largest electric furnace producer with an output in 1989 of 3.4 million tonnes of raw steel, virtually the same as Nisshin Steel, an integrated producer. Other large producers include Daido, the leading specialty steelmaker, and Hichi, a newly formed company, the result of a merger between Toshin and Azuma, both subsidiaries of NKK, Inc. Hichi has a capacity of over 2 million tonnes, and as a result of the merger, some individual furnaces may be eliminated.

Another merger, which took place in early 1990, involved Kyoei Steel. Four related companies were incorporated into Kyoei Steel Limited. The new company has a raw-steel capacity of more than 2 million tonnes, which makes it Japan's fourth largest electric steel producer. It is an affiliate of Sumitomo Metal Industries.[17]

Another of the larger producers is Yamato, with approximately 600,000 tonnes. This company has entered into a joint venture with Nucor in the United States to produce wide-flange beams. The plant, recently put in operation in Arkansas, has a capacity of 650,000 tonnes.

There have been plans to restructure the electric furnace steel manufacturers as far back as 1978. The minimills were designated structurally depressed by the government, along with a number of other industries. In 1983, some 3.8 million tonnes of electric furnace capacity were marked for dismantlement. By 1988, however, only 2.1 million tonnes were scrapped, leaving 1.7 million tonnes still considered surplus. The current plan is not to scrap any of this capacity but to cut production, reducing the number of shifts. This was deemed necessary since many of the approximately fifty minimill companies have just one furnace, and scrapping it would put the company out of business.

There are several estimates of the electric furnace capacity in Japan, although all are quite similar. It seems that a figure of 30 million to 32 million tonnes is reasonable, and although there may be a reduction in production in the 1990s, capacity will remain virtually intact. If there is a reduction in total steel output to 90 million tonnes of raw steel, it is estimated that the electric furnace segment will contribute about one-third of the tonnage, or 30 million tonnes. The largest specialty steel producer, Daido, with a capacity of approximately 1.5 million tonnes, anticipates a 10 percent cut in production in the 1990s but no cut in capacity.

The largest electric furnace company in Japan, Tokyo Steel, with approximately a 3.6-million-tonne capacity, has made a decision to enter the flat-rolled products segment of the steel industry by installing a hot-strip mill with a capacity to produce 1 million tonnes per year at its Okayama plant in southern Honshu. The cost is approximately 40 billion yen ($300 million). The continuous caster to feed the mill will not be a thin-slab caster but a conventional caster producing thick slabs. (This is presupposed since the president of the company stated that only conventional technology will be employed, and the plant will contain nothing new.)

The project will require the construction of one additional electric furnace, as well as a slab caster and hot-strip mill. The strip mill will be 48 inches wide. The management stated, "We have no intention of competing against the major integrated mills in high-quality material for the automobile or electric appliance manufacturers. . . . Our customers will be mainly small consumers. We know our limits: we start from scrap recycling and this limits our business field."[18] The mill will compete with the lower-grade hot-rolled coils imported into Japan, which in 1988 represented 3 million tonnes. Tokyo Steel believes that by the time the mill is ready to start up in 1992, there will be enough scrap generated in Japan to satisfy its needs.

In 1989, a record 33 million tonnes of electric furnace steel were produced, of which 8.7 million were specialty steel and the remainder carbon steel. In the very early 1990s, many electric furnaces over fifteen years of age will be replaced since depreciation is limited to fourteen years. A number of these will switch to direct current (DC), particularly if the units now under construction, and recently in operation, prove to reduce costs.

There are two types of DC furnace systems, one developed by NKK and Topy Steel and the other by Nippon, Daido, and Usinor. Claims are made that there will be a reduction in electrode costs as well as power costs. Further, the Japanese electric steel operators have decided that the electric furnaces should produce 70-tonne heats to be effective economically, so many of the furnaces with less than 70 tonnes will be replaced by those that are over 70 tonnes.

The stainless steel segment of the electric furnace industry has grown significantly in the last four years. In 1985, it was 1.5 million tonnes chrome nickel and 679,000 tonnes chrome. By 1988, chrome nickel was 2 million tonnes and 777,000 chrome.

The quantity of scrap generated generally has been increasing. In 1987, it was 30.5 million tonnes and, in 1989, 34 million. This increase has made a decided change in imports. In 1983, they constituted 10.5 percent of electric furnace consumption and in 1988 4.3 percent. In order to improve scrap, two steps have been taken: to devise a new technique in melting to remove impurities and to improve screening by the use of mechanical devices in place of visual examination.

Although the Japanese steel industry is projected to shrink in size and to diversify, it will continue to be a dominant worldwide force. Current plans to modernize equipment and develop a process for ironmaking that will reduce its dependence on the blast furnace and coke ovens will help maintain its position during the 1990s and on into the next century.

There are no new integrated plants planned into the foreseeable future because of declining world demand. The Japanese, with the lack of land as well as the need to import almost all ore and coking coal, will continue to engage in joint ventures in other countries as they did in the late 1980s. Exports will be centered on steel products with a high value-added, a trend already evident. Thus, although the tonnage of exports will decline, the value received will remain high. The Japan Iron and Steel Federation states:

> The Japanese steelmakers have been pressing ahead with restructuring as an industrywide effort in accordance with their medium- and long-term forecasts of economic activity, implementing rationalization measures such as equipment consolidation and employment adjustment. These measures were continued in 1988, irrespective of the economic recovery. Furthermore, the steelmakers stepped up their moves to rise up to the challenge of the 21st century, making entries into such fields of business as urban development, biotechnology, information and telecommunications electronics. In their overseas advances, Japanese integrated steel mills formed joint ventures with U.S. steel companies—a step taken to respond to Japanese automakers' advances into North America.[19]

This restructuring and these adjustments will continue into the 1990s.

Western Europe

The EEC was organized in 1950 with six members: West Germany, France, Italy, Belgium, Luxembourg, and the Netherlands. In 1970, the United Kingdom, Ireland, and Denmark were added. Greece obtained admission in 1981. In 1983, Spain and Portugal petitioned for admission, which was granted in 1986. Thus, steel production in Western Europe had varied not only in terms of individual companies but also for the community in terms of the number of countries involved.

In 1974, the year of peak production, nine countries, exclusive of Greece, Spain, and Portugal, produced 155.6 million metric tonnes of crude steel. Since that time, production has been considerably lower, declining to 110 million tonnes in 1982 for the nine countries. With the addition of Spain, Portugal, and Greece, output for 1989 stood at 140.0 million tonnes, considerably below the 1979 figure of 154 million for the twelve countries. Much of the decrease in raw steel can be attributed to the sharp increase in continuous casting, which rose from approximately 32 percent in 1979 to 84 percent in 1988. The total amount of steel continuously cast was 115 million tonnes, as opposed to 43 million in 1979. With a higher yield from continuously cast steel, less raw steel is needed to satisfy finished product demand.

The drop in capacity of the EEC for the production of raw steel has been substantial when one takes into account that 30 million tonnes were closed down between 1980 and 1983. In 1987, the High Commission of the EEC called for an additional reduction in capacity of 30 million tonnes: 20 million, including plates, heavy structurals, and flat rolled, from the integrated mills and 10 million of long products of the minimill type. Late 1987 witnessed a revival in steel demand, particularly for light, flat-rolled products, so that the various companies and countries resisted the closure of strip mills for the production of sheets, although some plate mills and structural mills were shut down.

The EEC has been subject to significant fluctuations in its raw-steel output since 1974. Currently the amount of capacity seems to be much more in line with demand than it has been since 1974. However, a recent report of the EC High Commission indicates that there could be an overcapacity in plate and structural mills in the early 1990s.

A considerable investment involving billions of dollars has been made in the last few years, and more will be forthcoming in the years ahead, certainly through the mid-1990s. For the integrated companies, virtually all of the funds have and will be directed to improving quality, reducing costs, and increasing productivity. Virtually nothing has been or will be invested in expansion per se, particularly in view of the fact that the High Commission has called and is calling for a reduction in capacity.

Reductions in capacity were required of Spain to fulfill the conditions of its entrance into the Common Market. The capacity of the electric furnace segment in Spain, which at its peak stood at between 13 million and 14 million tonnes, is to be reduced to a maximum of 10 million tonnes. Much of this has already been carried out. The basic-oxygen segment, which is operated by the two integrated producers, Ensidesa and Altos Hornos de Viscaya, stands at 6.5 million to 7.0 million tonnes.

The steel industry throughout the Common Market underwent radical changes in the late 1980s that will affect future capacity and operations:

1. Privatization, which has developed into a trend in a number of countries, the most outstanding of which was the United Kingdom where British Steel was privatized in late 1988.

2. Mergers, which have taken place in both France and Germany, with the result in France of the formation of Usinor-Sacilor, the second largest steel company in the world.

3. Joint ventures, which abound and are continuing at a rapid rate. Almost every major company in Europe has entered into a joint venture, either with another steel company or with service centers, both domestically and internationally.

4. Acquisition of steel companies as well as steel service centers. Many of these arrangements are in the formation of joint ventures, although some involve complete absorption.

5. Structural changes of a technological or corporate nature. Perhaps the most significant is the complete restructuring of the major Italian steel company, whose name was changed from Italsider to Ilva.

6. Technological breakthroughs that have affected virtually every phase of steelmaking.

These changes will continue in many areas as the future plans of the steel companies in the European Community indicate.

United Kingdom

The most significant development in the United Kingdom was the privatization of British Steel, which took place from 1988 to 1989 after twenty-one years of state ownership. The privatization consisted of issuing 2 billion shares in November 1988 at 125 pence per share. These were entirely taken up, and thus the company passed out of government hands. The company at that time had some 17 million tonnes of capacity, 14 million of them in operation. The facilities included integrated plants at Port Talbot and Llanwern in Wales, Ravenscraig in Scotland, and Scunthorpe and Teeside in northeastern England, as well as a number of plants with electric furnace steel capacity and some that did not produce steel but formed it into various products, such as tinplate, pipe, and galvanized sheets.

During 1987 and 1988, British Steel was highly profitable, registering a net profit of £410 million for the fiscal year ending April 1988. As a consequence, it was able to finance major capacity improvements made in that year. Total investment in plant and equipment amounted to £253 million. The facilities included ladle furnaces at Teeside and Scunthorpe, provisions for injecting coal in the Ravenscraig blast furnaces, and the construction of a sinter plant at Scunthorpe. Capital invested in the facilities that have been completed and were under construction during fiscal year 1988 and 1989 amounted to £307 million.

In the future, major investments will be made in a plate mill, currently under consideration, although the site has not been chosen. Other projects include vacuum degassing and a hot-dipped galvanizing line at Llanwern, a coke oven rebuild at Scunthorpe, a second continuous-casting facility at Port Talbot and Llanwern, modernization of a universal beam mill at Teeside, and several blast furnace rebuilds.

The continuous caster at Llanwern will be installed at a cost of £83 million and will be in operation at the end of 1993. A press release in June

1990 concerning continuous casting stated, "This development, together with a similar investment currently under construction at Port Talbot Works, will enable the company's strip products division to take full advantage of the competitive facilities in its South Wales works." The Port Talbot casting machine will be commissioned at the beginning of 1991.

As part of the restructuring of the sheet division, the hot-strip mill at Ravenscraig will be closed during the first half of 1991. This is two years beyond the commitment date made in 1987, when it was announced that the Ravenscraig hot-strip mill would be kept in operation for two years. The entire situation at Ravenscraig will be reviewed after the closure of the strip mill. There has been considerable political discussion about Ravencraig's hot-strip mill since 1987, when it was declared surplus capacity.

With privatization came the desire to acquire facilities on the Continent in order to increase British Steel's activity there. After considerable negotiations, British Steel announced that it had reached an agreement with Klockner to purchase that company's Mannstaedt division, a major portion of which is located at Troisdorf near Cologne. This facility produces 200,000 tonnes annually of hot-rolled special sections and 120,000 tonnes of hollow and cold-formed sections from hot-rolled coil. In addition to the main plant, two small subsidiary companies fabricate mining arches. The purchase price was $180 million. The plant will ultimately be furnished with semifinished by British Steel and provides a significant outlet for British Steel on the Continent looking toward 1992.

British Steel also has been involved in negotiations for other facilities, particularly distribution outlets on the Continent. These were successful when British Steel acquired 35 percent to 40 percent of Aristrain, a major distribution center and minimill in Spain.

In 1989, total raw-steel output in the United Kingdom was 18.7 million tonnes, of which British Steel produced 14.2 million, or 76 percent. The remainder was produced by a number of companies operating electric furnaces, the largest of which was United Engineering Steels, which produced 2.3 million tonnes of raw-steel in its several plants. United Engineering Steels is owned 50 percent by British Steel, and between the two companies, they accounted for 85 percent of the United Kingdom's raw-steel output in 1989.

France

Usinor-Sacilor was formed in 1988 by a merger between Usinor and Sacilor, both government owned. Other facilities were subsequently added, so that the resultant entity accounted for more than 92 percent of the raw steel produced in France in 1989. In that year, the entire output of France was

19.3 million tonnes; the production of Usinor-Sacilor in France accounted for 17.9 million tonnes. Adding the production of 5 million tonnes at its facility in Germany brings the output of the entire complex to 23 million tonnes. This output placed the company second in terms of world raw-steel production, topped only by Nippon Steel of Japan.

The Usinor-Sacilor Corporation has five basic divisions: Sollac, which produces flat products; Unimetal, producing long products; Ugine, producing stainless steel, both flat and long products; a metallurgy division, which consists in great part of Creusot Loire; and a transformation and other activities division.

The principal plants under the jurisdiction of Sollac are Dunkirk, Fos on the Mediterranean, and Lorraine. The principal producer for Unimetal is also located in Lorraine. Stainless operations are at Ugine Savoie and L'Ardoise. Creusot Loire operates a plant with electric furnaces. In addition, there are two minimills that were operated as joint ventures with Riva Industries of Italy. A 66 percent interest was held by Riva; Usinor-Sacilor held the remaining 34 percent. In early 1990, this was sold to Riva, so that it now has 100 percent ownership of the minimill formerly operated jointly with Unimetal.

In addition to hot- and cold-rolled sheets, Sollac has a number of galvanizing lines located in its three main plants, as well as additional lines in smaller finishing units. The three hot-strip mills, located one each at the major integrated plants, have been equipped with the latest technology, including roll-bending and side-shifting equipment. Another development has been the injection of coal into the blast furnace at the Fos plant, reducing its dependence on coke.

In 1990 as well as the late 1980s, Usinor-Sacilor acquired a large number of companies—steel producers, specialty producers, and distribution outlets—either entirely or in part. It also entered into a number of joint ventures in several countries, including Germany, Belgium, Italy, Spain, the United States, Turkey, and the United Kingdom.

In Belgium, there is a joint venture in a bar mill with Arbed and Cockerill. In Italy, La Magona d'Italia was acquired in part. The company produced approximately 110,000 tonnes of tinplate, 200,000 tonnes of galvanized, and 250,000 tonnes of prepainted sheets. It is owned 50 percent by Lutrix, which sold 24.9 percent of its interest to Usinor-Sacilor and a similar amount to Ilva. In Spain, Usinor-Sacilor entered into an agreement with Ensidesa to work together in a number of areas, including the modernization of Ensidesa's coated-steel-production line. Usinor most probably will hold a 25 percent share and will supply steel from its Solmer plant in Fos to Ensidesa's plant at Sagunto on the Mediterranean.

In the United States, Usinor acquired a number of companies in whole or in part. It bought 50 percent of Georgetown Industries, a rod producer.

The venture involves technological assistance and information to be given by Usinor for the production of high-quality rods. In the specialty steel field, Usinor acquired J&L Specialty Steel, a spin-off from LTV. In addition, a number of distribution outlets were acquired.

In Italy, through its subsidiary Ugine, it has made a foray into the stainless steel market with the acquisition of three companies, which gives it 20 percent of the market. These include Alessio Tubi and an additional share in Terninoss, which, as a consequence, expands its share in Terninoss to 66 percent. Ugine also acquired Castek, a leading service center.[20] As of mid-1990, the company was negotiating with Falck of Italy for joint ventures in long products and wide strip. These discussions came to nought.

In Germany, in addition to the purchase of SaarStahl, it has entered into a joint venture with Thyssen and SMS to produce a thin-slab caster. Its holdings in Germany are so extensive that a large portion of its employment—over 20 percent—is currently in that country. Usinor's activities in acquisitions and joint ventures are unprecedented in extent. They also include a cold-reduction mill in Turkey in conjunction with Ilva, as well as some Turkish interests.

In the last few years, the company has moved up to become the second largest in the world steel industry, some 5 million tonnes behind Nippon Steel. Its attempt to acquire part ownership in LTV in the United States, which has some 10 million tons of steelmaking capacity, would move it into first place. (LTV, however, has a problem with a pension liability, and Usinor is not anxious to involve itself in this matter.) In the early 1990s, acquisitions will continue, as will facility upgrading, and it is estimated that some $500 million will be spent each year, principally by the Sollac and Unimetal divisions.

Usinor, whose growth has been by acquisition, was profitable in 1988 and 1989 and has had the funds to make these many acquisitions. It is a government-owned company that has not announced any plans for privatization.

West Germany

West Germany is by far the largest steel producer in the Common Market. Its major company, Thyssen, with 11.6 million tonnes of raw-steel production in 1989, ranks seventh among the world's steel producers. Unlike Britain and France, West Germany has a number of major steel producers, including Krupp with 4.6 million tonnes, Peine Salzgitter with 4.4 million, Hoesch with 4.1 million, Klockner with 3.6 million, and Mannesman with 3.6 million in 1989.

The German industry has reduced its steelmaking capacity from 55 million to 60 million tonnes at its peak in the mid-1970s to approximately

47 million tonnes in 1990. The principal company, Thyssen, cut back from 18 million to 19 million tonnes in the 1970s to 11 million to 12 million tonnes in 1990 by closing a number of its plants to bring capacity into more realistic alignment with demand.

Thyssen. Thyssen is a highly diversified company, with approximately 50 percent of its revenue coming from steel and the rest from other sources—engineering, trading, capital goods, manufacturing, and construction, which includes bridges and railroad car systems. In recent years, it has been involved in new transportation technologies, termed the Maglev System, which will produce revolutionary railroad cars.

In terms of developments for the future, the company is constructing a continuous hot-dipped galvanizing line as a joint venture with Hoogovens. The facility is to be located at Thyssen, where 75 percent of the output will remain, with 25 percent going to Hoogovens. In addition, a painting line will be built to go into operation in 1992. Thyssen is also developing laser welding of sheets, whereby coils will no longer be shipped to the automobile industry; they will be replaced by first operation blanks that will consist in part of sheets welded together, most likely of different quality and different thicknesses. The coating line's output will be principally for appliances. In addition, Thyssen, in partnership with SMS and Usinor, is developing a thin-slab caster, which will produce a 1-inch-thick slab. Currently a pilot plant is in operation. The speed of the caster, now 5 or 6 meters a minute, will be stepped up to 10 meters, and the exiting slab, which will be 1 inch thick, will be fed into the rolling mill without reheating, where it will be reduced in one pass. If this is successful, it will revolutionize the thin-slab casting process, as well as the rolling required to reduce the slab to a sheet. Since Thyssen has reduced its capacity from 18 million or 19 million tonnes to 11 million or 12 tonnes, there is no thought of increasing steel melting. The funds to be expended will be directed to projects to improve quality and productivity and to increase capacity in finished products.

In terms of capital investment, the 1989 Thyssen *Annual Report* states, "The capital invested in fixed assets by Thyssen WORLDWIDE in the year under review totaled DM 1,703 million." Of this amount, 1,393 million deutsche marks was invested in the Federal Republic of Germany. Expenditures for the next few years are expected to be in the same range.

Thyssen is engaged in a number of projects outside the country, one of which is a joint venture in Taiwan and South Africa for the production of stainless steel. A hot-strip mill will be erected in South Africa with Highveld and Samancor of South Africa and Yieh Loong of Taiwan as partners. The same group will also construct a cold-reduction mill in Taiwan to process the coils from the South African mill. The project is now in question.

In anticipation of the situation as it will exist in the EEC in 1992, Thyssen is moving into other countries in the EEC by acquiring distribution centers. For example, it has taken a 30 percent stake in the stockholder, Garfield Lewis, in the United Kingdom. This company specializes in the distribution of aluminum and stainless steel.[21] Thyssen has also formed a joint venture with a Spanish stockholder, Francisco Ros Casares, in which it will hold 50 percent of the capital. This will require the construction of a new service center facility. Ros Casares is a substantial distributor of steel with more than twenty outlets.[22] Thyssen in conjunction with Acinerox, a Spanish specialty steel producer, has acquired one-third of the Mexican stainless steel strip producer, Mexinox. Both Thyssen and Acinerox have one-third of the company, with the remaining third in the hands of the Mexicans. Mexinox is a cold roller of stainless and plans to install a melt shop.

Thyssen will continue to move aggressively into the worldwide picture. It already has outlets in the United States and Canada, where it has a series of service centers, in addition to ownership of the Budd Company, a producer of transportation equipment with sales in 1988–1989 of $1.5 billion. Thyssen's core business will remain steel, although it will continue to make acquisitions in other fields that appear attractive.

Klockner. One of the major German companies, Klockner has its principal plant in Bremen. The Klockner organization consists of two principal parts, the steel company and the trading company. A third part, dealing with engineering, has been divorced from the other two and is under the direction of Deutchbanke.

Klockner's future plans do not include any increase in steel production but rather an improvement in facilities to increase quality and productivity and reduce costs. It is upgrading the continuous caster at Bremen to allow it to produce a wider slab that can be rolled on its hot-strip mill, which is 90 inches wide, making it the widest mill in Europe. Another project that will help reduce costs is the expansion of the harbor facilities to accommodate larger iron ore carriers.

The company is also involved in a joint venture with Sidmar of Belgium to produce a hot-dipped galvanizing line, which will be located at Sidmar. A second hot-dipped line with a capacity of 350,000 tonnes annually will be installed at the Bremen plant. Recently Klockner agreed to sell its Mannstaedt division to British Steel for some $180 million. The plant produces special hot-rolled sections, as well as hollow cold-formed sections.[23]

Klockner will continue to supply the semifinished steel to this mill, although in the not-too-distant future, British Steel will take over the supply function.

Peine Salzgitter. In West Germany, the only government-owned plant was Peine Salzgitter. It was purchased by Preussag in 1989 and privatized. At one time Preussag was state owned but was privatized in the 1970s. Salzgitter is a shipbuilding and steelmaking operation, and its purchase by Preussag makes it part of a larger industrial organization with less dependence on steel. Both Preussag and Salzgitter are involved in the exploration and production of oil and gas and have active trading segments.

The steel operations are conducted by Peine Salzgitter and will be unaffected by the merger. Thus, it will remain one of West Germany's largest steel-producing companies, with an annual output of 4.5 million tonnes. The diversification will protect the new firm against a downturn in the steel market.[24]

Krupp. Krupp is one of Germany's oldest steel producers, with plants in the Ruhr region. In 1989, its raw-steel output was 4.6 million tonnes, placing it twenty-second among the steel producers of the world.

To bring its capacity into line with demand, Krupp announced in 1987 that the plant at Rheinhausen, with a 3-million-tonne capacity, would be closed. This will be accomplished in several stages. Steel, which was produced at the plant, will be obtained from the Huckingen plant, which will be a joint venture with Mannesmann. The plant, now owned fifty-fifty by both companies, has a capacity for 4 million tonnes. Two million tonnes of slabs will be used by Krupp and 2 million by Mannesmann. The slabs will be sent to Krupp's plant at Bochum, where they will be rolled into finished products.

The Rheinhausen plant's finishing facilities have been closed down; what remains are two blast furnaces, a coke oven battery, oxygen converters for steel production, and a continuous caster. In early 1990, one of the blast furnaces was shut down. The remaining furnace produces 170,000 tonnes of iron per month; however, Krupp's requirement is 60,000 tonnes to help service the Bochum plant's finishing facilities. If the 110,000 extra tonnes can be sold, the furnace will remain. Possibly some of the ventures planned between Krupp and East Germany steel producers could require additional tonnage. If these projects materialize, there is a strong possibility that the furnace at Rheinhausen will remain in operation, producing iron that will be turned into slabs.

Krupp is a major producer of stainless steel and is seeking joint ventures outside Germany to produce this product.

Luxembourg

Arbed, the largest steel manufacturing company in Luxembourg, expanded its ownership considerably during the early 1980s, securing a major share of Saar Stahl. Recently, however, it divested itself of this, and current steel operations include those in Luxembourg, which amount to 4.5 million tonnes of raw steel, which are principally rolled into structural sections. In addition, it has a majority share (67 percent) in Sidmar in Belgium, which has a capacity of 3.5 million tonnes, and a 22 percent holding in a Brazilian steel company with 1 million tonnes of capacity. Thus, the total productive capacity of Arbed is in the area of 8 million tonnes. A very high percentage of Arbed's steel made in Luxembourg—almost 90 percent—is exported, since the size of the country offers a very limited market.

During the next few years, there are no plans for major investments in steel mill facilities; however, during the past year, a new type of structural beam, named Histar, has been developed, which has a number of advantages over the standard wide-flange beam. Among them are high-yield strengths, outstanding toughness properties, and extremely low carbon equivalent, ensuring excellent weldability. The excellence of the beam comes from the finishing process. The company describes the product as a jumbo shape of outstanding quality. It is "the result of new in-line quenching and a self-tempering process . . . which allows the production of rolled shapes that contain a combination of mechanical, chemical, and technical properties ensuring greater performance and economy in steel construction."[25] This new product has been available for about a year.

Arbed in the last decade has constructed a new furnace and two continuous casters, as well as modernizing much of its steel works and rolling mills. This has increased productivity considerably and reduced the work force. In the future, more emphasis will be placed on specialty steel which now constitutes 40 percent of the company's output. Further, it plans to diversify into areas that will be complimentary to ironmaking and steelmaking rather than opposed to them. Steel will remain the most significant operation in the company.

Currently, there are discussions between Arbed and Cockerill of Belgium to form a joint venture in flat rolled products which will be significant in size compared with the flat product segment of such companies as Thyssen, Usinor-Sacilor, and British Steel.

Spain

The two principal steel companies in the Spanish industry are both fully integrated facilities making steel with the basic-oxygen process. The others, which are numerous, are electric furnace plants. The two integrated mills, Ensidesa and Altos Hornos de Viscaya (AHV), have a combined capacity to produce between 6.7 million and 7.0 million tonnes. AHV has one plant with 2.2 million tonnes, while Ensidesa operates two plants—one at Aviles for flat products with a capacity of 2.5 million tonnes and the other at Verina for long products with a capacity to produce 2.2 million tonnes. Each of these companies has recently upgraded its hot-strip mill for sheets. Both companies have comprehensive programs for modernization, which will improve quality, increase productivity, and reduce costs. A fourth mill, Altos Hornos de Mediterraneo at Sagunto, formerly operated as an integrated plant under the joint ownership of AHV and United States Steel, is now a wholly owned subsidiary of Ensidesa with its blast furnaces and steelmaking facilities abandoned. It operates a tandem cold mill for which hot-rolled bands are supplied by Ensidesa from its Aviles works.

In 1983, when Spain expressed a desire to enter the Common Market, it needed a substantial revision of its steel industry in order to meet the requirements for entrance. The Spanish steel industry had grown rapidly from 1966, when its raw-steel production was 3.8 million tonnes, to 1983, when output was 13 million tonnes. Most of the capacity was in the electric furnace segment of the industry, which in that year constituted 52 percent of the output as against 45 percent for the basic-oxygen furnace and 3 percent for the open hearth. In 1986, the year of Spain's entry into the Common Market, the open hearth was discontinued so that output from the electric furnace and the basic-oxygen furnace constituted total production. In that year, electric furnace production was 59 percent (versus 41 percent for basic oxygen).

One of the means of restructuring the Spanish industry was to reduce its electric furnace capacity, achieved between 1985 and 1990, when it fell to approximately 9.5 million tonnes. Total capacity is 16.5 million tonnes, with basic oxygen constituting approximately 7 million tonnes.

The electric furnace segment consists of a large number of individual furnaces, some of which have been closed and others consolidated into five major groups. The largest of these is the Celsa Group, which controls three plants and owns a fourth in conjunction with the Marcial Usin Group, which also operates two other plants. Metgasa operates a single plant, while Riva of Italy has a large 800,000-tonne plant. The fifth group, Aristrain, operates three plants, one of them recently purchased.

In terms of the future, the Spanish steel industry investment in plant and equipment will be directed to improving quality, reducing costs, and increasing productivity. Having reduced the size of its capacity considerably between 1985 and 1990, it has no intention of increasing the capacity of any existing plants.

AHV plans to invest $400 million in the five-year period between 1990 and 1994. This includes a continuous-annealing line for tinplate production, which will improve its quality and will be installed at a cost of $126 million. There will also be more coating and prepainting capacity, as well as cold, narrow strip. Further, a considerable amount of investment will be required to meet environmental requirements.

Ensidesa will also install a continuous-annealing line for tinplate to upgrade, and a new galvanizing line, as well as facilities for organic coating, will be installed. The cold reduction plant at Sagunto, which has a 1.6-million-tonne capacity, will update its electrolytic galvanizing line.

There is a strong possibility that after 1992 there will be some alliance between Usinor-Sacilor and Ensidesa involving the cold-rolling mill at Sagunto. It now receives most of its hot-rolled bands from Ensidesa, which requires lengthy transportation, by water or by land. A much closer source would be the Usinor plant at Fos, about 350 kilometers away by sea. This would be a more logical source for the Sagunto plant's requirements of hot-rolled bands.

In the electric furnace segment, the Celsa group is continually looking for advantageous acquisitions in Spain or possibly Portugal.

The Spanish steel industry has arranged several international joint ventures. The first is an agreement signed between Ensidesa and Usinor-Sacilor to work together in a number of areas, including the modernization of Ensidesa's coated-steel production line. Most probably Usinor-Sacilor will hold a 25 percent minority share and will supply some steel from its Solmer plant in Fos to Ensidesa's plant at Sagunto on the Mediterranean. The second involves a stainless steel producer, Acerinox, which plans a joint venture with Armco Advance Material Corporation of Middletown to produce stainless steel sheets 60 inches wide. The plant will be located in Spain and is scheduled to start production in 1992.

In mid 1990, British Steel acquired 40 percent of Aristrain, which will give it access to the production of structural beams in Spain, as well as the distribution network, which Aristrain operates in a number of countries in the EEC.[26] Ultimately British Steel may acquire 45 percent.

Portugal

In early 1990, an announcement was made that Siderurgia Nacional, the Portuguese national steel company, would be privatized. The company consists of two plants, an integrated unit, Seixal, with one blast furnace, and an oxygen converter, as well as an electric furnace. Total capacity is about 600,000 tonnes. The second plant, Maia, is an electric furnace operation with 200,000 tonnes of capacity. Total production in 1988 was 800,000 tonnes. Both plants have continuous-casting machines. The company produces some flat-rolled as well as long products.

A number of interests, both inside and outside Portugal, are considering the mill, among them the Celsa private-sector group from Spain. Possibly the Portuguese may sell only a share of the company and maintain a continuing interest.[27]

Netherlands

The only integrated steel plant in the Netherlands is Hoogovens, which has a capacity for some 5.5 million tonnes of steel and is a modern unit in virtually every respect. Much of the mill has been replaced and updated in the last few years, including blast furnaces, basic-oxygen steelmaking facilities, and continuous casting, which is now applied to 100 percent of the output. The hot- and cold-strip mills were renewed in the 1980s, when the hot mill was upgraded from 3.8 million tonnes to 4.5 million.

The hot-dipped galvanizing line at Hoogovens has a 260,000-tonne capacity, with a second line planned to produce in excess of 200,000 tonnes of hot-dipped galvalume for the automobile industry. This will be 72 inches wide. Hoogovens expects the growth in coil coating to be between 8 and 12 percent a year.

The company is also bullish on the automobile industry in Europe, expecting it to produce 14 million to 16 million vehicles, with 1 million cars made by the Japanese in England and Spain. As a result, cold-rolled sheet output for Hoogovens will increase from 1.2 million to 1.6 million tonnes. Its total of two and a third galvanizing lines, since it has a one-third interest in a venture with Cockerill and Arbed, will provide a production of 800,000 tonnes of galvanized steel in the future. In spite of this increase in sheet products, there will be virtually no increase in raw-steel capacity.

In addition, Thyssen and Hoogovens are engaged in a joint venture to construct a hot-dipped galvanizing line, which will be located at the Thyssen plant in Duisburg. Hoogovens will take 25 percent of the output and Thyssen 75 percent. The line will be in operation in late 1991.

Hoogovens has bought an interest in Norsk Jern, a Norwegian state-owned company producing tinplate. It was formerly owned by Norsk. Hoogovens participation is now 40 percent. The arrangement gives Norsk greater access to the Common Market and gives Hoogovens an outlet for cold-rolled steel, as well as a participation in the American market, which Norsk enjoys.

Belgium

The principal company in the Belgian steel industry is Cockerill, which has two integrated plants with an aggregate capacity of 5 million tonnes. In the early 1980s, there were four plants with a 10-million-tonne capacity, which was reduced by management to bring capacity more into line with market conditions. There were two plants in Liège and two at Charleroi. One in each location was closed. In Liège, the plant is located in several parts of town and therefore involves transporting steel back and fourth.

In 1976, the company installed a hot-strip mill and now has two—one at each location. The 5 million tonnes are divided almost equally between the two plants: 2.6 million tonnes at Charleroi and 2.4 million at Liège.

The principal product of the company is flat-rolled steel, including 2 million tonnes of galvanized sheets produced on six lines, some of which are joint ventures, including one with Hoogovens and Usinor. A new line is also being installed in France with Usinor. The company also operates prepainting lines—three at Liège and one in France. In addition, there are prefabricating plants where galvanized sheets are fabricated for construction purposes. It operates service centers in France, Belgium, Netherlands, United Kingdom, and Spain. The largest, Pum, is in France.

Three of the mills at Charleroi produce long products, including a rod mill owned 70 percent by Riva of Italy and 30 percent by Cockerill. Arbed owns 10 percent of a structural mill, and Usinor has a 40 percent interest in a third mill.

In terms of basic production, iron ore comes from Brazil, North Africa, and Australia. Eighty percent of its coal is provided by the United States, with the remaining 20 percent from Australia. There are two blast furnaces at each plant. Basic-oxygen steel is made in three 250-tonne standard converters and three Q-Bop 190-tonne furnaces.

Cockerill can roll more steel than it can melt and consequently purchases slabs. As much as 250,000 tonnes have been procured in some years, much of it from European companies, including Clabecq in Belgium. Currently there are three cold-reduction mills that will be reduced to two, which will be upgraded to maintain the same capacity. In addition to the 2 million tonnes of galvanized capacity, Cockerill produces 1.2 million tonnes of hot-rolled, pickled, and oiled sheets, as well as 300,000 tonnes of tin-plate. Cockerill has been in the coating business for twenty-five years and has established a preeminent position.

Cockerill plans to spend about $100 million a year during the 1990s, an investment that will be concentrated on modernizing the plant by upgrading hot-strip and cold-strip mills. Emphasis will be placed on improving quality. Also, a considerable investment will be needed to meet environmental standards. There is no intention of increasing capacity.

Recently the company engaged in developing its steel outlets by the purchase of a controlling 55 percent interest in YMOS AG, a major producer of car parts in Germany. This will allow Cockerill to penetrate the German automobile market and is particularly significant since the company will phase out its long-products production in Charleroi.

Another integrated company in Belgium, with about 2 million tonnes of steelmaking capacity, is Usiness Gustave Boel. The company produces flat-rolled steel and has recently revamped its hot-strip mill with electrical controls and hydraulic screw downs, as well as roll bending. There is no thought of increasing capacity. One of the major improvements, however, is the preparation of the blast furnace for coal injection. The principal products are galvanized steel and painted sheets.

Belgium exports a very large percentage of its steel production.

Italy

The Italian steel industry consists of Ilva, a major integrated government-owned steel operation with some 13 million to 14 million tonnes of capacity. In addition, there are a number of electric-furnace companies. Ilva is a new creation, having replaced Italsider, which was substantially restructured in the late 1980s.

Italsider ran into financial problems when the steel boom of 1974 turned into a depression, which lasted with varying degrees of intensity through 1987. Prior to 1974, Italsider made huge investments, including the construction of a 10-million-tonne plant at Taranto, the largest in Europe. Unfortunately, from 1975 to 1987, the company did not make a profit, in part because of the depression and its financial position. Total net losses from 1975 to 1987 reached $9.7 billion.[28]

The situation was desperate and required strong measures. Restructuring the company was not enough. It had to be a radical shakeup, which involved closing Italsider and transferring a certain number of the assets to the new company, Ilva, which was organized in mid-1988 and formally began business operations on January 1, 1989. Since that time, over 700,000 tonnes of steelmaking capacity and 1.5 million tonnes of rolling mill capacity have been closed, with a 25 percent reduction in employment.[29]

Ilva, a much more streamlined operation than its predecessor, and devoid of high-cost, obsolete facilities, as well as a cumbersome structure, has been a profitable operation. The decree creating Ilva was contained in a message to the High Commission in Brussels: "On 16 June 1988, the Italian Government advised the Commission of a plan to restructure the Italian public steel industry. Starting with the winding-up of the parent company, Finsider, and its main steel subsidiaries, the plan comprises a number of industrial, commercial, financial and social measures which should allow the new steel entity, Ilva, to achieve, from 1990, adequate operating results to ensure viability."[30]

Ilva absorbed most of the facilities previously operated by Italsider. These consisted of three principal integrated steel plants: Taranto with a capacity of 8 million tonnes, virtually all of which was converted into flat-rolled products and plate, with a small portion of the output in welded pipe; Piambino, a plant with a capacity of 1.5 million tonnes devoted to long products; and Bagnoli, with 1.2 million tonnes of raw steel capacity feeding a modern hot-strip mill, which was constructed in 1983. As part of the restructuring, the steelmaking facilities at Bagnoli were to be closed down, although the strip mill would remain operative, fed by slabs from Taranto and Tubarao in Brazil.

Ilva also has a 40 percent interest in Cornigliano in Genoa, an integrated plant with approximately 1 million tonnes of raw-steel capacity. The Riva interests have acquired 51 percent of this plant. It produces principally semifinished products, which are distributed to finishing mills throughout the country. Most of these are minimills. There is a possibility that this plant may be closed in the future and the facility at Piambino expanded and operated as a joint venture with Ilva, Riva, and Luccini.

In addition to the integrated facilities, Ilva absorbed three electric furnace plants: Terni, with 600,000 tonnes; Dalmine, with 300,000 tonnes; and Aosta, with 200,000 tonnes. As a result of the reconstruction and the commitment to close melting facilities at Bagnoli, the EEC permitted the Italian government to help finance the new company with between $3 billion and $4 billion in equity exchanged for debt.

In 1990, Ilva has a raw-steel capacity of 11.5 million tonnes, which ranks it the eighth largest producer in the world and the fourth in the EEC. The company not only expects to invest capital in plant and equipment in the next four years in the amount of $2.5 billion but also plans acquisitions and joint ventures. Some $600 million has been earmarked for this purpose, to be used between 1990 and 1993.[31] Joint ventures will be considered not only with Italian companies but also on an international basis.

Capital improvements will include a hot-dipped galvanizing line, the site of which will be determined in late 1990. In addition, two other projects, each involving electrolytic galvanizing lines of 150,000-tonne capacity, will be installed at Turin and Genoa. The hot-strip mills at Taranto will be upgraded and the rolling capacity improved. Novi a nonsteelmaking plant, will receive a continuous annealing line.

Ilva has purchased an interest in Margona, a producer of flat-rolled products, including sheets, galvanized material, and tinplate. A recent joint venture concluded with Falck is comprehensive in nature, involving a number of conditions, including a 5 percent interest in the Falck company, as well as provisions to supply Falck with 500,000 tonnes of steel.[32] Another joint venture has been entered into with Usinor-Sacilor to build a cold-reduction plant in Turkey. This will involve a mill with 300,000 tonnes of capacity to be put in operation in early 1993. In addition to Ilva and

Usinor, which share equally in 49 percent of the ownership, two Turkish groups, Eregli and Borusan, hold the other 51 percent, divided 17 percent and 34 percent, respectively.[33] Other joint ventures have been entered into in Italy, including a wire operation and a tube mill. Thus, Ilva has expanded principally through acquisitions.

In 1990, Ilva announced a plan to sell a minority of its shares to the public to raise funds. Given the activity of the newly created company during its first two years of operation, which have been profitable, the future looks much better than it did under the previous organization.

The second most significant company in the Italian steel industry is controlled by the Riva interests. In addition to six plants in Italy, three of which produce steel by the electric furnace method and one, the joint venture with Ilva in the Cornigliano plant, Riva also owns Sevillana SA, an 800,000-tonne facility in Spain, acquired in 1976. The plant has a large, modern bar mill, six electric furnaces, and two continuous-casting lines, each with six strands. Production capacity is 1 million tonnes, although under the agreement admitting Spain to the Common Market, production has been reduced to 800,000 tonnes. In addition, Riva has a virtual monoploy on rebar production in France with the ownership of three mills, two purchased from the Unimetal division of Usinor. The latest acquisition was Laminoirs de Bretange. Riva also has a 70 percent interest in a rod mill in Belgium, with Cockerill holding 30 percent. The mill has a capacity of 500,000 tonnes, and Riva is building electric furnace capacity to feed this facility.

Riva's future plans are flexible insofar as the company takes advantage of opportunities as they arise to expand their acquisitions. The entire steel complex operated by the Riva organization currently embraces 3.5 million tonnes of crude steel, and with the acquisition of the third French rebar mill, as well as the completion of the new mill in Belgium, the figure will rise beyond 4 million tonnes.

Another active participant in the Italian steel industry is Arvedi, which is part of Finarvedi. This company is installing a new hot-strip mill with a thin-slab caster. The mill is based on Mannesmann's design and will be known as In-line Strip Production (ISP). It involves a thin-slab caster that will cast slabs 60 millimeters thick. They are squeezed down by rolls in the caster to 40 millimeters and then immediately pass through three four-high rolling mill stands that reduce the thickness to 15 millimeters. After passing through a sheer, the slabs go through a reheating furnace and a coil box. Emerging from the coil box, the slab passes through a four-stand, four-high strip mill to be reduced to the required thickness before coiling.

The mill is different from that installed by Nucor insofar as it reduces the slab in the caster and has three four-high stands immediately at the exit of the continuous caster. There are seven stands in all. Widths will be 650 millimeters to 1,330 millimeters (26–53 inches). The mill will have a capacity for 500,000 tonnes annually—300,000 tonnes of it carbon steel and 200,000 tonnes stainless steel—and should be in operation by late 1991 or early 1992. The installation cost will be approximately $200 million.

The Italian steel industry is one of the largest producers in Europe. Further, the Italian economy is a large consumer of steel, so that the future production should remain relatively close to that achieved in the past, when the production of raw steel was consistently the second largest in the EEC, at an average of 23 million to 24 million tonnes per year.

Turkey

Turkey is one of the fastest-growing steel industries in Western Europe. In 1974, the year in which the European Community reached its all-time high in raw-steel production, the tonnage produced in Turkey was 1.6 million. This grew slowly through 1980, when it reached 2.5 million tonnes. In the early 1980s, growth was steady but modest, reaching 4.9 million by 1985. Since that time, growth has been rapid. Between 1985 and 1988, some 3 million tonnes were added, as output of raw steel reached 8.1 million tonnes in 1988. Much of this came from the electric furnace segment of the industry, which produced 3.8 million tonnes in 1988, as compared with 3.6 million from the basic-oxygen furnace and 700,000 from the open hearth.

The integrated segment of the industry consists of three plants: Eregli, with a capacity of 1.8 million tonnes; Isdemir, the most recently constructed plant in the integrated segment, with a capacity of 2.2 million tonnes, and Karabuk, the oldest integrated facility, with a capacity to produce 600,000 tonnes. At Karabuk, steel is produced by open-hearth furnaces, and there is no continuous casting. Thus, the plant is outmoded. There are plans to expand the plant by expanding its ironmaking capacity from 600,000 to 900,000 tonnes. This will be accomplished by upgrading the blast furnaces, replacing the open hearth, and installing continuous casting. Both Isdemir and Karabuk are under the jurisdiction of TDCI, the General Directorate of Turkish Iron and Steel.

The electric furnace segment, with a capacity of 5.2 million tonnes, or some 53 percent of the country's potential output, has more than tripled in its output since 1984, when its capacity was 1.5 million tonnes. The total industry capacity for that year was 4.3 million tonnes, which expanded to 9.9 million tonnes by 1988. The industry is, in a sense, out of balance since the production of long products far exceeds flat-rolled products. In 1988, production of flat-rolled products was 1.8 million tonnes, while long-product production was 5.1 million tonnes, much of it exported.

There is a plan to expand the country's capacity to 11 million tonnes by the mid-1990s. The possibility of reaching 11 million tonnes not only of capacity but of raw-steel production by 1995 is reasonably good since the country was able to increase its output from 1985 to 1988 by more than 3 million tonnes. The increase, however, will require investment principally at the integrated plants. Eregli proposes to move from 1.8 million tonnes to 3.7 million, which alone would bring the nation's capacity to some 12 million tonnes. Another increase, which has not yet been approved and which will add further capacity, involves the blast furnace at Karabuk. There will also be additional electric furnaces. These are not nearly as necessary as the increase in Eregli's capacity, which will provide flat products.

In the last five years, investment in the electric furnace segment of the industry has been so great that it now constitutes 53 percent of steel output as opposed to 25 percent in 1982. There is not a large enough market in Turkey to absorb the electric furnace output of long products, as well as those of Karabuk and Isdemir. This accounts for the export tonnage, which amounted to 2.8 million in 1988. Since 1982, when electric furnace production began to expand, Turkish exports have increased dramatically. In that year, they were a mere 174,000 tonnes; by 1988 they were 2.8 million.

Turkey's export market for a number of years has been the Middle East and North Africa. However, in the late 1980s, significant tonnages were exported to a number of other countries, including the United States. In 1987, 407,000 tonnes were shipped to the United States. The major products were wire rods, concrete reinforcing bars, standard pipe, structural pipe, and galvanized sheets. In 1988, exports to the United States dropped to 284,000 tonnes. Nevertheless, wire rods doubled, and there was a significant increase in concrete reinforcing bars. Galvanized sheets represented a very small 6,500 tonnes.

Imports have also increased. In 1982, they were 900,000 tonnes and in 1988, 1.6 million tonnes. A significant part of this total was 482,000 tonnes of slabs from Brazil to be rolled at Eregli, which has more finishing than melting capacity.

Turkey is one of the few countries in Europe, or for that matter in the industrialized world, with plans to increase its capacity during the 1990s. It could reach 20 million tonnes during the latter part of the decade, since there has been discussion on the possibility of adding 10 million tonnes to Turkey's capacity between 1994 and 2000. The need for this is based on the per capita consumption of steel, which is considerably below the average of industrialized countries. Flat products accounted for some 23 percent of the output as of 1989. This to some extent reflects the current demand. However, as the country's economy progresses, there will be a greater need for flat products.[34]

Eregli is involved in a $1.8 billion program for expansion and modernization. A five-stand, tandem cold-rolling mill will cost $500 million, along with additional facilities, such as pickling and annealing. The mill will have a capacity of 1.5 million tonnes. The steelmaking capacity, currently 1.8 million tonnes, will be raised to 3.7 million by enlarging two blast furnaces, as well as three oxygen converters, which will be upgraded from 90 tonnes per heat to 115 tonnes. On the hot-strip mill, one finishing stand will be added to increase its capacity to 3 million tonnes. Two continuous casters are also in the program, which will raise the casting rate to 98 percent. Before the expansion is completed, the company will import slabs so that its shipments can amount to 3 million tonnes. These are obtained from Brazil and South Africa. It is contemplated that 600,000 tonnes will be imported annually for the next two years.

The company has two hot mills, one a Steckle mill and the other a semicontinuous mill. Current shipments of these mills are 1.9 million tonnes, which will be raised to 3 million tonnes. Eregli produces plates, as well as hot- and cold-rolled sheets.

In early 1990, a decision was made to allow private participation in the ownership of Eregli. When the shares were made available, 5.5 percent were sold to the general public.[35]

Since 1984, Isdemir has increased production from 831,000 tonnes to 1,849,000 and Karabuk from 500,000 tonnes to 582,000, while Eregli rose from 1,544,000 to 1,816,000 tonnes. Thus, the total for the integrated plants increased over the five-year period 1984–1988 from 2.9 million to 4.3 million tonnes.

Austria

The steel industry in Austria consists mainly of Voest-Alpine, with approximately 4.5 million tonnes of capacity. In addition, there is a small minimill with some 200,000 tonnes of capacity. Voest-Alpine has undergone an extensive corporate reconstruction since 1986 and is a much more comprehensive organization under the broader heading of Austrian Industries.

The steel company consists of two plants, one at Linz and one at Donawitz. The Linz plant has been updated and is modern in every respect. The steel is made entirely in the No. 3 LD shop, with its three 150-tonne converters, which replaced the other shops that have been closed down. Total capacity of the works at Linz is 3.5 million tonnes. The second plant at Donawitz has a capacity of 1 million tonnes, and a study is being conducted on the possibility of changing the steelmaking process, while another alternative is to eliminate the iron and steelmaking facilities and operate the rolling mills with billets and blooms obtained outside the plant.

Donawitz makes long products, including rails, and Linz is confined to flat products. Its hot-strip mill and cold mill have been upgraded, and the emphasis has been placed on quality. The electrolytic galvanizing line has been upgraded, and a new hot-dipped galvanizing line is being added. It is possible that a fourth stand will be added to the cold mill with roll shifting at the hot-strip mill. The company produces parts for the automobile industry, which it will continue to do for the remainder of the decade.

Austria is an exporting country. In 1988, it exported 3.1 million tonnes of steel products, 75 percent of its total product output. Imports were 1.3 million tonnes. This ratio will most probably continue through the 1990s. If Donawitz is closed, however, 1 million tonnes of steel capacity will be eliminated. Raw-steel production will then be in the area of 3.5 million tonnes, and exports will be curtailed. However, the company can be quite profitable due to the fact that it is concentrating on higher-quality products and the production of automobile parts.

In terms of iron ore, needed for the blast furnaces at Linz and those still operating at Donawitz, domestic production in 1988 was 3.2 million tonnes, which was supplemented by 4.2 million tonnes of imports. This situation will continue through most of the 1990s unless the furnaces at Donawitz are shut down, in which case there will be a decided reduction.

Sweden

Raw-steel production in Sweden has been relatively stable since 1977, when it was about 4 million tonnes, which represented a decline from the 1974 high of some 6 million tonnes. Since 1977, it has been in the 4.0-million- to 4.8-million-tonne range, although during that time there was a substantial restructuring of the industry. In 1978, the three principal steelmakers—Stora-Koppargarg, Granges, and Norrbottens—were combined to form Svenskt Stal Aktiebolag (SSAB). The combination operated plants at Domnarvet, Lulea, and Oxelsund.

As of 1990, the largest plant in Sweden is operated by SSAB at Lulea with 1.6 million tonnes of semifinished products. Another company, Ovako Steel, owned 50 percent by the Swedes and 50 percent by the Finns, has a 50 percent interest in the Lulea plant and takes liquid steel from it, puts it through casting machines to form billets and blooms, and uses them in the rolling mill, which it owns, to produce long products.

Of the 1.6 million tonnes of semifinished products produced at Lulea, 1.2 million tonnes of slabs are sent to Domnarvet. Domnarvet also receives 600,000 tonnes of Oxelsund's total production of 1.2 million tonnes. These tonnages feed the hot-strip mill at Domnarvet, which has been improved through the introduction of new walking-beam furnaces and other modifications that increased its capacity from 1.2 million tonnes to 2 million tonnes, making it Sweden's prime rolling and finishing mill. The plant will also put in a galvanizing line. Lulea has installed a new slab caster to facilitate supplying the Domnarvet plant.

Oxelsund, the other SSAB steelmaking plant, rolls 600,000 tonnes of slabs at its own facility.

Of SAAB's three plants, Lulea and Oxelosund have a capacity to produce 2.8 million tonnes of basic-oxygen steel, while Domnarvet produced approximately 500,000 tonnes of electric furnace steel. However, this has been shut down and the shop sold to the North Koreans.

Another steel producer is the Fundia group, made up of several plants with a total capacity of 600,000 tonnes. Other electric furnace operations include the special steel company, Avesta, with a capacity of 800,000 tonnes.

In 1988, 52 percent of Sweden's steel was made by the oxygen process, as compared with 48 percent by the electric furnace process. Since the closure of Domnarvet, this ratio has been changed. It will be reduced further when the plant at Hellefors, with 200,000 tonnes of electric furnace capacity, is closed in 1991.

In terms of the future, in addition to the galvanizing line planned for Domnarvet, a ladle furnace will be installed at Lulea, and the plate mill at Avesta will be converted to a strip mill, thus allowing it to roll more of the raw steel it produces rather than have it done by other companies. The mill will be constructed by a West Germany consortium and will also be a factor in improving the quality and increasing productivity of the plant. It is scheduled to go into operation by the third quarter of 1991.

No expansion in capacity is projected for the Swedish steel industry. In fact, there will be some reduction during the first few years of the 1990s, amounting to as much as 500,000 tonnes.

Sweden has exported a substantial amount of its steel output. In 1988, some 3.0 million tonnes of steel products were shipped out of the country, as opposed to 2.1 million tonnes imported. Of the exports, a significant quantity was in the form of semifinished slabs. This proportion will most likely continue for the 1990s.

Australia

Broken Hill Proprietary (BHP), with a capacity to produce 6.7 million tonnes of raw steel in 1990, is by far the largest steel company in Australia. In addition, there are two small minimills, Commonwealth Steel Company and Smorgon Steel, with a total capacity of less than 500,000 tonnes. BHP operates three steelmaking plants, Port Kembla, Newcastle, and Whyalla. There are also a number of other finishing mills which do not have steelmaking facilities.

In the late 1970s, BHP had a capacity of some 8 million tonnes of raw steel. However, with the depression which overhung most of the industry on a world basis from 1982 to 1986, BHP reduced its capacity following the drastic drop in production to 5.7 million tonnes in 1983 from a high of 8 million tonnes in 1979. In the remainder of the 1980s, production was in the area of 6 million tonnes.

In 1989, it was recognized that steel demand had increased and that BHP should likewise increase its capacity to meet the country's needs. Thus, it made plans to add tonnage at its three steelmaking plants. Port Kembla, the largest of the three with a capacity of 3.8 million tonnes, is being expanded to 4.5 million, principally through increasing the ironmaking capability of the blast furnace. With the improvement at No. 2 blast furnace, more hot metal will be provided to the basic-oxygen converters, which have adequate capacity to absorb it as do the finishing facilities. Newcastle, with a capacity of 1.1 million tonnes, will be expanded to 2 million tonnes through minor investments in a number of areas.

Whyalla, located near Adelaide, currently has a 1.1-million-tonne capacity. It will be expanded to 1.25 million through the installation of a continuous caster. In addition, a minimill with a capacity of 250,000 tonnes will be built near Sydney. This plant, to begin with, will not have a rolling mill but will continuously cast billets. Plans also call for the installation of a new galvanizing line.

When the expansion is completed, total capacity will be in the area of 8 million tonnes. Total investment for the expansion program will be $889 million(AUS). In addition to the aforementioned facilities, the program includes upgrading a number of other units such as the tin mill.

This program comes on the heels of a five-year program instituted in the mid 1980s that represented an investment in excess of $1 billion(AUS). This involved a complete renovation of the hot-strip mill, a continuous caster, improvements to the basic-oxygen steel shop, an upgrading of the plate mill, and an investment in coke facilities. As a result of the two programs, BHP will have a world-class plant in every respect with a total capacity of 8 million tonnes and 100 percent continuous casting. BHP will be in a position to serve its domestic market and export more steel than it has in the past few years.

Australia will continue to be the second largest exporter of iron ore in the world with Japan as its principal market, although ore is also sold to a number of European countries.

South Africa

In 1989, raw-steel production in South Africa reached an all-time high of 9.6 million tonnes, 7 million tonnes of it produced by Iscor, the largest steel company in the country. Additional tonnage came from companies such as Highveld, which has a 1-million-tonne capacity, and smaller electric furnace operations like Scaw Metals, with a capacity to produce some 400,000 tonnes. In 1988, South Africa imported 100,000 tonnes; exports were 2.6 million tonnes.

Iscor adopted new technology by installing at its Pretoria works a unit of the Corex method of producing iron, capable of 300,000 tonnes. After a number of start-up problems, the unit has worked smoothly in 1990, and it is expected that by 1991 it will be operating at full capacity and should produce hot metal at a cost well below the Pretoria blast furnace. In the future, a Corex unit will be installed at either the Newcastle or Vanderbijlpark works.

There will be no increase in the 1990 capacity of 7 million tonnes. Finishing facilities will be installed at Vanderbijlpark, including a tin-free steel line and an electrolytic galvanizing line. This is part of the program to add more value-added products to the company's output. There is also speculation that a Corex unit, possibly with a 500,000-tonne capacity, will be installed at Saldana Bay, along with steelmaking facilities to produce semifinished for export.

In the mid-1970s, there was a plan to build a joint venture plant at Saldana Bay, but, with the collapse of the steel boom, it was quietly shelved. The idea, however, is not dead and could well be revived by the mid-1990s.

Iscor has entered into a joint venture with Dorbyl, an engineering group, to produce seamless tubes. The company is Tosa Seamless Tubes, owned 60 percent by Dorbyl and 40 percent by Iscor, which will provide the steel.

Iscor was privatized as of the end of 1989 through issuing 1.5 billion shares, which were sold to the general public, with some 90 million shares placed in trust for the employees. The price per share was 2 rands, yielding a total of approximately 3 billion rands. Purchase of the shares was very rapid.

Highveld, a company that produces steel as well as vanadium, has a capacity to produce 1 million tonnes of steel. This will be increased by some 200,000 tonnes with the installation of a pellet plant to pelletize iron ore before it goes into the smelting process. The higher-grade pellets will increase the iron output by some 20 percent, which will be passed along through the steelmaking process to account for the extra 200,000 tonnes. In the mid-1990s, Highveld might install cold-rolling facilities so that it can produce cold-rolled sheets. Currently its product line is limited to hot-rolled sheets, plates, and wide-flange beams.

South Africa's steel capacity will be increased by approximately 200,000 tonnes, a small percentage of the 9.6 million tonnes produced in 1989.

Notes

1. *IISI, 1970 Report of Proceedings*, Fourth Annual Conference, p. 12.
2. OECD, *The Iron and Steel Industry in 1980* (Paris: OECD, 1982), p. 33.
3. National Steel Corporation, *1979 Annual Report*, p. 4.
4. National Intergroup, brochure 1983, pp. 3, 4.
5. National Steel Company, press release, February 1984.
6. *American Metal Market*, February 9, 1990, p. 2.
7. Robert Wilthew, "Mini/Market Mills Look to the '90s" (paper presented at Steel Survival Strategies, June 1989).
8. *American Metal Market*, January 1, 1990, p. 1.
9. Japan Iron & Steel Federation, *The Steel Industry of Japan 1987*, p. 4.
10. Ibid.
11. Personal interviews.
12. *Nippon Steel Annual Report*, 1987.
13. Inland Steel, news release, December 18, 1989.
14. *Steel Times International* (March 1989): 31.
15. *Metal Bulletin*, April 9, 1990, p.29.
16. *Nisshin Steel Annual Report 1988*, p. 12.
17. *Metal Bulletin*, January 4, 1990, p. 25.
18. Ibid, June 19, 1989, p. 23.
19. Japan Iron & Steel Federation, *The Steel Industry of Japan 1989*, p. 7.
20. *Metal Bulletin*, December 4, 1989, p. 25.
21. *Ibid.*, October 5, 1989, p. 25.
22. *Ibid.*, October 19, 1989, p. 35.
23. *American Metal Market*, June 22, 1990, p. 2.
24. *Metal Bulletin*, October 5, 1989, p. 25.
25. Announcement by Arbed, September 1959.
26. Conversations with executives of Aristrain.
27. *Metal Bulletin*, February 1, 1990,. p. 23, February 26, 1990, p. 29.
28. Giovanni Gillerio, paper delivered at Steel Survival Strategies, June 1990. "International Steelmakers' Strategies for the 90s"
29. Ibid.
30. *Restructuring of the Italian Public Steel Industry* (Communication from the Commission to the Council), Commission of the European Communities, Brussels, October 25, 1988, p. 1.
31. Gillerio, paper delivered.
32. *Metal Bulletin*, July 12, 1990, p. 19.
33. *Ibid.*, March 19, 1990, p. 25.
34. *Ibid.*, November 6, 1989, p. 27.
35. *Ibid.*, January 29, 1990, p. 21.

3
Steel Capacities in Third World Countries

T he keynote for Third World steel development was sounded at the second general conference of the United Nations Industrial Development Corporation (UNIDO) held in Lima, Peru, in March 1975. One of its principal actions was the adoption of the Lima Declaration on Industrial Development and Cooperation. It calls attention to the fact that "the developing countries constitute 70 percent of the world's population and generate less than 7 percent of industrial production." In order to remedy this situation, the declaration states, the developing countries should increase their industrial production "to at least 25 percent of total world production by the year 2000, while making every effort to insure that the industrial growth as achieved is distributed among the developing countries as evenly as possible."[1]

The delegates recognized that a 25 percent share could not be achieved in every industry; consequently, to compensate for this, some industries were targeted for a higher percentage of world production. Steel was one of these; the target was placed at 30 percent of the world's steel output by the year 2000.

In 1975, Third World steel production, including the People's Republic of China, was 61 million tonnes. Projections made in the mid 1970s for steel production in the year 2000 placed the production figure for raw steel on a global basis at 1.4 billion to 1.7 billion tonnes. Thus, the target for the developing countries would be somewhere between 350 million (at 25 percent of the lower number) and 525 million (at 30 percent of the higher figure).

In 1975, a number of countries undertook programs to increase their output while the industrialized countries, suffering from an abrupt drop in steel production in that year as compared with the record output of 1974, put a hold on their expansion plans in steel. This persisted in the industrialized countries with few exceptions until 1990. The Third World countries, however, installed new capacity to the extent that their aggregate production by 1980 had advanced to 101 million tonnes. In Latin America, aggregate output rose from 18.6 million tonnes in 1975 to 29.2 million in 1980, an increase of 65 percent. Other countries with significant growth included

China, India, South Korea, and Taiwan. The projections of the Third World countries were to develop as much steel capacity as could be financed in order to supply their own needs and to have additional tonnage available for export.

In spite of the depressed conditions of many of the countries in the world steel industry, as total output in the industrialized world fell from 463 million tonnes in 1974 to 400 million in 1977 and recovered to 442 million in 1979, only to drop to 338 million in 1982, Third World production continued to grow to 130 million in 1982. By 1988, a year of record output up to that time, Third World production stood at 163.6 million tonnes. The possibility of reaching 25 percent by the year 2000 seems to be well within range, since in 1988, the developing countries produced 21 percent of the world's total raw steel output. This possibility is partly a result of a sharp decrease in the amount of raw-steel production projected for the year 2000. In place of the 1.4 billion to 1.7 billion tonnes, it is more likely that it will be in the area of 850 million to 900 million tonnes, and plans for increasing capacity in the Third World call for an addition of 50 million to 55 million tonnes, which would bring its potential to approximately 220 million out of a probable world steel production of 850 million to 900 million tonnes. In terms of potential, the Third World would be capable of producing 25 percent of the total.

The difference in philosophy between the Third World countries and the industrialized countries is sharp. The industrialized countries feel that their capacity to melt steel is adequate for much of the next decade. There is a possibility that they may add some tonnage through the installation of minimills or other electric furnace operations; however, this will be minimal compared to the existing capacity. In the United States, for example, there could be an addition of minimill capacity in the area of 4 million to 5 million tonnes. Third World countries, on the other hand, have extensive plans by which their capacity will be augmented during the next ten years. The most serious hurdle to the realization of this increased tonnage is the availability of capital, particularly in countries such as Brazil and Mexico.

The Third World has many electric furnaces in operation and consequently used most of the tonnage of direct-reduced iron (DRI) production in the world in 1989. Total production was 16 million tonnes produced in twenty-four countries. Of the twenty-four countries, seventeen are in the Third World, with an output of 10.7 million tonnes. The largest producer in the Third World was Venezuela, with 4.5 million tonnes, followed by Mexico, with 3 million. The output of the industrialized countries was only 5.3 million tonnes, with the Soviet Union accounting for 1.6 million, the largest amount.

Brazil

The steel situation in Brazil has been in a state of flux since March 1990 when the government announced that it had decided to privatize the integrated plants. The immediate plan is to sell Tubarao and Usiminas, the two most profitable units in the complex, and use the funds received to improve the other integrated plants so that they will become desirable purchases. As a corollary, the elaborate plans drawn up in 1989 for the modernization, improvement, and expansion of the coke-based integrated plants have been put on hold. It is a question as to when Tubarao and Usiminas will be sold. The monetary situation in Brazil has been drastically overhauled, and this could delay their sale. Siderbras, the steel holding company, will be abolished, as will Interbras, the government trading company. However, CVRD, the ore-mining unit, will not be sold, particularly since it is a profitable operation and the world's leading supplier of iron ore, having exported some 105 million tonnes in 1988.

In a number of comments made on this plan, Siderbras is said to have a debt of $12 billion, which has been somewhat reduced from $17 billion as a result of government-issued debentures. Further, it has been stated that Siderbras posted a very large loss of $2.3 billion in 1988 and $2 billion in 1987. In 1989, however, a number of Siderbras operations were profitable. Usiminas had profits of $190 million and Tubarao $116 million. Acominas registered profits of $10 million and Cosipa $88 million, while CSN neutralized much of this with a loss of $205 million.[2] One of the principal reasons for Siderbras's huge debt is the fact that it absorbed the debt of a number of its subsidiaries, thus altering their financial structures.

When the Siderbras steel mills are privatized, the new owners might undertake much of the modernization plan set down by Siderbras in 1989. The total cost for the five plants concerned is estimated at almost $11 billion. Table 3–1 presents capital requirements, broken down into three categories, designated A, B, and C. A represents the investments required to maintain the current facilities' capacities. B represents the investments needed for the modernization and improvement considered essential to maintain quality competitiveness without increasing capacity. C indicates investments that are required to expand capacity to meet the growth anticipated by the market projections. B also includes expenditures for environmental facilities associated with B and C.

Since the plants will be privately owned, there will be a need to exercise financial restraint, and as a consequence, some of Siderbras's elaborate plans may well be cut back. In spite of the fact that this is a possibility, it will be interesting for the record to detail the improvements and expansion

Table 3-1
Capital Investment Requirements
(millions $U.S.)

	CSN	Cosipa	Usiminas	CST	Acominas	Total
A	589	235	102	32	42	1,000
B	1,417	1,512	1,196	632	772	5,529
C	285	336	169	2,139	1,462	4,391
Total	2,291	2,083	1,467	2,803	2,276	10,920

Source: Study issued by Siderbras in 1989 on the restructuring the steel industry.

Siderbras planned. This will serve as a road map for the future, although there may be a number of detours.

Siderbras, as it is constituted as of April 1990, consists of six plants. Five are integrated, coke-based plants that account for the country's entire coke-based, integrated production: Usiminas, Cosipa, Tubarao, Acominas, and CSN. In addition, Piratini uses direct-reduced iron as its raw material and will probably be sold to the Gerdau interests, the largest private steel group in Brazil. Cofavi, an electric furnace operation, was sold to Durferco, basically a trading company that plans to increase the capacity of the plant.

In 1989, the plans for the expansion of Siderbras amounted to some 8 million tonnes—from its then current 17 million to 25 million tonnes—by the year 2000. Some 3 million tonnes were to be added at Tubarao, along with a continuous caster and a hot-strip mill by 1994. By 1995, Acominas was to be doubled with the addition of 2 million tonnes. The last 3 million were to come from expansion activity at the other three integrated plants.

A Siderbras report issued in 1989 gives the plans for the five integrated plants in great detail:

A) CSN

CSN will raise its liquid steel production capacity to 5.3 million mt per year through coke oven and blast furnace improvements, a new sinter plant and retirement of a small old one, and bottom blowing and sub-lance installation in the BOFs. Continuous casting will increase to 100 percent through improvement of existing machines. The conventional ingot practice and the slabbing-blooming mill will be retired. Non-flat finishing facilities will be shut down when no longer required and no longer profitable as ACOMINAS's come on stream. Hot strip mill capacity, using both mills would increase to over 5 million mt per year through relatively modest investment improvements. A new cold tandem mill and a new processing line for metal sheets is planned. In 1998 start-up of an electro-galvanizing line is planned.

B) Cosipa

COSIPA plans to increase steelmaking capacity to about 4.2 million mt per year through some blast furnace improvements and increase scrap purchases. The addition of a new continuous slab caster in each BOF shop will provide 100 percent continuous casting capability and conventional ingot and primary mill practice will be retired.

A major expansion is planned for the plate mill in two steps. Hot strip mill capacity will be modestly increased along with quality improvements. A new cold tandem mill facility including pickler, continuous annealing, skin passing and finishing facilities is planned. An electro-galvanizing line to serve the automotive sector is also planned.

C) Usiminas

USIMINAS plans to increase its liquid steel capacity to 4.2 million mt per year through relatively minor improvements in the primary facilities and increased scrap purchases. As in the cases of CSN and COSIPA, USIMINAS plans to replace its conventional ingot/slab practice by continuous casting 100 percent of its liquid steel. An extensive modernization for improving quality (some capacity increase expected) is planned for the hot strip mill. A new cold tandem mill facility will be built and Brazil's first electro-galvanizing line is planned for start-up in 1991. The capacity of the heavy plate mill will be maintained at the current level.

D) CST

CST plans to double its steel production by 1994 and continuously cast about 4.4 million mt per year, or 67 percent of its liquid steel. A slab caster will be installed in 1991, increasing crude steel tonnage through improved yield as ingot casting is partially substituted. The production of slabs for export would be essentially maintained and a new hot strip mill, expandable to 4 million mt per year, would be installed. No. 2 blast furnace start-up is planned to precede a full scale reline requirement of the existing furnace. Hot rolled product is planned for both domestic and export markets.

E) Acominas

ACOMINAS anticipates start-up of Brazil's first medium and heavy structural mills in 1991. A doubling, essentially in kind, of its steel capacity and continuous slab casting of just under 50 percent of its liquid steel is planned for 1995. A hot strip mill of about 2.0 million mt per year capacity at the same time will utilize the cast slabs. Semi-finished products, (slabs, blooms and/or billets) will round out the product line.

. . . . These increases are connected with market projection which are revised yearly. And the plan is flexible enough so that as market projections change, so will the Installation Plan.[3]

Siderbras constituted approximately 70 percent of Brazil's output; the remaining twenty-four plants, many of them electric furnace operations and some charcoal-based blast furnace plants, plan modernization and some increase in capacity during the 1990s.

In 1988, Siderbras produced 17 million tonnes of the country's 24.7 million total and in 1989 17.4 million tonnes of the country's 25.2 million. Siderbras plants produced all of Brazil's flat-rolled products. Consequently, the private sector was limited to long products, of which it produced about 8 million tonnes.

The plans for the future, which now seem to be indefinitely postponed, included two greenfield-site plants—one in the north with 3.5 million tonnes of capacity and another in the south with 1.5 million tonnes. There is still hope that the integrated plant in the north near São Louis, capital of Maranhão State, will be undertaken by private interests. In fact, the hope was so strong that the plant was given the name *Usimar*. Comments on the project described the location as "an extraordinary favorable location for the new steel project in the country whenever market conditions called for it in the future."[3] It would use Carajas ore and would have an excellent ocean port to ship the product overseas.

If the plans for the five integrated mills are carried out by private interests, the investment would be some $11 billion over a period of ten years. Currently it cannot be provided by the state and will have to be raised privately by the future owners. The privatization will take the government of Brazil out of the steel business completely, although it will still maintain its interests in CVRD, the iron company.

Brazil's plans for the 1990s have been adjusted twice in the last three years. In 1987, they called for an increase in steel capacity of 20 million to 25 million tonnes by the year 2000 to bring the total to 45 million to 50 million tonnes of raw steel. This was scaled back to a total of 35 million to 38 million tonnes and now, in terms of government participation, has been abandoned. The country was the sixth largest producer in the world in 1988 and 1989 but will not continue in that position in the early 1990s because of privatization. It will remain the principal exporter of iron ore, which surpassed 100 million tonnes in 1988 and will most probably continue at that level for the early 1990s.

The plan announced the day after the new president was inaugurated came as a surprise, although it was known for some time that privatization was intended; however, it was not expected so soon. This is evident from the fact that Siderbras announced in January that the government planned to invest $700 million in the Siderbras plants to improve facilities. Further, the installation of an electrolytic galvanizing line at Usiminas was also planned. However, the new plan, which involved drastic changes in the monetary situation in Brazil, cancelled the expenditure of the $700 million for the present.

One of the developments that will be postponed is the expansion of Tubarao. This plant, which went into production in late 1985, was built at a cost of almost $3 billion and owned jointly by Kawasaki (24.5 percent), Italsider (24.5 percent), and Siderbras (51 percent). The ownership of Kawasaki and Italsider, now Ilva, has subsequently been reduced to 5.5 percent each.

Tubarao is the only large, integrated plant in the world that was constructed to produce and sell semifinished steel exclusively. In this respect, it has been successful and should continue to be so since slabs will be in demand worldwide. Late in 1988, for example, it secured an order for the year 1989 for 482,000 tonnes of slabs to be delivered to the Eregli Steel Works in Turkey. It also recorded a profit of $116 million in 1989, to be the second most profitable of Siderbras's units. The plan to double the size of Tubarao and include a caster and hot-strip mill will not be carried out for another year or two due to privatization. However, with a continuous caster, it will be an attractive project, since more and more slabs will be required in a number of industrialized countries throughout the world, particularly if they are forced to shut down some of their integrated steelmaking operations should the production of coke be reduced due to environmental regulations.

The capacity to produce cold-rolled sheets is somewhat limited in Brazil, so eight steel distributors have developed a plan to build a privately owned cold-reduction mill. The site for the mill is adjacent to the Cosipa plant near São Paolo. The land is expected to be donated by Cosipa, in return for which hot-rolled bands to be cold reduced will be purchased from that company. The new mill will be built by either the Japanese or West Germans.[4]

In general, the situation in regard to the availability of funds, which have been severely curtailed, is an emergency measure that may last for as long as a year and possibly more. This will delay most of the plans for investment in the steel industry. It should, however, be considered a delay rather than a cancellation. Much of which has been planned will probably be under construction by 1991 or 1992 when the plants are privatized.

The private sector of Brazil's steel industry accounted for approximately 30 percent of total national production. In 1988 and 1989, its output was 7.7 million and 7.4 million tonnes of raw steel respectively. The largest of the private producers is the Gerdau Group, which within the last two years purchased the Usiba mill, formerly owned by Sidermex. It also purchased the Courtice Steel minimill in Canada for some $52 million. These two plants added 500,000 tonnes of steel capacity to the group's total.[5]

The private sector also operates blast-furnace plants that are based on charcoal as a fuel. In some years, as much as 35 to 40 percent of the iron produced in Brazil comes from charcoal furnaces. A number of these have been planned for the Amazon rain forest area where wood from charcoal is plentiful. Four of these have been built and eighteen more have been planned. However, a problem has arisen in respect to these furnaces. Environmentalists objected to the use of trees in the rain forest to produce charcoal and maintained that the area would be destroyed within a matter of twenty years. The furnaces were constructed along the right-of-way of the railroad which carries ore from Carajas to the sea, and thus, it was planned that they should use Carajas ore. The objection of the environmentalists has been so strong that there is doubt that the other eighteen plants will be built.[6] As of 1989, the plans of the private sector involved the expenditure of $1.3 million during the 1990s.

The state of the Brazilian steel industry in the year 2000 is now a matter of some conjecture. However, it can be said with some degree of certitude that the industry can be somewhat larger than it is currently and more efficient. This will depend, in great part, on the amount of investment made by the new owners of the privatized, integrated plants.

Chile

Chile has one integrated steel mill, CAP, with a capacity to produce less than 1 million tonnes; however, with a planned investment of $400 million, capacity will be increased to 1 million tonnes. This will be achieved by installing a new coke oven battery with 500,000 tonnes of capacity as compared to the previous battery capacity of 280,000 tonnes. The coke oven will allow the blast furnace to produce more iron to feed the BOF, whose capacity is adequate to produce a million tonnes of steel.

A continuous caster, which has been on the premises for some time, will be installed. Improvements will be made to the hot mill, possibly adding another stand, and the same will be done with the cold mill. Further, a galvanizing line producing galvalume will be installed to replace the present facility, and a temper mill will be added.

This plant was privatized in the last few years, with the workers owning 30 percent of the capital. Mitsubishi has 6.5 percent, and the Swiss own 20 percent.

People's Republic of China

The modern Chinese steel industry dates back to the early 1950s, when production of raw steel passed the 2-million-tonne mark in 1954. With assistance from the Soviet Union the industry developed rapidly; by 1960, output stood at 18.7 million tonnes. A few large plants were operating, but a significant amount of iron production in the early 1960s came from the small so-called back yard furnaces, which were producing a few tonnes per day. Many of them had an annual capacity of less than 300 tonnes and were abandoned in the mid- to late 1960s.

When the Russians withdrew in 1960, production of steel dropped precipitously to 8 million tonnes in 1962. It recovered slowly, and by 1970, it reached an estimated 18 million tonnes. In 1977, the continual increase in plant construction raised steel production to 23.7 million tonnes. From that point, it continued to grow consistently. By 1983, it was 40 million tonnes, and in the next six years, the increase was a dramatic 50 percent, raising steel output to 61.3 million in 1989. The goal set in early 1989—100 million tonnes by the year 2000—has been reduced to 90 million tonnes, and the 1995 objective has been cut from 80 million tonnes to 75 million. Plans for increasing the production of major steel plants, such as Ashan and Baoshan, remain intact.

The Chinese industry has erected greenfield-site plants in some places, such as the Baoshan plant, whose first phase was 3 million tonnes, to be augmented in the second phase to 6.7 million to 7.0 million tonnes. In a number of other cases, the Chinese have bought used steel mill equipment from companies throughout the world. For example, a rod mill was purchased from USX of the United States and shipped to the Anshan plant, where it was installed in a matter of eighteen months after it was dismantled. There were also two hot-strip mills from Japan, one from Nippon Steel's Sakai Works for a reported $13 million. The mill will be installed in the Meishan Steel Works near Nanjing. Currently the plant is producing pig iron. The installation of the mill will require the purchase of slabs for a number of years before the company can fully integrate.[7] A second hot-strip mill was purchased from Nisshin Steel, where it was in operation at the Kuri Works. The mill has a capacity to produce 2.6 million tonnes per year and will be transferred to the Taiyuan Iron and Steel Corporation.[8]

There are a number of fully integrated plants in China. These include Anshan, which is the largest producer, with an output of 8 million tonnes in 1988. The plant is large by any standards, with ten blast furnaces, fourteen open hearths, and three oxygen converters. It employs 220,000 people directly.[9] It was originally planned to increase the plant to 15 million tonnes

by the year 2000, principally through the addition of a new plant immediately adjacent to the present facility. The present facility will be expanded
through blast furnace rebuilds.

Wuhan Iron and Steel Company had its origins in the closing years of
the last century. It became a modern plant in the late 1950s and 1960s. The
steelmaking equipment was open-hearth furnaces. Since then, three oxygen
converters have been installed. The facility operates four blast furnaces,
making iron to produce approximately 4.5 million tonnes of steel in 1988.
It is expected that the plant will produce 7 million tonnes by 1993, with the
possibility of an increase of 4 million tonnes more by the year 2000. The
increase will be accomplished through the addition of another blast
furnace, more oxygen-converter capacity, as well as vacuum degassing and
continuous casting.

The Shou Du steel plant, built in 1919, continued as a pig iron producer
until 1949, after which it was rebuilt as an iron and steel plant and
subsequently enlarged to the point where it produced some 3.6 million tonnes
of raw steel in 1988. Much of this expansion took place in the 1980s. It was
able to increase production from 1.4 million tonnes in 1979 to 3.6 million
tonnes in 1988 through the acquisition of two used oxygen steelmaking
converters from Cockerill of Belgium. In addition, a used slab caster was also
purchased from Belgium and a cold-rolling mill from Sollac of France. Plans
for expanding the plant have not been completed, although there is talk
about the possibility of 7 million tonnes of production by the year 2000.

Taiyuan Iron and Steel Company is one of the smaller integrated plants,
with a production of 1.6 million tonnes of raw steel in 1988. The plant's
steel is produced in two used oxygen converters bought in Austria, with a
50-tonne heat capacity, and an argon furnace bought from Sweden. There
are also several electric arc furnaces with continuous-casting machines. The
plant will be increased in capacity to 2.5 million tonnes by 1995, adding
blast furnace capacity and a third oxygen converter, as well as more
continuous casting.

A major step in the development of the Chinese steel industry was the
construction of the Baoshan Steel plant near Shanghai. In May 1978, Nippon
Steel signed a letter of intent with the Chinese government outlining the scope
of responsibilities that Nippon had agreed to undertake. These involved
engineering, construction, and the initial operation of a 6-million-tonne
integrated plant at a site called Baoshan on the Yangtze River. The plant, to
be built in two stages, was to consist of two large blast furnaces, each capable
of 9,000 to 10,000 tonnes of iron production per day with supporting coke
ovens and sinter plants. Steelmaking equipment would ultimately consist of

three 300-tonne basic-oxygen converters, with part of the output continuously cast and part poured into conventional ingots, to be rolled down on a blooming-slabbing mill. Finishing facilities would consist of a hot-strip mill, a cold-strip mill, and a seamless-pipe mill. In addition to the finished products, a substantial tonnage of semifinished was to be produced to feed other plants.

The first phase, on which construction was begun in 1979 providing 3 million tonnes, consisted of one blast furnace, two oxygen converters, a blooming mill, and a seamless-pipe mill. During the construction of the first phase, hundreds of Japanese were sent to construct the facility, and at the same time, hundreds of Chinese were sent to the Kimitsu Works of Nippon for training, since this plant closely resembled the Baoshan works. The first phase was put in operation in September 1985 with a raw-steel capacity of 3.2 million tonnes, slightly more than was anticipated. The first 3 million tonnes provided 500,000 tonnes of blooms for seamless pipe, 1.5 million tonnes of billets to supply rerollers, and 1 million tonnes of slabs for the Wuhan Steel works hot-strip mill. Nippon contracted to supply all the facilities with the exception of the seamless mill.

The second phase, with 3 million more tonnes, is to include a second blast furnace, additional coke ovens, a sinter plant, a third oxygen converter, a continuous-casting unit, a hot-strip mill, and a cold-strip mill. This phase will bring the mill into the production of flat-rolled products and will make it modern in every respect. It includes CVC (continuously variable crown) in order to roll as consistent a gauge as possible throughout the strip. The second phase, which will probably be completed in 1991, will bring the capacity to 6.2 million tonnes.

The third phase is to bring the output of the Baoshan works to 10 million tonnes by the year 2000. This would require a third blast furnace, additional coke and sinter capacity, and added oxygen converters. Finishing capacity would consist of a plate mill and more hot- and cold-strip mill capacity, as well as galvanizing lines. There is a report that financial problems will delay this phase of the Baoshan steel mill program.[10] When it will be completed is a matter of conjecture.

In addition, there are a number of other integrated facilities of lesser capacity and a large number of electric furnace plants spread throughout the country. A recent book on the steel industries of China and India lists sixteen small-size integrated iron and steel plants and fourteen semi-integrated steel plants, the former with 100,000 to 300,000 tonnes per year and the latter with 125,000 to 550,000 tonnes per year.[11]

In the 1990s, the Chinese industry will undoubtedly increase its production. It is doubtful that its goal of 90 million tonnes will be reached by the year 2000, since this will require considerable financial resources, although it is more than possible that an 85-million-tonne figure could be attained. With additional continuous casting, the yield from raw steel to finished products will be substantially increased. The International Iron and Steel Institute reports a 14.7 percent rate of continuous casting in 1988. If this increases to 60 to 70 percent, it will add considerable tonnage to the finished products and obviate the necessity to reach 90 million tonnes.

Steel imports for China declined sharply in the late 1980s from a high point of 19.6 million tonnes in 1985 to an estimated 9 million tonnes in 1988. Japan, which was the principal supplier, with 10.9 million tonnes in 1985, saw its exports to China dwindle to 3.9 million tonnes in 1989. It is conceivable that as China's production increases to beyond 70 million tonnes and the yield grows accordingly because of increased continuous casting, it will enter the export market. Up until 1988, its exports were minimal, at 150,000 tonnes.

The current need for steel at home is illustrated by the fact that the Chinese have cut down on the export of coking coal and pig iron to Japan. In 1990, the tonnage of pig iron shipped to Japan will be reduced from 1.3 million tonnes in 1989 to about 300,000 tonnes. Further, the price of exported coking coal has been raised by some $2.40 per tonne.

China is the outstanding example of expansion in the past ten years, having increased from a production of 37 million tonnes in 1980 to 61 million tonnes in 1989. It will continue to lead the world in growth during the 1990s. The demand for steel in this country of 1.2 billion people is great.

The Chinese are developing their ability to produce steel mill facilities, some through joint ventures with the Japanese. In early 1990, two Chinese companies—Chongqing Specialty Steel Works and Chongqing Design Company—took the initial steps to form a joint venture with two Japanese companies—Sumitomo Metals and Mitsubishi Heavy Industries—to produce continuous-casting machines. The arrangement will be directed to produce continuous-casting units for many of the electric furnace producers throughout China. The Japanese will provide the technology and design engineering, and the Chinese will provide the hardware. The possible market is extensive and includes most of the electric furnace plants in China.[12]

The Chinese are also interested in developing specialty steels and, in this respect, have invited a team from the Japanese specialty steelmakers to examine the possibilities of developing specialty steel plants in China. They are particularly interested in the Nanjing No. 2 steel plant to see if it is adaptable for this use.[13]

One area in which the Chinese had very little activity is the production of DRI. Thus far, there are only two units under consideration throughout all of China. These will be modest in size so that the combined production, if it materializes, would be approximately 1 million tonnes.

Taiwan

Taiwan is one of the countries in the Third World that has achieved considerable progress in building up its steel industry. In 1966, steel production was very small: 326,000 tonnes produced in electric furnaces. This figure grew slowly to 535,000 tonnes in 1973. A considerable advance was made in 1974 to 900,000 tonnes, and, in 1976, the integrated plant of China Steel came into production. It was constructed on a greenfield site with a capacity of 1.5 million tonnes to produce rods, bars, and plates.

In the early 1980s, China Steel's capacity was increased to 3.2 million tonnes by the addition of another blast furnace, and a hot-strip mill was installed for the production of sheets. An additional expansion was under-taken in the late 1980s with the erection of a third blast furnace, as well as a second BOF shop, which brought capacity up to 5.6 million tonnes. Improvements were made to the hot-strip mill and an additional cold-reduction mill was installed, as well as a continuous-annealing facility and an electrolytic galvanizing line. In addition, there was a new bar mill, as well as improvements to the existing plate mill.

The plant at Kaohsiung was originally planned for 8 million tonnes. However, there are limitations, including process water shortage and environmental considerations. Thus, it is quite probable that the fourth phase, which would bring it up to 8 million tonnes, will not be installed at the original site. The company is looking elsewhere to establish an integrated plant of 2.5 million to 3.0 million tonnes. The possibilities were eastern Canada and Malaysia. Feasibility studies were conducted to determine the future site. Malaysia was chosen for a plant of 2.5 million to 3.0 million tonnes. It is hoped that construction will start in 1992.

In addition to China Steel, there are a number of other steel operations in Taiwan, including several electric furnace plants. As of 1990, an additional hot-strip mill with a 2-million-tonne capacity was completed by the An Feng Group. This is a privately owned steel company that will secure slabs from overseas, as well as from China Steel, to feed the mill. China Steel can provide some 200,000 tonnes a year, so 1.8 million must be secured elsewhere. The hot-rolled sheet output will be used domestically by a number of steel processors and the shipbuilding industry. Currently the company does not plan to install any steel-melting capacity.

In March 1990, the An Feng Steel Company entered into a three-year contract with Acominas of Brazil to supply 200,000 tonnes of slabs per year. The mill went into operation in the third quarter of that year, when slabs from the Brazilian steel company began to arrive. An Feng is holding talks with a number of steel companies throughout the world, including Tubarao, to ensure a supply of additional slabs.

Another project in the form of a joint venture is being organized in Taiwan with the participation of Highveld and Samancor of South Africa, as well as Thyssen Steel of West Germany and Yieh Loong of Taiwan, to install a cold-rolling mill in Taiwan with a capacity for 200,000 tonnes. The hot bands will be rolled in a new South African plant. The output of the cold mill will be used principally in Taiwan. Yieh Loong is also contemplating the installation of a thin-slab caster.

Taiwan is one of the Third World countries that will add to its steelmaking capacity, although the addition is located in another country. It is also updating existing capacity in its own country so that there will be an improvement in quality and productivity.

India

The steel industry in India consists of three companies with integrated units and a host of small electric furnace operations. The largest company, by far, is SAIL (Steel Authority of India, Ltd.). This company has five integrated plants, with a nominal capacity of 11.2 million tonnes. The most recently built is Bokaro, with 4 million tonnes. Bhilai also has a 4-million-tonne capacity. Both of these plants were built with the help of the Soviet Union. Ruorkela, built with the help of the Germans, has a 1.8-million-tonne capacity, and Durgapur, with 1.0 million tonnes, was constructed with assistance from the United Kingdom. The fifth plant, IISCO, was established in India as a private operation but was taken over by the government and made part of SAIL in the early 1970s. Currently its capacity is listed at 1 million tonnes, although production in 1988–1989 was less than 500,000 tonnes. Its peak of 970,000 tonnes was achieved in the early 1960s.

In addition to SAIL, a private company, Tata, has a current rated capacity of 2 million tonnes, which by 1993 will be increased to 3 million tonnes. There is also a newly constructed government plant, Visakhapatnam, not included in the SAIL complex. It has been under construction for a number of years and in early 1990 produced its first steel. Current capacity is 1.5 million tonnes. Originally the plant called for 3.5 million tonnes. It is still under construction and will be finished, it is hoped, in the early 1990s.

Currently it has one coke oven battery feeding the blast furnace, which provides iron for the basic-oxygen converter. There is a continuous caster for blooms, which are to be converted into a series of long products, including merchant bars, wire rods, and structurals.

The electric furnace segment of the industry consists of numerous companies with relatively small production capabilities. Many of these operate furnaces with 10- to 12-tonne heats, although in a few cases, the furnaces are as large as 50 tonnes per heat. Total nominal capacity of the electric furnace segment is somewhat in excess of 4 million tonnes; however, there is a chronic shortage of scrap and electric power, which confines the output of these units to approximately 3 million tonnes.

Raw-steel production in India in 1989 was 14.4 million tonnes, a slight increase over the previous year's figure of 14.3 million but nevertheless a record. SAIL's contribution to this output was 9.7 million tonnes, with the remaining production coming from Tata and the electric furnace segment.

Plans for the Indian steel industry are ambitious by national standards. During the 1990s, there will be at least three blast furnaces built and several continuous casters installed for slabs as well as blooms. SAIL's capacity of 11 million to 12 million tonnes will be expanded to about 15 million by the mid-1990s. The program includes bringing Bhilai and Bokaro up to the 4-million-rated-tonne mark. The 1988 output at Bokaro was 2.8 million tonnes of raw steel. This will be increased by upgrading the blast furnaces as each comes due for relining, as well as installing a continuous caster and a second cold-reduction mill. The hot-strip mill will also be upgraded to improve quality, as well as to increase output. It is hoped that in addition to the increased production, man-hour output productivity will also be increased.

The 1988 output of raw steel at Bhilai was 3.1 million tonnes, short of its rated capacity of 4 million tonnes. There are plans for Bhilai that extend into the second half of the 1990s, including a second basic-oxygen steelmaking shop, which will eliminate its open hearths, and an additional continuous caster. It is hoped that this will bring its capacity above 5 million tonnes. For the first half of the decade, however, the objective is to produce 4 million tonnes or the rated capacity.

Rourkela was one of the three original plants of SAIL, then known as Hindustan Steel Company in the 1960s. It has a rated capacity of 1.8 million tonnes, with a production in the 1988–1989 fiscal year of 1.2 million tonnes. It is planned to increase the capacity to 3 million tonnes with the construction of a blast furnace and additional oxygen steelmaking capacity.

Durgapur, also one of the first three original Hindustan plants, currently has a rated capacity of less than 1 million tonnes. In the late 1980s, it achieved an output of 1 million tonnes. There are plans to increase capacity to 1.6 million to 1.8 million tonnes, which will be achieved, to a great extent, by replacing the open-hearth capacity with oxygen steelmaking. Vacuum degassing and ladle refining facilities will also be added. A higher yield from raw steel to finished product will be achieved by the installation of continuous-casting units for billets.

The IISCO steel plant, although rated at one time at 1 million tonnes, now has an actual capacity of some 600,000 tonnes. This unit will be replaced in great part with a new blast furnace, oxygen steelmaking, and continuous casting, so that its capacity will be increased to 2 million tonnes. The current rated capacity of SAIL is 11.2 million tonnes and, with the planned increase, will be advanced to 14.8 million tonnes. The total increase will involve a large investment in continuous casting, as well as a shift from open-hearth steelmaking to basic oxygen.

Tata Steel Company was the first integrated plant built in India in the opening decade of the century. In 1947, it produced approximately 1 million tonnes of steel. Currently it is rated somewhat in excess of 2 million tonnes, and expansion activities should bring it to 3 million tonnes by 1993. The additions consist of a new blast furnace purchased from Portugal, the installation of the energy-optimizing furnace developed by Korf, and an additional oxygen converter. There will also be a new hot-strip mill with a 1.5-million-tonne capacity to be fed by continuous casters for slabs.

The new plant, Visakhapatnam, which went into operation in early 1990, will be expanded through the installation of additional coke ovens, another blast furnace, and added oxygen steelmaking. The ultimate capacity will be 3.5 million tonnes.

The electric furnace segment of the Indian steel industry, which is heavily dependent on scrap, will reduce its dependence through the installation of a number of DRI plants, the capacity of which in India in 1989 was 600,000 tonnes. If current plans to increase this are realized, it can reach 9 million tonnes within five years. Almost 2 million tonnes are under construction, with 1.5 million contracted for and 5 million under study. If instead only half of this is achieved, a 4.5-million-tonne figure will be most helpful to provide feed for the electric furnace segment of the Indian industry. The expansion of the electric units, however, could be curtailed by the shortage of electric power.

Essar Steel, an Indian group, is building a DRI plant and proposing to establish a plant to produce 800,000 tonnes of hot-rolled coils for export. The DRI plant will feed an electric shop, which includes ladle refining. The steel will be put through a slab caster and a hot-strip mill. The plant will have a coastal location at Hazira in Gujurai State.[14]

Another interesting development is in the state of Orissa, where the chief minister plans to build 2.7 million tonnes of steel capacity with the help of POSCO, which it is hoped would take 40 percent of the investment.

The Indian government is optimistic and enthusiastic about increasing its steelmaking capacity. Recently the country's secretary spoke of 24 million tonnes by 1995—a considerable achievement when one considers that the output for 1989 was 14.4 million tonnes. The additional tonnage would come from the new integrated mill, Visakhapatnam, as well as improvements in SAIL. TATA is expected to add 700,000 tonnes, and the minimills will provide upwards of 1.5 million to 2.0 million tonnes.[15]

India, like most of the other Third World countries, will expand its steel-producing capacity during the 1990s. Virtually all of this added tonnage will be consumed in India, which has a deficiency of steel. Exports may increase by a modest amount, since India would like to have its products sold, at least to a limited extent, on the international market.

Mexico

Mexico is one of the countries that recently declared it will privatize the government segment of its steel industry. This currently consists of two large integrated plants and several small ones. The larger of the integrated plants is Altos Harnos, with a capacity to produce some 3.3 million tonnes of raw steel. In 1989, production was somewhat above 3 million tonnes.

Prior to the announcement of privatization, a significant reconstruction of the mill had been planned. Steel capacity from the BOFs was set at 3 million tonnes, and a small tonnage of open-hearth steel raised the total for the plant to 3.3 million tonnes. Ladle furnaces were to be installed at the two BOF shops, and the continuous caster was to be upgraded. The hot-strip mill was to be completely renovated, starting with the reheating furnaces and proceeding through the coilers. The cold mill was also to be upgraded. The cost for the hot-strip mill is in excess of $200 million, which has been provided by a World Bank loan. There are no plans for the plate mill. Indeed except for the hot-strip mill, most of the program has been put on hold, anticipating the plant's sale to private industry.

The other government plant is Sicartsa, with a capacity of 3.6 million tonnes. The first phase, built in the 1970s, consisted of coke ovens, a blast furnace, basic-oxygen converters, a continuous caster, and a rod and bar mill. The second phase, begun in the early 1980s, includes a direct-reduction facility, four electric furnaces, two ladle furnaces three continuous casters, and a fully modern plate mill. As of 1990, the plate mill has not been installed but is on the premises. It will have a capacity for 1.5 million tonnes when and if installed.

There was considerable delay in constructing the second phase of Sicartsa due to government's financial problems when the price of oil dropped sharply. The first phase of Sicartsa will not require any restructuring. The second phase represents an attractive investment opportunity since it is producing continuously cast slabs for sale.

The third integrated company, HYL, is in the private sector. It has two plants, one in Monterrey and one in Puebla. Both are fed by direct-reduced iron made by the HYL process. Finished products include flat and long products. The Puebla works is confined to the production of long products, including merchant bars and wire rods, while the Monterrey plant concentrates on the production of flat products. This plant will undergo an extensive renovation, which will include the installation of a continuous caster, as well as the modernization of the hot-strip mill and upgrading the cold-reduction mills.

In 1986, the government closed its plant in Monterrey, which had been taken over in the early 1980s and was formerly known as Fundidor. Much of the plant is being dismantled; however, the sheet-producing facilities, which have been mothballed since 1986, can be reactivated, and it is quite possible that they may be sold, either to HYL or a foreign investor.

In addition to the integrated plants, there is one large producer of pipe, Tamsa, which operates electric furnaces fed by direct-reduced iron. There are also some twenty small electric furnaces spread throughout the country operating principally on scrap, although some direct-reduced iron is used.

The situation in Mexico is fluid as of 1990 with the government's announcement of privatization of the industry. Mexico's production was quite static in the 1980s. In 1980, it was 7.2 million tonnes, and it remained in the 7-million- to 8-million-tonne range, reaching 7.7 million tonnes in 1989, a slight decrease from the record output of 7.8 million in 1988.

Mexico was given an increase in its voluntary restraint agreement for exports to the United States for the years 1989 through 1992, and it hopes to increase exports in accordance with this agreement. Because of the uncertainty hanging over the industry, the future of the government steel plants is not now predictable. When and if these plants are sold, plans for modernizing and restructuring Altos Hornos will undoubtedly be put into operation, and the plate mill at Sicartsa will be installed or sold.

Venezuela

In 1947, a very large, rich deposit of iron ore was discovered in Venezuela near Puerto Ordaz, located on the Orinoco River. Both United States Steel Corporation and Bethlehem Steel developed mines in the area, and in the late 1950s, the Venezuelan government organized a steel company located near the ore deposits. It was a government-owned and -operated facility known as Sidor (Siderurgica del Orinoco). The initial capacity, and that which functioned through the 1960s and most of the 1970s was 1.2 million tonnes. It operated four open-hearth furnaces based on hot metal produced in Tysland-Hole electric-reduction furnaces. In addition to Sidor, a small electric furnace producer, Sivensa operated two plants, with a total capacity of approximately 200,000 tonnes.

Steel production was considerably below capacity in the 1960s; however, it improved significantly in the 1970s, and in 1975, a large addition was planned for the Sidor plant. The expansion involved the installation of several direct-reduction units to produce DRI for two large electric furnace shops with a total capacity of 3.8 million tonnes, one with six 200-tonne furnaces and the other with four 150-tonne furnaces, raising the total capacity of the plant to 5 million tonnes. The furnaces were the first large installation in the world to be based on DRI as a furnace feed. As a matter of practice, DRI constitutes about 80 percent of the furnace charge, with scrap making up the remainder. For a number of years the plant at Sidor failed to produce at capacity. For most of that time, it operated between 1.5 million and 2.0 million tonnes. In the late 1980s, particularly from 1986 through 1989, it produced over 3 million tonnes. There are no plans to expand the plant.

The objective of the early 1990s is to raise production to capacity and to improve the operation of facilities. The plant will undergo substantial modernization in the early 1990s. The highest priority is a seamless-pipe mill, which will be completely modernized by 1991. In addition, the hot-strip mill will be revamped to increase its capacity by a half-million tonnes from 2.1 million tonnes to 2.6 million annually. The work will consist of modernizing the furnaces and the mill stands by introducing roll bending and side shifting. The direct-reduction facilities, which consist of four Midrex units and three HYL units, will be upgraded to increase their capacity. The object is to reach 4.2 million tonnes. They are now some 300,000 tonnes short of the goal, and this amount must be purchased during the next two years while the revamping is taking place. A continuous-casting machine will be installed at the open-hearth facility for rods and billets. When the modernization is finished, employment will have fallen because of retirements and attrition so that the current level of employment—18,000 employees—will be somewhat reduced.

The principal activity in Venezuela in relation to the iron and steel industry will be the construction of a number of DRI plants. These are intended to produce the material for export. Currently, in addition to the seven units at Sidor, there is a 400,000-tonne plant using the Fior process and a plant that has been converted, which was originally built by United States Steel. This plant has just been started up with the Midrex process and a capacity of 830,000 tonnes. It is owned by CVG, a government-owned company, and leased by Kobe Steel for eleven years. Kobe expects to export some 650,000 tonnes of its output. Sivensa is building a 600,000-tonne Midrex plant and expects to export 400,000 tonnes of its output.

There are currently feasibility studies to build a 1-million-tonne Fior plant for Sidor. From a practical point of view, it is doubtful that this should be one plant producing 1 million tonnes; rather it will probably be two units, each producing one-half million tonnes. The ownership of the plant will be 51 percent by Davy McKee and 49 percent by the Venezuelan government. It is planned that some 80 percent of the product will be exported.

Consigua, a consortium of three partners—CVG, Kobe Steel, and Midrex—is planning two Midrex plants of 1 million tonnes each, one of which will be used to feed electric furnaces, which will then produce continuously cast slabs for export. The other will produce 1 million tonnes of DRI pellets for export. This is expected to start by 1994. Thus, the total amount of new capacity, including the redone United States Steel plant, will be 4.4 million tonnes.

One of the principal motivating forces behind this expansion is the judgment that electric furnace plants, particularly in the United States but also elsewhere, will need more DRI as the quality of scrap deteriorates, particularly for minimills that intend to produce sheet products. It is not desirable to have a 100 percent scrap charge in the electric furnace for the production of sheets because tramp elements in the scrap make it impossible to produce a high-quality product. DRI will dilute these elements to a point where good-quality sheets can be produced from electric furnace steel.

Venezuela is richly endowed with iron ore and gas. Consequently, it is a perfect location for the production of DRI, a product that will be in demand increasingly in the 1990s.

South Korea

South Korea is an outstanding example of a Third World country that developed a modern steel industry in fewer than twenty years. In 1966, output was approximately 185,000 tonnes, produced in a small, obsolete open hearth furnace. In 1970, production, which was entirely from non-integrated plants, amounted to 481,000 tonnes. By 1989, the country was the eighth largest producer in the world, with an output of 21.9 million tonnes. Its production in that year surpassed such industrialized countries as France, United Kingdom, Canada, Spain, Australia, and South Africa.

The move to establish an integrated steel plant began in the mid-1960s when a consortium of companies from several countries was organized to prepare a comprehensive project development plan. This was part of the country's second five-year economic development plan, covering 1967 through 1971. Prior to the organization of this consortium, the government of South Korea had approached the International Bank for Reconstruction and Development (World Bank) for assistance, including a review of studies and feasibility reports on the Korean iron and steel projects. The Korean government was also referred to United Nations Industrial Development Organization (UNIDO) for further studies.

Doubts were expressed by the World Bank, which believed that since the economics of an integrated steelworks in South Korea were questionable considering its requirements for foreign capital, it would be better first to develop a machinery industry that would be intensive in labor and technology. Another agency, USOM, expressed the opinion in 1969 that an integrated steelworks would threaten the survival and expansion plans of existing steel mills and would disturb the price structure for steel products. It therefore recommended that electric steelmaking be adopted rather than an integrated plant. This recommendation was rejected, and work was started on an integrated plant using Japanese war reparation funds. In 1968, in spite of doubts as to the feasibility of constructing a fully integrated plant in South Korea, Pohang Iron and Steel Company (POSCO) was formed.

POSCO's first plant at Pohang, built in four stages, has five blast furnaces and a steelmaking capacity of 9.1 million tonnes. Construction on the first stage at Pohang began in 1970 and was completed in 1973. The plant proceeded by stages through 1983 when the second phase of the fourth stage was dedicated and the plant's capacity reached 9.1 million tonnes.

In the early 1980s, there was considerable discussion within the management of POSCO concerning the construction of a second integrated steel plant. The decision was made by chairman Tae Joon Park to proceed with the construction of a plant at Kwangyang, in the southern part of South Korea. The first phase of the plant was dedicated in May 1987 with a 2.7-million-tonne capacity. Immediately after, the second phase, with an equal capacity, was under construction, bringing the total potential to 5.4 million tonnes. The third phase will be finished in late 1990, adding 3 million tonnes. A fourth phase now in the planning stage will add a further 3 million tonnes, bringing the total of the plant's capacity to 11.4 million tonnes. At that point, the plant will contain four sinter plants; four coke oven batteries; four blast furnaces, each with a total output of 8,500 tonnes of iron per day; two basic-oxygen shops, with a total of six vessels; seven continuous-casting units; three hot-strip mills; three cold-reduction mills; two hot-dipped galvanizing lines; and one electrolytic galvanizing line. The cold-reduction mills are six-high and are the most modern units available.

The two mills, one at Pohang and the other at Kwangyang, will have a combined capacity in 1993, when the fourth phase of Kwangyang is completed, of 20.5 million tonnes. As of 1989, POSCO was the third largest steel company in the world, surpassed only by Nippon Steel of Japan and Usinor-Sacilor of France. The Kwangyang plant will be devoted to the production of flat-rolled products, and the Pohang facility, in addition to flat-rolled products including sheets and plates, produces rods and stainless steel. At its full future capacity, Kwangyang will provide sheets for the Korean economy to a point where imports will be sharply reduced. Both Pohang and Kwangyang are equipped with the most modern facilities.

In addition to POSCO, nine electric furnace plants and some thirty-five companies make products from purchased steel. The total production of the electric furnace group in 1989 amounted to 6.4 million tonnes, which, added to POSCO's output of 15.5 million, gave a total for the country of 21.9 million tonnes.

The electric furnace segment of South Korea's steel industry, whose capacity is 6.5 million tonnes, has grown considerably in the last decade. Three of these companies each has a potential to produce a million or more tonnes. The largest company, Inchon Steel, increased its capacity between 1987 and 1988 by 300,000 tonnes, so that its present potential is 2 million tonnes. Dongkuk also expanded its capacity by 150,000 tonnes between 1987 and 1988. Two of the other electric furnace companies, Sammi and Kangwon, expect to add 500,000 tonnes each by 1991. The latter will also add 120,000 tonnes by increasing the capacity of one of its transformers. Total addition to the electric furnace capacity between 1987 and 1991 will be 2.2 million tonnes.

South Korea, through Pohang Steel as well as its electric furnace plants, will be close to self-sufficient in terms of steel supply by the mid-1990s. The electric furnace capacity as of 1990 is 6.5 million tonnes, and with the added capacity planned by several of these mills, including that of Pohang, total capacity for the country by 1995 will be very close to 30 million tonnes. A significant portion of this—possibly as much as 8 million to 10 million tonnes of steel products—will be exported.

South Korea shares the same problem as Japan in terms of raw materials, since it has neither iron ore nor metallurgical coal and must import both. Its two integrated plants requiring these materials are located on the seacoast where there is deep water, so that large bulk cargo carriers can bring in the needed raw materials. Imports of raw materials will be required in the future. Pohang has invested in coal mines in several countries, thus ensuring itself of a supply. Ore is imported predominantly from Australia.

The South Korean industry, both Pohang and the electric furnace companies, have entered into joint ventures outside the country. The most notable is the joint venture in the United States between Pohang and United States Steel Corporation, which resulted in a cold-reduction mill in California. This is a most modern facility, with a six-high mill and continuous annealing. Pohang will supply most of the hot-rolled bands to the joint venture from its Kwangyang mill. These coils are high quality since the strip mill at Kwangyang embodies all of the most modern equipment.

Sammi, a producer of stainless steel, purchased three North American speciality steel plants: one, AlTech Specialty Steel Corporation, located in the United States, and two Canadian companies, Atlas Stainless Steels in Quebec and Atlas Specialty Steel in Ontario. It also will expand its capacity in South Korea to 1 million tonnes.

South Korea's progress has been remarkable over a short period of time and will continue to the mid-1990s, when it will have one of the most modern steel industries in the world.

Eastern Europe and the USSR

Eastern Europe

Recent dramatic changes that have taken place throughout the countries in Eastern Europe, as well as the USSR, will have a distinct bearing on their steel industries in the 1990s. These countries, including Poland Czechoslovakia, Rumania, Eastern Germany, Hungary, and Bulgaria, have increased their production from 40 million tonnes of raw steel in 1970 to 57.9 million in 1989, a growth of slightly less than 50 percent. This growth, in terms of total tonnage, was much less than the USSR which increased its raw steel output from 116 million tonnes in 1970 to 160 million tonnes in 1989. Much of the growth in the Eastern European countries took place between 1970 and 1980. There was very little growth between 1980 and 1989 as table 3–2 indicates.

Table 3–2
Steel Output* in Eastern Europe, 1970, 1980 and 1989

	1970	1980	1989
Bulgaria	1.8	2.6	3.0
Czechoslovakia	11.5	14.9	15.5
Eastern Germany	5.4	7.3	7.8
Hungary	3.1	3.8	3.3
Poland	11.8	19.5	14.8
Rumania	5.5	13.2	13.4

Source: International Iron and Steel Institute
*In millions of tonnes.

The facilities in the Eastern European countries are by no means world-class. The percentage of continuous casting is decidedly short of that in countries in the Western World. Continuous casting, which is considered essential to quality steel production, is far below the percentage in other major steel producing countries. For example, in 1989, Japan cast 93 percent of its steel, while the European Community cast some 88 percent, the United States 65 percent, and South Korea 94 percent. In the Eastern European countries, progress has been made between 1980 and 1989. However, results are still most unsatisfactory. Table 3–3 shows the percentage of steel continuously cast in 1980 and 1989. As is evident from the table, Rumania, Hungary, and Eastern Germany have made the most progress.

In terms of the oxygen process as a source of steelmaking, the Eastern Europeans are also considerably behind and are still making a large percentage of their steel by the open hearth, as of 1989. The figures in Table 3–4 compare with an average of 70 percent basic oxygen in the European Community, where the open hearth has been completely eliminated. Thus, for the Eastern European countries to become competitive, it will require a significant investment both in continuous casting and basic-oxygen steel production. These investments are necessary to reduce costs, increase productivity, and improve steel quality.

In addition to obsolete facilities, a complete change in management philosophy will be needed for the Eastern European countries to compete on a world basis. Over a period of forty-five years, this industry has operated in a managed economy where steel was allocated much more than marketed. As a result, there was little incentive to install the most modern equipment, since the facilities that were there were able to produce steel. It will take several years before the industries in these countries will be able to

Table 3–3
Percentage of Steel Continuously Cast in Eastern Europe, 1980 and 1989

	1980	*1989*
Bulgaria	0%	15%
Czechoslovakia	2%	9%
Eastern Germany	14%	41%
Hungary	36%	56%
Poland	4%	7%
Rumania	18%	34%

Source: International Iron and Steel Institutre

Table 3–4
Percentage of Basic-Oxygen and Open-Hearth
Raw Steel Production in Eastern Europe,
1980 and 1989

	Basic Oxygen	Open Hearth
Bulgaria	51%	10%
Czechoslovakia	47%	40%
Eastern Germany	31%	39%
Hungary	47%	43%
Poland	49%	36%
Rumania	48%	28%

Source: International Iron and Steel Institute

install modern equipment to compete on a world basis. Capacity will, most probably, be reduced. However, as much of the present equipment is replaced, the picture should brighten. Further, recognizing the fact that management has lived for at least forty-five years under circumstances completely foreign to a market economy, it will be necessary for those involved to adapt themselves to a philosophy necessary to compete in a market economy.

Much of the adjustment will be made through joint ventures, as well as consultations with Western World countries. There has been a decided movement on the part of Western European countries, particularly Western Germany, to establish relations with the steel industries in Eastern Europe. This has been particularly notable in the East Germany/West Germany relationship. Almost all of the Western German major integrated companies are involved in some sort of relationship with the Eastern German steel industry. Companies such as Thyssen, Krupp, Klockner, and Salzgitter have entered into agreements or joint ventures with those of Eastern Germany and elsewhere. Hungary has been the recipient of several joint ventures, particularly one involving Korf and Metallgesellchaft in which each group has taken a 30 percent share in an Hungarian company which will be restructured with modern facilities to produce 650,000 tonnes of wire rods and bars.

Thyssen is involved in several arrangements including a joint venture involving a new company to produce and process special steels. Krupp has made an arrangement with VEV Oranienbarg, a cold-reduction producer. Klockner has an agreement with Henningsdorf to provide semifinished steel which will replace the open hearth at that plant.

Soviet Union

Prior to World War II, the Soviet Union was a significant factor on the world steel scene. In 1939, it produced 18.6 million tonnes of raw steel, which ranked it third among steel producers. Much of its industry was destroyed during the war, and rebuilding was necessary. This was accomplished in a relatively short period; production rose to 51 million tonnes in 1957, which placed it second to the United States in terms of raw-steel output. In 1974, the Soviet Union took over the leadership in world raw-steel output, passing the United States. Since that time, it has increased its steel production significantly, unlike many of the other industrialized countries, including the United States, Japan, and Western Europe, which have seen their raw-steel output decline.

In 1989, 161 million tonnes of raw steel were produced, an amount far greater than the 108-million-tonne output registered by Japan, the second largest producer. Some 16 percent of the raw steel was continuously cast, and as a consequence, the yield from raw steel to finished products left something to be desired.

In terms of raw materials for steelmaking, the Soviet Union is reasonably well endowed. It has large reserves of iron ore, much of which ranges in iron content from 55 to 63 percent. In 1987, some 251 million tonnes were mined, of which 47 million, including 11 million tonnes of pellets, were exported to Eastern bloc countries, such as Czechoslovakia, Poland, and Rumania. These three countries took over two-thirds of the exports. Large quantities of coal are available. However, the supply of metallurgical coal for coke is supplemented by metallurgical coal shipped in from Poland.

Scrap imports are negligible since the country is relatively self-sufficient with respect to this essential steelmaking material. In fact, it exports significant tonnages annually, much of it to Yugoslavia, Japan, and Italy.

A large quantity of scrap was needed in 1988 for an electric furnace production of 22 million tonnes, or 14 percent of total steel output. This will increase to some extent in the next decade, with the charge being made up not only of scrap but also DRI. The Soviet Union increased its capacity to produce this material fourfold between 1985 and 1987 and will expand further in the future. In 1989, it ranked third in the world in DRI production behind Venezuela and Mexico.

The Soviet Union carries on a relatively active trade in steel with a number of countries. In 1987, exports of steel products were slightly over 9 million tonnes, with East Germany, the largest customer, importing 3.4 million. Other significant recipients were China and Hungary, each with 800,000 tonnes, Yugoslavia with 700,000 and Bulgaria with 600,000 tonnes. A relatively small amount went to countries in Western Europe, among them Italy with 200,000 tonnes.

Steel imports totaled 10.8 million tonnes, with pipe accounting for 5.2 million. The principal suppliers were Western Germany, with 2.5 million, and Japan with 1.4 million. Smaller amounts, ranging from 800,000 tonnes downward, came from such countries as Poland, Italy, France, China, Austria, and Rumania.

Future plans call for improving the efficiency and productivity of the finishing and processing segments of the industry. Very little additional tonnage is contemplated. Current capacity is in the area of 175 million to 180 million tonnes, which indicates that the operating rate in 1989 was over 90 percent.

Efforts to improve the industry's efficiency will center on continuous casting and the replacement of open-hearth furnaces by basic-oxygen converters. Continuous casting will provide not only a better steel but a much higher yield of finished products from raw steel. Currently 24 million tonnes are continuously cast. If this figure is increased to 80 million, or 50 percent of raw steel, the yield of finished products would advance substantially without any additional melting capacity. Such a program will take several years to complete.

The Soviet Union produces about one-half of its steel by the open-hearth method. This will be changed in the years ahead. One of the largest plants, Magnitogorsk, produced open-hearth steel in 1988. By the mid-1990s, this will be changed to 50 percent BOF and 50 percent open hearth. A similar change is planned for other large plants, including Krivoi Rog.

Several factors challenge the future growth of the steel industry in the Soviet Union:

1. It is expected that per capita consumption of steel will decrease somewhat due to a more rational utilization.

2. The challenge from nonferrous metals, particularly aluminum and plastics, is significant.

3. Steel quality must be improved to reduce rejection rates. [16]

Steel growth, which was rapid in the 1960s at 5.4 percent annually, had slowed to 2.7 percent in the 1970s and 1.5 percent in the 1980s. In the decade ahead, there will be very little increase, if any, in raw-steel production; however, shipments should increase with the growth in continuous casting.

The recent liberalization movement in Soviet industry will have a widespread effect, although this may take several years before it is accomplished. Among the new products is the installation of a galvanizing line at the Magnitogorsk Works, one of the largest mills in the country. This unit will be a hot-dipped line with a capacity in excess of 300,000 tonnes. [17]

There have been some difficulties in the reorganization of the Soviet steel industry, in great part because of financial restraints. One of these was the postponement of a fully integrated plant in Komsomolsk.[18]

The Soviet steel industry has not been a major factor in world steel trade, particularly since its exports were confined principally to the Eastern bloc, a condition that may change.

Middle East and North Africa

The growth of the steel industry in the Middle East and North Africa is a post–World War II development. The steel-producing countries in that area are Algeria, Egypt, Iran, Israel, Nigeria, Qatar, Saudi Arabis, and Tunisia. Total production in 1973 amounted to 1.25 million tonnes, which grew gradually and by 1980 had reached 3.7 million tonnes. Output by 1988 had grown to almost 8.0 million tonnes.

Egypt was the leading producer in 1988 with 2 million tonnes, followed by Saudi Arabia with 1.6 million. Algeria is estimated at 1.4 million tonnes. Iran, with 978,000 tonnes, is the only other significant producer. Most of the others turn out 500,000 tonnes or less.

Egypt uses virtually all of its steel at home, having exported only 66,000 tonnes in 1988. Qatar, on the other hand, with a production of 527,000 tonnes in 1988, exported an estimated 480,000 tonnes, virtually all of its output, while importing approximately 100,000 tonnes. Egypt, with the largest production in the area, imported an additional 2.2 million tonnes. Algeria was the third largest producer with 1.4 million tonnes and imported an estimated 1.25 million tonnes. The region is heavily dependent on imports; in 1988, total imports amounted to 6.75 million tonnes, while exports were an estimated total of 670,000 tonnes, or more than a ten-to-one ratio in favor of imports. The region will continue to be heavily dependent on imports throughout the 1990s.

Egypt has gradually expanded its production from 500,000 tonnes in 1974 to 1.0 million in 1981, followed by an increase to 1.4 million tonnes in 1987, and finally to 2.0 million in 1988. This was the result of the installation of a new steelworks that came into production in late 1986. The mill, a joint venture with Japan, included a direct-reduction plant with a capacity in excess of 700,000 tonnes and an electric furnace steelmaking plant with approximately an 850,000-tonne capacity. The electric furnace feeds continuous casters, which were supplied by the Japanese. In addition, a 300,000-tonne rod mill went into operation in 1987. The Japanese are minor partners, holding some 10 percent of the ownership. It is particularly interesting to note that in spite of Egypt's increase in production, it imported as much as it produced in 1988.

In terms of the future, Egypt plans to produce more rebar, since there is a deficiency of it in the country. As of 1989, domestic production was considerably short of demand, so that the companies, including National Metals, Delta Steel, and Alexandria Iron and Steel Company, adopted programs to increase their production.

Egypt plans to reduce its dependence on imports considerably, if not totally, by the year 2000. As part of the increase, additional direct-reduction plants will most probably be installed to reduce the dependence on imported scrap.

Saudi Arabia entered the steel business in 1983 with an initial production of 275,000 tonnes. In the next year, with equipment operating full time, production increased to 840,000 tonnes and moved up significantly in 1987 to 1.4 million tonnes and in 1988 to 1.6 million tonnes.

In the 1990s, Saudi Arabia plans to install an additional 1.5 million tonnes of flat-rolled products. This will consist of additional Midrex units, as well as electric furnaces and a thin-slab caster with a strip mill. The company, located in Al-Jubail, operates its electric furnaces on DRI, which is produced on the plant premises with two Midrex units. Its principal products currently are bars and wire rods.

Because of the abundance of gas in countries such as Qatar, Kuwait, and Saudi Arabia, DRI production will increase significantly in the 1990s due, in part, to a tendency to use more DRI in electric furnaces.

A project conceived in the 1970s that never was realized consisted of shipping ore from Brazil to Saudi Arabia, where it would be converted into DRI and the ships would return to Brazil with oil. There has been considerable discussion about reactivating this in the 1990s as the demand for DRI increases, particularly since the composition of electric furnace steel must be improved. Consequently, the Middle East can become an important source of raw materials for steelmaking in the last half of the 1990s.

Scrap will be available in abundance on a world basis, however, high-quality scrap, for which demand will increase in the years ahead, will be limited, and with the increase in demand, the price will rise. Consequently DRI will be competitive costwise, so that the combination of an increase in the price of high-quality scrap, as well as its limitations in relation to steel made from it, will make DRI a most attractive material for electric furnace operations.

In 1979, Nigeria, enjoying prosperity from the sale of its oil, made a decision to build a steel industry. As a result, the 15,000 tonnes of production for 1979 rose to 229,000 tonnes in 1984 with the construction of Delta Steel. This plant, located near the seacoast, hit a peak of 321,000 tonnes in the following year, but dropped off to 234,000 tonnes in 1988.

The country was dependent on the outside for most of its steel during the 1980s, as imports averaged better than 2 million tonnes through 1987.

However, in 1988, there was a very sharp drop to 171,000 tonnes. Much of the steel that was imported was in the form of pipe for oil-production activities.

In 1980, Nigeria undertook the task of building an integrated steel mill with coke ovens, a blast furnace, basic-oxygen converters, continuous casters, and bar mills. The location was in the interior at Ajaokuta. In the course of the ten-year period, both Soviet and French construction teams were involved in the operation. Currently, the plant is approximately 80 percent finished. It is barely functioning, since the remaining 20 percent is necessary for it to go into full operation. There have been financial problems since the oil revenues for Nigeria have declined, as the price-per-barrel fell in the 1980s. An estimated $5 billion has been spent thus far on the integrated mill, which will have a nominal capacity of 1.3 million tonnes.

There has been pressure brought on the Nigerian government to abandon the project at several stages along the way. However, this has been resisted because of the amount of funds already expended. The problems connected with the plant involve iron ore, which, although located nearby, is low in iron content and must be upgraded, while coking coal must be imported. As of 1990, there is some uncertainty as to when the plant will be finished. Presumably, it will be sometime in the early 1990s.

The Nigerians are conducting a study on the feasibility of producing flat-rolled products at Ajaokuta. This would require the installation of equipment to roll sheets which would be expensive.

Delta Steel, the other integrated steel mill in Nigeria, is based on direct-reduced iron for its electric furnace. The mill has a nominal capacity to produce 1 million tonnes. However, it has never operated at more than 30 percent of its capacity, due to a number of items including the lack of working capital, as well as the scarcity of electricity. Although significant, this latter problem can be solved.

There are a number of mills, principally rerollers, scattered throughout the country that must be supplied by Delta or possibly later by Ajaokuta.

Under ideal conditions, granting that the financial and other problems can be solved, by the year 2000, Nigeria might have the nominal capacity to produce more than 2 million tonnes of raw steel. However, a number of hurdles must be gotten over before this can be realized.

Far East

During the past two decades, the smaller steel producers in the Far East have expanded production considerably. These include Indonesia, Malaysia, Philippines, Thailand, Bangladesh, Pakistan, Hong Kong, and Singapore. In

1970, production in these countries was 674,000 tonnes. In 1980, the figure increased to 2.1 million tonnes. Indonesia was responsible for a substantial amount of this increase, with its output going from a mere 10,000 tonnes in 1970 to 543,000 tonnes in 1980. The Philippines grew to 331,000 tonnes from 118,000 tonnes, and Singapore increased from 107,000 tonnes to 340,000. In 1988, output in this region increased substantially to 5.1 million tonnes, with Indonesia again accounting for the largest increase to 1.85 million tonnes. Other producers with significant tonnage were Malaysia with 550,000 tonnes, Pakistan with 1.2 million, Singapore with 425,000, and Thailand with 435,000 tonnes.

A number of these countries are planning to increase their capacity and also diversify their product lines. Several have also begun to export small tonnages. In 1988, Hong Kong, Singapore, and Indonesia led the group with 850,000, 568,000, and 700,000 tonnes, respectively. In terms of imports, in the same year, the total indicates a substantial dependence on the steel made in other countries. Hong Kong imported 2.7 million tonnes, Singapore 2.1 million, Thailand 2.5 million, and Malaysia 1.1 million tonnes, while Indonesia fell from a high of 2.1 million tonnes in 1981 to 300,000 tonnes, which reflects the shift away from imports in favor of domestic production.

Malaysia

In terms of the future, Malaysia is planning an added DRI plant to supply its electric furnaces with feed material and lessen its dependence on scrap. The plant will have a designed capacity of some 720,000 tonnes a year, which will feed the electric furnace at Perwata to allow it to produce 600,000 tonnes of raw steel.[19] Construction has also started at its second tinning line, which will double its capacity to 180,000 tonnes. The black plate to be tinned will be supplied by three Japanese companies: Nippon, Kawasaki, and NKK.[20]

It seems certain that Malaysia will become a greater producer of steel when the China Steel Company of Taiwan builds its 2.5-million-tonne integrated steel mill there. The decision to do this has recently been made.

Pakistan

Pakistan began to produce steel on a very small scale in the early 1980s. This grew gradually until 1985 when it was 750,000 tonnes. In 1988, it produced an estimated 1.2 million tonnes. There are several small companies, with limited steel production, and one large company, Pakistan Steel Mills Corporation, a fully integrated blast furnace operation with two oxygen converters with 1 million tonnes of capacity. The plant produces predominantly flat-rolled products. Its expansion has taken place in the past three years; plans are for further growth in the 1990s.

Pakistan has drawn up plans to increase its steelmaking to 3 million tonnes by 1996. This will be accomplished through the installation of several minimills. Part of the expense will be deferred by a $100 million loan from the Soviet Union. The production will consist principally of long products.[21]

Indonesia

Indonesia has grown steadily in terms of raw steel production from 1979 when it stood at 182,000 tonnes to 1987 when it exceeded 2 million tonnes. There was a modest drop to 1.9 million tonnes in 1988. It has a number of nonintegrated steel producers that operate pipe mills, a product needed for the extensive oil operations in the country.

A significant item that marks the growth of steel production is the amount of steel exported and imported. In 1983, there were no exports; by 1988, they stood at about 700,000 tonnes. In terms of imports, the figure stood at 2.1 million tonnes in 1980 and declined to 300,000 tonnes by 1988.

Krakatau is the largest integrated plant, with a capacity of 2 million tonnes. There are some electric furnace plants in the country, although their production is minor compared to Krakatau. There is also a tin mill operated by one of the smaller companies.

Krakatau produces it steel in electric furnaces with a DRI charge that constitutes 80 to 85 percent of the material used, with the remainder being scrap. The company operates four HYL direct-reduction units and eight electric arc furnaces, as well as continuous casters, a hot-strip mill, and bar and rod mills. Part of the output of the hot-strip mill is sold as hot-rolled sheets and part to the CRMI mill, which operates a fully modern six-stand cold-reduction mill with a capacity to produce 1 million tonnes.

Krakatau plans to add 1.5 million tonnes of steel in the early 1990s. This will be based on DRI and the electric furnace process. The expansion plans will include additional DRI capacity, as well as added electric furnaces. In addition, a ladle furnace and a new bar mill will be installed. Ore for the direct-reduced process is imported in the form of pellets from Brazil and Sweden. Since it has an abundance of natural gas, Indonesia relies on the direct-reduction process.

Expansion plans at Krakatau call for switching three of the four HYL II units to HYL III. In addition, the electric furnaces will be upgraded by adding water-cooled panels and roofs. This will provide more tonnage; however, much of the additional tonnage will come from the installation of the ladle furnace. The rod mill, which is reasonably modern, will be upgraded to increase output, and one more caster will be added for slabs. The hot-strip mill will add one more coiler as well as additional finishing stands. Currently the World Bank has called for a feasibility review, which is underway and may result in some changes in the program.

Thailand

Thailand has an ambitious program to increase its steel output. In 1989, the Sahaviriya Group proposed to construct a hot-strip mill with an initial capacity of 500,000 tonnes to be completed in 1993, after which it was to be extended to 1.8 million tonnes by 1996. For at least three years, this mill is to be fed by imported slabs. In addition, a cold-rolling mill with a capacity of 200,000 tonnes was to be completed by 1995. This will be extended to 670,000 tonnes. Another project to be completed by 1993 is a 135,000-tonne electrogalvanizing line. There has been some delay in starting this project, although it appears that construction may well start in 1991.

Another development is the construction of a 300,000-tonne-per-year plant for the production of bars, to be installed by the Siam Iron and Steel Company. An additional project that has been proposed will be a joint venture between the National Iron and Steel Mills of Singapore and Bangkok Steel. This will consist of a minimill with a capacity of approximately 400,000 tonnes of bars and rods, set to begin operations in 1992.

In addition to steel projects, there has been activity in the service center segment of the industry, where Nippon Steel of Japan and Bangkok Coil Center have joined to build a service center with a sheer, a roller leveler, and a slitter. A further participation of Nippon Steel into Thai's steel industry is in the form of a joint venture to product tinplate, organized in conjunction with Siam Tinplate and expected to go into operation in 1991. It will consist of facilities to produce both tinplate and tin-free steel. The ownership is 40 percent Unicord, a Thai cannery, and 40 percent Japanese interests, divided among Sumitomo, Mitsubishi, and Nippon.[22]

Notes

1. *Proceedings of the Second General Conference of the United Nations Industrial Development Corporation (UNIDO)*, Lima, Peru, March 1975.

2. *Metal Bulletin*, March 22, 1990, pp. 19, 22.

3. *Ten Year Investment Plan for the Siderbras System*, 1989. Siderbras Siderurgia Brasilerra, S.A.

4. Metal Bulletin.

5. *American Metal Market*, October 19, 1989, p. 2.

6. *American Metal Market*, February 19, 1990, p. 4.

7. *Asian Wall Street Journal*, March 13, 1990.

8. *Metal Bulletin*, July 13, 1989, p. 27.

9. Gilbert Etienne, Jacques Astier, Hari Bhushan, and Dai Zhong, *Asian Crucible: The Steel Industry in China and India* (Geneva: Modern Asia Research Center, 1990), p. 81.

10. *Metal Bulletin*, April 26, 1990, p. 27.

11. Gilbert Etienne, ed., *Asian Crucible: The Steel Industry in China and India*, Graduate Institute of International Studies (Geneva: Modern Asia Research Centre, 1990).

12. *Metal Bulletin*, January 25, 1990, p. 19.

13. Ibid., February 19, 1990, p. 22.

14. Ibid., September 18, 1989, p. 39.

15. Ibid., May 14, 1990, p. 44.

16. Ernest Sharipov, paper on "Soviet Steel Industry: Steel Survival Strategies IV," New York, 1989.

17. Ibid., January 22, 1990, p. 21.

18. Ibid., July 16, 1990, p. 21.

19. Ibid., December 14, 1989, p. 27.

20. Ibid., January 11, 1990, p. 23.

21. *Steel Times International* (January 1990): 6.

22. *Metal Bulletin*, October 19, 1989, p. 29.

4
Raw Materials

hree of the raw materials required for steel production—iron ore, coal, and scrap—are highly important since they are essential to steel production and involve large tonnages. In addition, there are a number of other items used in various operations to impart qualities to the steel according to its final use, including manganese, chromium, nickel, titanium, vanadium, tin, and zinc. This study, however, will concentrate on the three major raw materials.

Iron ore is basic to the production of steel; it provides the fundamental element, iron, from which steel is made.[1] Coal, for the most part, is transformed into coke, which is necessary in the blast furnace to smelt the iron ore to produce pig iron. Scrap is not strictly a raw material in the same sense as iron ore or coal since it is drawn from previously manufactured items. But it is used in almost every type of steelmaking, including the basic-oxygen converter, the electric furnace, and the now-obsolete open hearth.

Iron Ore

Fortunately for the steel industry, iron ore is available in abundance; it constitutes 4 to 5 percent of the earth's crust. It is not evenly distributed, however, since large, rich deposits are found in some countries and virtually none in others. Japan, the second largest steel producer in the world, must import over 99 percent of its iron ore. Brazil, which is sixth in world steel production, has enough rich iron ore reserves to supply the entire world for more than thirty years.

On a global basis, there are some thirteen locations with large enough iron ore deposits to constitute a significant factor in iron ore world trade. The iron content of these deposits varies considerably, from 66 percent in Brazil to 28 percent in China. All of the major producers, with the exception of France and China, mine ore with 60 percent or more iron content. Table 4–1 indicates 1988 production for the leading areas, along with the average iron content of the ore.

Total world production in 1988 was 966.1 million tonnes. For the previous fifteen years, output had increased from 898 million tonnes in 1974, when world steel production was 703 million tonnes, to 931 million

Table 4–1
Iron Ore Production, 1988

Country	Production (millions of tonnes)	Iron Content
Australia	99.5	65%
Brazil	145.0	66%
Canada	40.7	63%
China	164.0	28%
France	12.0	33%
India	49.4	61%
Liberia	12.8	68%
Mauritania	9.5	65%
South Africa	23.0	65%
Sweden	20.4	63%
United States	56.4	60%
Soviet Union	249.7	60%
Venezuela	18.2	64%

Source: International Iron and Steel Institute, *Steel Statistical Year Book 1989*, p. 53.

tonnes to support 747 million tonnes of steel production in 1979. Since that time, the 900-million-tonne mark has been surpassed several times, reaching a record high of 966 million tonnes in 1988. It seems unlikely in view of projections for steel output, particularly blast furnace, iron-dependent steel output, such as the BOF and open hearth, that iron ore production will not often exceed 1 billion tonnes by much during the 1990s. Thus, in terms of the future availability, known proved reserves of over 250 billion tonnes will be adequate to provide for the steel industry's requirements indefinitely.

The Soviet Union, by far the largest ore producer, in 1988, mined 250 million tonnes, greatly exceeding Brazil, the second largest producer, with 145 million tonnes. However, some of the Soviet tonnage is low grade (for example, 55 percent iron), and therefore, there is a need to produce more tonnes of ore to extract the needed iron; virtually all of the Brazilian ore is high grade, containing an average of 66 percent iron. Thus, Brazil does not have to mine as much tonnage as the Soviet Union does to obtain an equal quantity of iron.

The Soviet Union exported some 43 million tonnes in 1988, leaving 207 million tonnes for domestic use. Iron production was 114 million tonnes, so on a calculated basis, it would seem that the average ore used has less than a 60 percent iron content.

Production in China was estimated in 1988 at 164 million tonnes. Iron content was quite low at 28 percent, requiring China to import 12.4 million tons of high-grade ore.

Australia and Brazil have been exporting larger and larger tonnages of ore for over two decades. In 1973, Brazil exported some 45 million tonnes, and Australia shipped 74 million tonnes. Brazil's ore· exports increased rapidly to reach 105 million tonnes in 1988, and Australia rose to 98 million tonnes. The Australian figure had been relatively stable until 1988, when it rose sharply, while that of Brazil has grown steadily. Other major exporters of ore in 1988 were Canada, with 31 million tonnes, Sweden with 18 million, Liberia with 14 million, and Venezuela with 12 million.

World trade in ore in 1988 was 404 million tonnes, or more than one-third of global ore production. Thus, transportation has become a significant item. Where ports will allow it, huge ships have been put in operation, many of them carrying up to 250,000 tonnes of iron ore in one voyage. The tonnage contained in the ship has a significant bearing on the transportation price. A 160,000-tonne ship carrying ore from Brazil to Europe will charge $5.75 to $6.00 a tonne, whereas a smaller ship of 80,000 to 100,000 tonnes will require $7.50 to $7.75 a tonne. There are, however, some advantages to the smaller carriers since not every port in the world can accommodate the vessels carrying 150,000 to 200,000 tons. The smaller vessels of 60,000 to 80,000 tonnes can move into a much larger number of ports. This is one advantage that the Venezuelan ore carriers have over those of Brazil.

Iron Ore Processing

Iron ore during the past thirty years has been upgraded or beneficiated to a very great extent. The two principal means of accomplishing this improvement are sintering and pelletizing. Sinter, used widely in Western Europe and Japan, is produced by mixing fine ore with coke breeze or coal dust to produce a clinker-type substance, which allows for a much smoother blast furnace operation. Pellets are small, round balls, usually less than 1 inch in diameter, made from concentrates of varying qualities of ore. In the United States, taconite, which has a low iron content of 25 to 30 percent, is crushed and concentrated before being pelletized. Ore that in raw form was 25 to 30 percent iron has 60 percent or better as a pellet. Pellets are also made from high-grade iron ore.

Sinter is used to a great extent in Japan and Western Europe; blast furnace operators in the United States prefer pellets. As a result of beneficiating iron ore in the past two to three decades, as little as 5 percent of the blast furnace charge in the United States currently consists of raw or untreated ore.

The extensive use of sinter in Western Europe and Japan can be seen from the production of that material in these countries. In Western Europe, an annual average of somewhat over 100 million tonnes of sinter was produced during the 1980s. In the United States, the average was approximately 17 million tonnes. In Japan in the past decade, the average sinter production was more than 90 million tonnes annually.

Western European production of pellets in the past decade averaged less than 12 million tonnes, although the figure has risen to 15 million in the last five years. In the United States, pellet production averaged somewhat less than 50 million tonnes during the past five years, while in earlier years with greater iron and steel production, it was somewhat less than 70 million tonnes.

In addition to blast furnace feed, iron ore has been converted into DRI by several processes. Two principal processes, Midrex and HYL, dominate the field. Both use gas as a reducing agent. There are a number of others that use a solid reducing agent, such as the Lurgi process, which is in operation in South Africa.

DRI is generally made by passing gas through iron ore pellets in a shaft furnace so that the oxygen is removed from the pellet and what was charged at 60 percent iron is finished at about 85 to 90 percent iron, since the gas takes off much of the oxygen. The process has been in operation since the 1950s, when a plant was installed in Mexico. Subsequently it has expanded throughout the rest of the world in areas where natural gas is abundant and cheap. Venezuela, Saudi Arabia, Indonesia, and Mexico have been fruitful areas for its growth. Plants have been installed in twenty-four countries throughout the world (table 4–2). Table 4–2 shows a capacity of 25.11 million tonnes and production in 1989 of 15.9 million. The Midrex and HYL processes constitute 22 million of the 25 million tonnes of capacity and 14 million of the 15.9 million tonnes of production.[2]

The pellets, with 88 to 92 percent iron, are used as feed for electric furnaces. They are particularly popular in Venezuela, where DRI pellets constitute some 80 percent of the charge into the electric furnaces at Sidor.

It is not surprising to find several installations in operation in Saudi Arabia and Indonesia, where gas is plentiful and cheap. By far, the greatest amount of capacity is in Venezuela; the industry there plans to add over 4 million tonnes.

Future Developments

DRI will expand in the future. However, since for most of the production, natural gas is required, it will be prohibitive to install it in any country where abundant, cheap gas is not available. It is expected that countries with the gas and capacity at the present time are those in which it will be

Table 4–2
DRI World Production and Capacity
(millions of tonnes)

Country	1989 Capacity	Production			
		1986	1987	1988	1989
Argentina	0.93	0.95	1.04	1.07	1.17
Brazil	0.31	0.30	0.20	0.20	0.26
Burma	0.04	0.03	0.02	0.02	0.02
Canada	1.00	0.69	0.73	0.77	0.71
Egypt	0.72	0.03	0.47	0.77	0.82
Germany, Federal Republic of	0.40	0.17	0.20	0.27	0.35
India	0.60	0.17	0.19	0.19	0.36
Indonesia	2.00	1.32	1.03	0.98	1.30
Iran	0.73	0.00	0.00	0.00	0.04
Iraq	1.47	0.00	0.00	0.10	0.20
Malaysia	1.25	0.58	0.59	0.50	0.64
Mexico	3.03	1.36	1.56	1.58	2.09
New Zealand	0.17	0.08	0.00	0.00	0.00
Nigeria	1.02	0.11	0.14	0.14	0.13
Peru	0.12	0.06	0.06	0.05	0.05
Qatar	0.40	0.49	0.47	0.50	0.53
South Africa	1.36	0.79	0.84	0.73	0.84
Saudi Arabia	0.80	1.17	1.04	1.08	1.21
Trinidad	0.84	0.38	0.49	0.59	0.70
United Kingdom	0.80	0.00	0.00	0.00	0.00
United States	0.40	0.16	0.21	0.29	0.29
Soviet Union	1.67	0.75	1.26	1.60	1.70
Venezuela	4.50	2.94	3.12	2.73	2.44
Total[a]	25.11	12.53	13.66	14.16	15.94

Source: Midrex Corporation.

[a]Following are earlier production figures: 1976: 2.90; 1977: 3.36; 1978: 4.83; 1979: 6.81; 1980: 7.36; 1981: 8.08; 1982: 7.31; 1983: 7.83; 1984: 9.23; and 1985: 11.16.

expanded. During the next decade, capacity might be increased by 20 million tonnes, bringing it up to 45 million tonnes. Output should increase by some 10 million to 12 million tonnes by the mid- to late 1990s.

During the next decade, steel output in the Third World will grow to some extent, particularly if the Chinese and the Brazilians succeed in their ambitious plans. However, this addition will not require much more than a total of a billion tonnes of iron ore for the industry, and with a conservative estimate of reserves at 250 billion tonnes, there is no concern about running out of ore.

The problem with iron ore is that mines must be developed in regions that are less accessible, and the cost of production will increase. An example is the Carajas mine in Brazil, which was opened in 1985. Total cost was in excess of $3 billion since a railroad had to be constructed, as well as a mining site town and a port terminal. With investments in new developments running high, ore will be plentiful, but in spite of new techniques, there is not much hope that it will be reduced in price.

The trade in ore in 1988 involved some 404 million tonnes, indicating that many steel-producing countries are and will be heavily dependent on imports.

Regional Movements of Iron Ore

EEC. Steel production in the European Community grew rapidly after World War II. In 1947, the EEC countries produced some 32 million tonnes of steel. At its peak in 1974, production rose to 156 million tonnes, with over 80 percent based on pig iron, the production of which stood at 111 million tonnes. Consequently a great deal of ore was required.

Ore reserves that had fed the European blast furnaces for many decades before World War II were either inadequate in terms of iron content or exhausted by the 1970s, so imports have constituted a large percentage of the iron ore needed to produce pig iron. This condition has persisted to the present since iron ore production within the EEC itself has declined significantly since 1974. In that year, it amounted to 67.7 million tonnes, and in 1988, it fell to 16.5 million tonnes. The major producer in both years was France, making a contribution of 54 million tonnes in 1973 and 12.0 million tonnes in 1988. The French ore is very low in iron content, averaging 33 percent. This is beneficiated so that the iron content as it is charged into the furnace is about 45 percent.

Sweden was a significant producer in 1973; some 34.7 million tonnes were mined, 32.9 million of them exported principally to European countries. In 1988, this production had fallen to 20.4 million tonnes, with 17.7 million exported to Belgium-Luxembourg, Finland, West Germany, the Netherlands, Austria, and France.

Total imports in 1988 for the EEC were 133.5 million tonnes. For most countries, this represented virtually the entire consumption of iron ore. The United Kingdom and West Germany produced insignificant sums—224,000 and 70,000 tonnes, respectively. Of the 12.0 million tons mined in France, 3.7 million were exported to Belgium-Luxembourg, and the remainder was consumed domestically. However, this tonnage had to be supplemented in 1988 by some 19 million tonnes, with significant amounts coming to France from Australia, Brazil, Canada, Liberia, and Mauritania. Western

Germany, the largest steel producer in the EEC, imported 44.5 million tonnes in 1988. Almost half came from Brazil, with substantial amounts from Australia, Canada, Liberia, and Sweden.

Italy is a resource-poor nation lacking iron ore and coking coal, which accounts to a great extent for the fact that 56 percent of its steel production is from electric furnaces using scrap. Italy produces no ore and in 1988 imported 18.9 million tonnes, about 6 million of it from Brazil. Other suppliers included Liberia, Australia, Canada, and Mauritania.

The United Kingdom imports virtually all of its ore. In 1988, this amounted to some 14 million tonnes. Canada was a big supplier—some 6 million tonnes, or almost one-third—since British Steel has large interests there. Brazil and Australia provided significant tonnages as did South Africa.

Belgium and Luxembourg are also resource-poor countries with respect to iron ore. Their entire requirement of 23.4 million tonnes was imported in 1988. Brazil accounted for 5.5 million tonnes, principally because Arbed has an interest in an ore mine in that country. France provided 3.7 million tonnes of low-grade ore, while Sweden, Venezuela, Australia, and Mauritania provided varying smaller amounts.

The Netherlands operates one integrated steel mill at IJmuiden. Its output in 1988 was 5.3 million tonnes of raw steel, which required imports of 7.6 million tonnes of iron ore. There were three principal sources: Brazil with 2.5 million tonnes, Sweden with 1.5 million, and Australia with 1.5 million tonnes.

Spain produced some 4.2 million tonnes of ore in 1988, of which 1.9 million tonnes were exported in relatively small amounts to the Netherlands, France, and the United Kingdom. Imports were 5.7 million tonnes, principally from Brazil, Venezuela, and Liberia.

The position of the EEC in regard to iron ore—heavy dependence on imports—will continue. The reserves of ore in most of these countries have been virtually exhausted, and it is doubtful that France will continue to produce ore much longer, since the low-grade quality has to be heavily supplemented by higher-grade imports, in both France and Luxembourg.

In the 1990s, most of the steel used in the EEC will continue to be produced there. However, in the decade beyond 2000, one can look for joint ventures with resource-rich countries to provide semifinished steel to plants in the EEC. These ventures will be sought out and entered into, particularly when blast furnaces and coke ovens, which involve heavy expenditures, are due for replacement. This will also reduce the amount of iron ore imported.

It is fortunate for a number of companies in Western Europe that some of the steel plants are located on the coast and can receive ore directly by ship. Some examples of these are Port Talbot, Wales, one of the largest plants of British Steel; Teeside, on the northeast coast of England; and Llanweren in Wales. Ravenscraig in Scotland is a relatively short distance from the coast, and thus ore must be transferred from ships to railcars. Scunthorpe is located near enough to the coast so that the transportation of ore is relatively cheap.

In France, the two major plants, Dunkerque and Fos, are located on deep water, as is the large integrated plant in Holland. In Italy, Taranto, in the southern part of Italy, is located on water and can receive raw materials by ship.

Germany, on the other hand, is handicapped; most of its plants, with the exception of the Klockner works in Bremen, are inland. And although the Klockner plant has access to the sea, it cannot accommodate ships over 40,000 tonnes. Most of the large steel-producing plants are in the Ruhr and are serviced by the Rhine River. This requires the transfer of ore at Europort or Rotterdam to small barges, with an additional freight charge of some $5 to $6 a ton.

North America. Canada supplies its industry in great part with domestic ores and exports more than twice the amount used in its blast furnaces. The United States produces large quantities of ore but must supplement them with imports.

In 1988, Canada produced 40.7 million tons of ore, exported 31.3 million and consumed 16.1 million tons. Despite its export tonnage, some 6.7 million tons were imported principally from the United States. This is a result of joint ventures that Canadian steel companies have entered into with steel companies in the United States that are operating mines in the Lake Superior region.

Both integrated companies of Canada, Stelco and Dofasco-Algoma, have participation in U.S. mining projects. Stelco has a 15 percent ownership in Hibbing Mining Company and 25 percent in the Eveleth Mines. Algoma has 30 percent participation in the Tilden Mine. Most of the Canadian production is located on the Quebec-Labrador border, where the Iron Ore Company of Canada, Wabush Mines, and Quebec-Cartier have large operations. There are other operations in central Canada, along Lake Superior, such as the Sherman Mine and the Adams Mine, both owned by Dofasco—but both have been closed.

In 1988, of the 31.3 million tons exported, Canada shipped almost equal amounts to the United States, the United Kingdom, and continental Western Europe, including Germany and the Netherlands, plus some to Japan.

The United States produced 56 million tons of ore in 1988, of which 5.3 million tons were exported to Canada. Much of the ore produced in the United States comes from taconite, a low-grade ore with 25 to 30 percent iron content. In 1988, 56 million tons of pellets were produced, some of this from imported ore. With few exceptions, the pellet plants are joint ventures. Some include several companies, such as the Hibbing operation of Bethlehem Steel, which also has Stelco and Pickands-Mather, now Cleveland-Cliffs, among its partners. The Tilden mine and Taconite plant is a joint venture of Algoma, Cleveland-Cliffs, LTV Steel, Stelco, Wheeling, and Sharon.

In addition to domestic production, the United States has to rely on imports from other countries. The principal source is Canada with 8.9 million tons in 1988. Brazil was second with 4.8 million, and Venezuela third with 3.5 million. Small amounts came from a number of other countries.

Imports, particularly those from Canada, come principally into the Great Lakes ports. There are only two U.S. integrated steel plants located on the seacoast: United States Steel's Fairless works near Trenton, New Jersey, and Bethlehem's Sparrows Point plant at Baltimore, Maryland. Ore from South America is delivered to these two plants, and some reaches interior plants by rail or the Mississippi River. This must be transferred from ships to barges for its journey north.

The United States could be self-sufficient since it has adequate reserves and pellet plants with enough capacity to supply its requirements; however, foreign commitments were made in the late 1940s and 1950s, when projections for the industry's growth were most optimistic, and it was felt that supplements to iron ore should be secured abroad. In the late 1940s, expeditions from United States Steel and Bethlehem prospected in Venezuela and found and developed huge quantities of ore. United States Steel also prospected in Brazil and was responsible for discovering the very large deposit at Carajas.

The Venezuelan ore deposits were nationalized in the mid-1970s, and United States Steel contracted to continue purchasing that ore. Consequently several million tons still come into the United States from Venezuela.

Although North America has more than adequate reserves and production to take care of its entire requirements, it will continue to bring in ore from Brazil and Venezuela into the 1990s. Brazilian ore will be purchased on quality and price; there is a contract between United States Steel and Venezuela with several years to run.

Far East. Steel-producing countries of significance in the Far East include Japan, by far the major producer; the People's Republic of China, which has grown rapidly in terms of steel output during the past decade and plans to continue to grow in the 1990s; South Korea, which also expanded rapidly in the past decade and will continue to grow although at a somewhat slower rate; and Taiwan, which has increased its steel production considerably and will show limited future growth. India, Indonesia, the Philippines, and Malaysia will have a small but, for them, a significant growth.

Some of the countries, particularly Japan and South Korea, are virtually devoid of iron ore deposits and must import almost their entire requirement. Japan, the second largest steel producer in the world, imports 99.7 percent of its iron ore. In 1988, Japan imported 123.4 million tonnes of iron ore: 52.4 million from Australia, 28 million from Brazil, and 21.8 million from India. These three countries accounted for more than 80 percent of Japan's imports, with others representing small amounts, such as Canada with 2.2 million tonnes. The Japanese have a vested interest in a number of Australian mines and have assisted the Indians in developing some of their iron ore deposits.

South Korea produced 21.9 million tonnes of steel in 1989, most of it the product of Pohang Iron and Steel Company, a fully integrated operation. Basic-oxygen steel production, which required blast furnace iron, accounted for over 15 million tonnes of steel, or 70 percent of the 21.9-million-tonne total. Iron ore imports, which amounted to 98 percent of the total requirement in 1989, were over 22 million tonnes, of which 7.3 million came from Australia, 5.3 million from Brazil, 3.3 million from India, 2.7 million from Peru, and small amounts from other countries.

The fastest growing steel industry in the world is that of the People's Republic of China, which increased its output from 20.5 million tonnes in 1976 to almost 60 million in 1989. In terms of ore supply, it has vast reserves, although the iron content is low. In 1988, some 164 million tonnes of ore were mined. Nevertheless, China needed to import 12.3 million tonnes of higher-grade iron ore in order to achieve its production goal. Principal sources were Australia and Brazil, with a small amount from India.

Future ore developments in China are not completely determined. There are some mines with higher iron content that will be opened; however, such projects involve a large investment and probably will not be undertaken until well into the 1990s or perhaps beyond. United States Steel Engineers had a tentative contract to open one of these mines at a cost somewhat less than $1 billion; however, it was cancelled. Considerable concentration and beneficiation of the low-grade ores will be required in the decade ahead.

Taiwan is devoid of iron ore resources and must import its requirements for blast furnace iron, which is converted into BOF steel. In 1989, 6 million tonnes of its total steel production of 8.6 million tonnes were produced in the basic-oxygen converter. Ore imports in 1988 amounted to 8.5 million tonnes, the bulk of it from Australia and Brazil.

India has a large reserve of iron ore. In fact, in the early 1950s, it was judged that India had the largest iron ore reserves in the world. Since that time, discoveries in Australia, Brazil, and elsewhere have greatly surpassed the Indian figures. In 1988, India produced some 49 million tonnes of iron ore, of which 31.6 million were exported. Japan was the principal recipient with about 20 million tonnes. Smaller amounts went to South Korea, Rumania, East Germany, and Italy. The iron content of India's ore—61 percent—is quite satisfactory, and there is little question that India will continue to be a significant supplier of Japan and Korea in the decade ahead. Some of India's ore deposits were developed with the aid of Japanese capital in the past ten to fifteen years.

Indonesia has had a rapid growth of its steel industry since 1977, when output was a mere 130,000 tonnes. In 1987, just eleven years later, output was 1.9 million tonnes. This was produced entirely from electric furnace facilities. At Kratkatau Steel Company, Indonesia's largest producer by far, there are direct-reduction facilities that provide iron pellets for the electric furnace charge. The ore for these pellets comes in great part from Brazil. Additional direct-reduction facilities will be installed in the decade ahead, requiring further imports of high-grade iron ore.

Latin America. Four countries in Latin America—Brazil, Venezuela, Chile, and Peru—have been exporters of iron ore for many years. The country with the oldest record is Chile, with deposits developed prior to World War II by a number of steel companies, including Bethlehem. Chile supplied iron ore to Bethlehem at its Sparrows Point plant for a number of years before and after World War II.

In 1947, a group of mineralogists from United States Steel went to Venezuela in search of ore deposits. In the mountainous region not far from Puerto Ordaz, the party made an astounding discovery when they found literally a mountain of iron ore. Its content was 58 percent to 60 percent iron, considered rich at that time, since most of the companies in the United States were using Lake Superior ores that had about 50 percent to 53 percent iron content.

United States Steel established the Orinoco Mining Company and began to mine the mountain of ore, which was about 21/2 miles long, a half-mile wide, and some 2,600 feet high. Venezuela also yielded ore from another deposit not far away that was discovered by Bethlehem Steel. With these facilities, Venezuela became the principal overseas supplier of ore to the United States in the 1960s and 1970s.

In subsequent years, discoveries were made in Brazil, which yielded reserves of billions of tons of high-grade ore—well over 60 percent in iron content. Subsequent to this discovery, Brazil dominated the Latin American scene in terms of iron ore exports.

Brazil exported 45 million tonnes in 1973, increasing this rapidly to 81 million tonnes in 1981. During the next two years, when the steel industry was in a slump, ore exports declined. However, they recovered to 88 million tonnes in 1984 and have increased annually since.

Until 1984, most of the ore exported from Brazil was mined in the state of Minas Gerais and shipped through the port of Tubarao, which was equipped to handle ore carriers of 250,000 tonnes.

Brazilian deposits are extremely large, and there is no concern about their depletion. In 1966, there were reports of ore deposits found at Carajas, a region located in the state of Pará in northern Brazil. Subsequent explorations uncovered a very rich and extensive ore deposit. The work was done by Vale do Rio Doce (CVRD) and United States Steel. United States Steel discovered the deposit, and CVRD subsequently negotiated with it to form AMZA (Amazonia Mineracao SA), which was organized to operate the Carajas ore body once it was put into production. CVRD held 51 percent of the shares and United States Steel 49 percent.

By the mid-1970s, various surveys indicated the extent of the deposit and the richness of the ore; however, the body was located in a relatively inaccessible area and would require the construction of a railroad some 550 miles long, much of it over difficult terrain. Furthermore, the port of São Luis had to be developed. The cost of developing the mine, building the railroad, and equipping the port was judged to be in excess of $1 billion. In July 1977, United States Steel decided to drop out, and its share was sold for $55 million to CVRD. Thus, the Carajas project became a 100 percent Brazilian operation.

The project lay dormant for several years. Finally, in April 1981, CVRD began planning, and work was started in earnest. The total cost by that time had risen significantly, and when the first ore was shipped in 1985, over $3 billion had been invested in the project. Funds came from Western European steel companies, Japan, and the World Bank.

Carajas is the largest known single deposit in the world, with 18 billion tonnes of high-grade reserves, having a 66 percent or more iron content. The ore is particularly suited after crushing for sinter feed and is therefore welcome in Europe and Japan, where sintering is popular among the blast furnace operators.

Brazil shipped some 88 million tonnes of ore from deposits other than Carajas in 1984. Since the mine opened, its production has increased rapidly, and, by 1987, some 25 million tonnes were produced, as compared with 12 million in 1985. This represented 13 percent of Brazilian exports in 1985 and 27 percent in 1986. In 1989, production reached 35 million tonnes and, in the longer term in the 1990s, plans are for it to be in excess of 50 million tonnes.

In 1987 and 1988, the financial picture improved, and CVRD is planning to increase the capacity of the mine. The bottleneck is the railroad, which will have to be expanded. It is hoped that the time required to ship a trainload of ore from Carajas to São Luis will be reduced from 28 to 21 hours. This improvement could increase the carrying capacity of the railroad over and above the current 3 million tonnes per month. Other equipment will have to be replaced and expanded, including front loaders and trucks to carry ore from the mine to the railroad. The investment needed to increase capacity is well worthwhile, since Carajas will be providing ore for the blast furnaces of the world for decades to come.

In Venezuela, the export of iron ore assumed significant proportions after the discovery in the late 1940s of large deposits of rich ore. The local steel industry was virtually nonexistent when the ore was discovered, and it was not until 1960 that work was begun on an integrated steel plant with more than 1-million-tonne capacity. Thus, by far, most of the ore mined in Venezuela was designated for export. The material was fine and provided good sinter feed, as well as feed for conversion into pellets.

Exports in the 1950s were in excess of 25 million tonnes a year, with markets principally in the United States, since United States Steel and Bethlehem owned the largest mines. In 1974, with the industrialized countries breaking records in steel production, Venezuela exported 26.3 million tonnes of ore to the United States and Western Europe. In 1975, the industry in Venezuela was nationalized, and plans were made to expand the Venezuelan steel industry to some 5 million tonnes through the installation of electric furnaces, which were to be fed by DRI made from Venezuelan ore. The management of the Venezuelan steel industry informed many of the European countries that after 1975 it would reduce its exports greatly since the iron ore would be needed at home. This need at home did not develop, and as a consequence, Venezuela lost much of its European market; export tonnage fell to an average of 11 million to 12 million tonnes in 1981 and declined drastically to 6 million in 1982. Further, United States Steel Corporation, which took some 7 million tonnes a year when it owned the ore mine, cut its import tonnage to less than 3 million after the mine was nationalized.

In the late 1980s, exports recovered to 11.6 million tonnes, most of it—2.7 million tonnes—to the United States, with 1.5 million to Belgium and almost 1 million tonnes to Italy. Other consumers took relatively small amounts (less than 1 million tonnes).

Venezuela has a disadvantage in dealing with the European market vis-à-vis Brazil. The Brazilian ore is shipped to Europe in cargo carriers as large as 200,000 tonnes, while Venezuela mines its ore a considerable distance up the Orinoco River, a waterway that can accommodate only ships of 50,000 to 60,000 tonnes. Thus, the freight rate is higher by as much as $2 a tonne.

A large expansion in DRI production is planned in Venezuela that will consume several million tonnes of its ore at home; however, the prospect for growth in exports of DRI is improving because electric furnaces in the United States require an upgraded charge.

Chile has a relatively small steel industry, which produced 900,000 tonnes of steel in 1988. One integrated company, CAP, is the source of virtually all of Chile's steel. Chile requires relatively little iron ore—approximately 1.5 million tonnes. The remainder of the 7.3 million tonnes produced in 1988 was exported, the bulk of it to Japan and a small amount to the United States. There is obviously an adequate supply of ore to meet the requirements of Chile's steel operations for decades to come.

Peru has a steel production even smaller than that of Chile—less than a half-million tonnes in 1988. However, the country does have ore deposits and exports a high percentage of its production. Its principal customer is South Korea, with Japan taking a small amount in terms of its total requirement. All other sales are in small amounts, making a total of 4.8 million tonnes. Peru's exports have been fairly stable—in the range of 4 million to 5 million tonnes.

The second largest steel producer in Latin America is Mexico, with an output of 7.8 million tonnes of raw steel in 1989. In terms of raw materials, Mexico is almost self-sufficient as far as ore is concerned. However, it imported small amounts from Brazil, much of it used for DRI production.

Brazil will continue to dominate the ore export situation in Latin America for the foreseeable future. With the exception of Venezuela, almost all other Latin American countries have relatively small reserves of iron ore.

One significant steel producer, Argentina, imports ore from Peru and Brazil. Brazil supplied almost 3 million tonnes in 1987.

Middle East and North Africa. There are several steel-producing countries in this area, four of which had significant outputs recorded in 1988: Algeria with 1.4 million tonnes, Egypt with 2.0 million, Iran with 1.0 million, and Saudi Arabia with 1.6 million.

Algeria has a supply of ore in the southwestern part of the country, and a significant tonnage has been produced over the last ten years. The high point was reached in 1982 with 3.9 million tonnes; the 1988 figure was 3.0 million tonnes. This country exported what might be considered a significant tonnage of ore in 1979 when it shipped 2.5 million tonnes; however, exports fell dramatically in the late 1980s when steel output increased.

Saudi Arabia has one steel plant with electric furnace production based on DRI; being devoid of ore, it must import this mineral. The principal source is Brazil, which accounted for 1.5 million tonnes in 1988. This is used to produce DRI, which now accounts for a production of 1.6 million tonnes of steel. The Saudi Arabians expect to increase steel output by approximately 1.5 million tonnes by adding direct-reduction units, which obviously will require more ore.

Egypt has increased its steel output in the past three years, reaching an estimated production figure of 2.0 million tonnes in 1989. In addition to small electric furnace plants, there are two larger operations, one with blast furnaces and the other using DRI. Both require iron ore, which seems to be well supplied from domestic sources. In 1988, 2.3 million tonnes of ore were produced. However, since an additional direct-reduction plant has been installed with a 700,000-tonne capacity, some ore has been imported from Brazil, amounting to 787,000 tonnes in 1987.

Ambitious plans were laid out for the Iranian steel industry in the early 1970s, with calculations that the country would be producing 15 million tonnes by 1985. However, the political unrest in the area rendered the attainment of this goal impossible. At the present time, Iran is producing an estimated 1.0 million tonnes. It operates a plant with conventional blast furnace equipment, as well as some direct-reduction facilities. Both require iron ore; however, statistics on production or imports are not available.

South Africa is self-sufficient in terms of ore for its steel production, which has varied from 7.9 to 9.6 million tonnes in the last ten years. The country is capable of producing 25 million tonnes of ore, of which it exported 11.2 million in 1988. The high point in exports was reached in 1979 when 14.2 million tonnes were shipped out.

In 1973, the Sishen-Saldanha Bay project was initiated by Iscor, which involved the expansion of the mine at Sishin, as well as the construction of a 570-mile railroad and loading facilities at the Saldanha Bay port. The facilities are equipped to handle 20 million tons a year. This figure has never been reached, but South African iron ore exports are significant. The principal consumer is Japan, followed by the United Kingdom. Other countries, such as Germany and Italy, take small tonnages.

Other Western Europe: Significant European steel producers, and consequently iron ore users, outside the EEC—Austria, Sweden, Finland, Norway, Turkey, and Yugoslavia—accounted for 25.6 million tonnes of raw-steel production in 1988. Switzerland had a production in 1988 of less than a million tonnes, all of it produced by the electric furnace.

The largest steel producer is Turkey with more than 8.1 million tonnes in 1988, 45 percent of it from the oxygen process requiring blast furnace pig iron and, consequently, iron ore. Turkey accounted for a production of 3.8 million tonnes of iron ore in 1988 and required a supplement of over 2 million tonnes in imports, principally from Brazil and Australia.

The next three largest producers are Austria, Sweden, and Yugoslavia. Austria had a production of 4.6 million tonnes of steel, virtually all of it—over 92 percent—from the oxygen process, whereas in Sweden, which has a production of 4.8 million tonnes, only half—51.9 percent—came from the oxygen process, with the remainder coming from electric furnaces.

Sweden is a large producer of iron ore. Production was 20.4 million tonnes in 1988, with exports of 17.1 million, so that approximately 3 million tonnes were used for domestic production.

Austria produced 3.2 million tonnes of ore, exporting nothing but importing 2.4 million tonnes, thus consuming a total of 5.6 million for its iron production in 1988. Imports came principally from Sweden and the Soviet Union each of which accounted for 900,000 tonnes. Other countries exporting to Austria include Brazil and Australia.

Yugoslavia had a steel production of 4.5 million tonnes in 1988, 43 percent by the oxygen process and 26 percent by the open hearth, both of which required molten iron from the blast furnace, which, in turn, required ore. Iron ore production was 6 million tonnes and imports 1.1 million tonnes, coming principally from India and Peru.

Norway's steel production in 1988 was approximately 900,000 tonnes, of which 42 percent came from the basic oxygen process. Norway, however, does not operate a blast furnace. Its ironmaking plant consists of six electric furnaces, which feed two basic-oxygen converters. Its iron ore production in 1988 was 2.6 million tonnes, of which 1.9 million tonnes were exported.

Finland's steel industry has remained relatively constant in output since 1980 when it recorded a production of 2.5 million tonnes. In 1988, output reached 2.8 million tonnes, with over 83 percent coming from the oxygen process. Iron ore production was 560,000 in 1988 and required a supplemental import of 2.3 million tonnes, principally from Sweden and Norway.

Future operations and requirements of these non-EEC Western European countries should not witness radical changes.

Australia. In the immediate post–World War II period, the Australian steel industry consisted of Broken Hill Proprietary (BHP), which in 1948 produced 1.3 million tonnes of raw steel. Not very much was required in the way of iron ore, which at that time was taken from two mines not far from Adelaide. The steel industry grew to an output of some 6 million tonnes by 1966, thus requiring more ore.

Since the only known deposits of ore were those near Adelaide, the legislature declared an embargo on exporting ore so that its industry would not become dependent on imports. In the mid-1960s, a number of large deposits of iron ore were discovered in northwestern Australia, as well as other locations, including Tasmania, a large island to the south of Australia. As a result of these discoveries, Australia became an exporter of iron ore. In fact, it is the largest single item that the continent exports.

Mines were developed in several locations and were joint ventures. The Japanese were involved in some, as were British and U.S. companies. By 1974, scarcely a decade after the major discoveries, exports reached 83.6 million tonnes, with the Japanese companies taking the bulk of this tonnage.

In the years following, as the steel industry declined in Europe and to some extent in Japan, ore exports fell and hit a low point of 72.7 million tonnes in 1982. In the 1980s, ore export tonnage remained relatively stable, fluctuating between a high of 85 million tonnes and a low of 74 million.

Along with Brazil, Australia, with a worldwide clientele, dominates the export trade in iron ore. The largest consumer is Japan, which gets 40 to 50 percent of its requirement from Australia. The tonnage varies depending on steel activity. In 1980, it represented 58.8 million tonnes. In 1988, the total was 52.4 million tonnes, or some 42.5 percent of the Japanese requirement.

In 1987, the European countries took 16.5 million tonnes, with Germany, at 5.3 million, the largest consumer. Other countries, such as the United Kingdom and France, took over 3 million tonnes each.

Australia exports a large amount of ore to South Korea. In 1988, it supplied 37 percent of Korea's total requirement of 19.7 million tonnes. Another large consumer was China, with 7.5 million tonnes.

There are five major producing locations in Australia as of 1989, four of them joint ventures. The fifth, the Hamersley complex, is 100 percent owned by CRA. The Mount Newman deposit is owned 85 percent by BHP, 10 percent by Mitsui, and 5 percent by CIMA. Robe River is owned 50.9 percent by Robe River Mine, 31.5 percent by Mitsui, 7 percent by Nippon, 7 percent by Sumitomo, and 3.6 percent by Lido Hair. Savage River has the largest participation in terms of partners in its ownership, with Sumitomo Metals having 17.4 percent, Nippon Steel 16.5 percent, Nisshin Steel 6.6 percent, Mitsubishi Corporation 3.8 percent, Kawasaki Steel 3.0 percent, Chemical International Finance 1.4 percent, NKK 1.4 percent, Sumitomo Corporation 1.2 percent, Seven Australian companies 12.4 percent, and Cleveland Cliffs 36.2 percent. The Seven Australian companies, Cleveland-Cliffs, and Chemical International Finance formed Northwest Iron Company, which has 50 percent of the operation. As of late 1990, Cleveland-Cliffs will acquire 100 percent ownership through a subsidiary.

Goldworthy, operating a relatively small deposit in northwest Australia, is in the process of opening a new mine since its original locations have been depleted. It is owned 70 percent by Consolidated Gold Fields and 30 percent by BHP.

The widespread ownership shares in the Australian iron ore industry are not surprising when one considers that the five companies mentioned were formed in the 1960s when Australian capital was limited so that operations were successful by virtue of Japanese long-term contracts. At that time, the steel industry was in a growth period, and a number of companies wished to share in the ownership of rich iron ore. There have been some changes since the original companies were established; however, the diversity of ownership, particularly in mines such as Robe River and Savage River, remains.

Australia, with its extensive deposits of more than 40 billion tonnes of ore, most of it proved and some inferred, will continue to supply a number of steel industries throughout the world with high-grade ore for the remainder of this century and beyond.

It is clear that the world steel industry does not face any crisis in terms of availability of iron ore. There is enough to care for the present and an increased volume of pig iron and DRI production for the future. Areas that are currently rich in iron ore will remain the principal suppliers for the world in the decade ahead.

Coal

Metallurgical coal, a form of bituminous coal and necessary for the production of blast furnace coke, is available in a number of locations around the world. Unlike ore, however, the total supply of metallurgical coal is somewhat limited. The other type of bituminous coal, referred to as steam coal, is available in much greater quantities.[3]

Recognizing that there is a potential shortage of metallurgical coal in the years after 2000, nations such as Japan, which must import 90 percent of its coal, and some European countries with high import ratios, are making efforts to develop processes that can use steam coals to produce pig iron.

Virtually every large integrated steel producer in the world is interested to a greater or lesser extent in the development of these processes. Japan is particularly involved; its six leading integrated companies are combining their efforts to reach a solution to the problem of using nonmetallurgical coal to make pig iron.

Although world reserves of metallurgical coal run into the billions of tonnes, they are not comparable in number to those of iron ore. Further, the deposits are much more limited in terms of high-grade metallurgical coal for coking purposes. Significant reserves exist in the United States, the Soviet Union, China, West Germany, India, Australia, South Africa, Poland, and Canada. Large portions of these coals, however, are inferior coking coals and expensive, almost uneconomical, to mine. For example, West Germany's coals are difficult to produce because of the depth of the mines. In order to keep them competitive, the German government must subsidize the production of coal to the extent of 150 deutsche marks per ton. The coal in India, where there is an estimated 33 billion tonnes of bituminous and anthracite coal, is high in ash content, running as much as 20 percent. South

African coal can be coked; however, it is inferior to the best coals available in the world, particularly those in the United States. The Soviet Union has a large quantity of bituminous and anthracite; however, a significant portion of this is not too desirable for coke.

Japan has poor and limited coal and must import virtually all of its coking coal. In 1988, it imported 65 million tonnes of coking coal, approximately the amount it consumed in manufacturing coke. This came principally from Australia, Canada, or the United States. Australia accounted for 26.4 million tonnes, or 40 percent of the total, Canada 17.4 million or 26.7 percent, and the United States 11.8 million or 18 percent. Most of the remainder came from the Soviet Union, South Africa, and China.

The Japanese hope to reduce their dependence on coking coal by blending it with inferior metallurgical and noncoking coals in small quantities and, more important, by developing a smelting process for iron ore that can use nonmetallurgical coal. This attempt, which is a concerted effort on the part of the major integrated producers, should succeed to a limited extent in the decade ahead; however, at best, it will account for a minor portion of the country's iron production. Blast furnaces and coke ovens will still be much in evidence at the turn of the century.

Trade in Coal

Like iron ore, metallurgical coal must be shipped from country to country since some countries that need it have very little and must import most of their requirement. The total international trade in 1988 in metallurgical coal amounted to 183.5 million tonnes. There were four principal exporting countries: the United States, Canada, Australia, and Poland. Other countries, such as West Germany, accounted for some exports, but, in terms of volume, except for South Africa, they were considerably less than the four leading exporters.

Statistics are available for exports from the United States, Australia, and Canada by destination, breaking down tonnage into metallurgical coal and other types (table 4–3). In regard to Poland, no such statistics are available, since coal exports to specific countries are not broken down in terms of metallurgical and other coals but rather given in a lump sum. There is, however, a breakdown for total exports (table 4–4). In 1988, they amounted to 32,174,000 tonnes, of which 11,062,000 were coking coal and the remaining 21,112,000 were steam coal.

In addition to the four countries mentioned, there is a considerable tonnage of coal shipped from South Africa. In 1988, the total amounted to 39,501,000 tonnes of bituminous coal. However, here again, there is no breakdown into metallurgical and other types of bituminous coals.

Table 4–3
Exports of Metallurgical Coal by Destination from the United States,
Australia, and Canada, 1988
(millions of tonnes)

	United States	Australia	Canada
Canada	6.6	—	—
Argentina	0.6	0.4	—
Brazil	4.6	1.7	1.7
Chile	0.05	—	0.186
Belgium-Luxembourg	5.1	0.8	—
France	3.9	2.4	0.5
Italy	5.8	1.9	0.025
Netherlands	2.5	1.1	0.5
Rumania	1.4	1.6	—
Spain	2.3	0.8	—
Sweden	0.5	0.7	—
Turkey	1.8	1.6	—
United Kingdom	3.2	1.9	0.5
West Germany	0.6	—	0.103
Yugoslavia	1.1	—	—
Taiwan	0.6	3.2	1.1
Japan	11.8	26.4	17.4
South Korea	2.6	4.2	3.2
Algeria	0.6	—	—
Egypt	0.4	0.3	—
India	—	3.8	—
Mexico	0.2	—	0.055
United States	—	—	0.773

Source: International Coal Report's Coal Year 1989, edited by Doyle, Johnson, and McCluskey, pp. 25, 27, 32.

The three principal countries for which complete statistics are available account for most of the exports of metallurgical coal. Of the 183.5 million tonnes shipped in 1988, the United States accounted for 56.2 million, Canada 27.4 million, and Australia 57.9 million, for a total of 141.5 million, or 77 percent.

In addition to the receipts from these three countries, a number of countries on the list had significant imports of metallurgical coal from elsewhere in 1988. Belgium imported 1,583,000 tonnes from West Germany. France imported 1.3 million tonnes from the same source. Although Japan's principal imports came from the United States, Australia, and Canada, there were 5.9 million tonnes from the Soviet Union and 3.9

Table 4–4
Exports of Coal from Poland 1988
(thousands of net tonnes)

Alvania	63.6
Czechoslovakia	1,677.4
German Democratic Republic	620.6
Hungary	668.3
Rumania	1,312.2
Soviet Union	11,725.6
Yugoslavia	171.1
Belgium	517.9
Denmark	1,658.4
Federal Republic of Germany	1,658.1
West Berlin	350.0
France	246.8
Ireland	722.3
Italy	846.2
Netherlands	789.7
Portugal	69.6
Spain	259.2
United Kingdom	1,277.5
Austria	1,846.0
Finland	2,038.3
Norway	124.9
Sweden	975.8
Switzerland	123.0
Other Europe	5,108.0
Algeria	153.0
Argentina	121.0
Brazil	1,949.1
India	135.5
Iran	59.0
Tunisia	3.1
Total coking	11,062.5
Total steam	21,112.0
Total coal	32,174.5

Source: *Coal Year 1989*, p. 30.

Note: The figure for each country includes both metallurgical and steam coals.

million from South Africa. China, under a recent agreement with the Japanese, shipped in 1.6 million tonnes in 1988, a figure that could increase in the 1990s. The published statistics often do not distinguish between steam and metallurgical coal.

Taiwan is resource poor for steelmaking. It imported 17.7 million tonnes of coal, 4.8 million of it from the United States. However, of the U.S. exports of metallurgical coal, only 622,000 tonnes are listed as going to Taiwan, thus leading one to assume that 4.2 million represented steam coal. Australia, on the other hand, is listed as exporting 7.1 million tonnes to Taiwan, of which 3.2 million are listed under coking coal, thus indicating that almost 4 million tonnes represent steam coal. In terms of Canada, coking coal exports from that country to Taiwan were 1.1 million tonnes, which represent virtually the entire export of Canadian coal to Taiwan.

West Germany in 1988 was both an importer and exporter of coal. Some 7.6 million tonnes of coal were imported, 4.8 million of them from South Africa and Poland, with no distinction as to how much was metallurgical coal and how much was steam coal. At the same time, West Germany exported 5 million tonnes of coal, which is not broken down by steam or metallurgical coal. This went principally to Belgium, France, and Italy.

It is clear that trade in metallurgical coal will continue actively through the 1990s, since the blast furnace will continue to account for the larger part of pig iron production. Most of the processes for making pig iron without the use of coke are in the early development stage and will take a number of years for them to represent a major portion of pig iron production. Japan is striving to develop noncoke ironmaking processes, since it is the largest importer of coking coal and will continue to be so during the 1990s.

Coke

Coking coal, as its name indicates, is used in the production of coke for blast furnace operations. Coke ovens, used to produce coke from coal, represent a substantial investment. In a number of steel-producing countries, these facilities will soon come to the end of their useful life and must be replaced in the late 1990s or early in the next century. It is, in part, to avoid this investment and the dependence on metallurgical coal, as well as to avoid the pollution problems connected with coke ovens, that the new ironmaking processes are being developed.

Coke capacity has declined in relation to the production of pig iron for a number of reasons, among them the improvement in blast furnace practice, so that much less coke is needed to produce a tonne of pig iron than was required in the 1960s. In the United States, for example, this has declined from 1,900 pounds of coke per ton of pig iron to 1,000 pounds. Japanese coke rates have been low for some time, requiring less than 1,000 pounds per tonne of pig iron. Improvements in blast furnace burden, particularly the beneficiation of iron ore by sintering or pelletizing, have also contributed significantly to the decline in the coke rate. The use of high-top pressure and higher blast temperatures are additional factors.

In the United States, coke oven capacity in 1960 was in excess of 71 million tonnes. Capacity in 1989 was 26 million to 27 million tonnes. The amount of consumption in the blast furnace has fallen from a high of 61 million tonnes in 1973, when pig iron production reached a record of 96.2 million tons, to 22.3 million in 1986, when pig iron production was at a low point of 44 million tonnes. In 1988, when pig iron production recovered to 55.7 million, the consumption of coke rose to 29.4 million tonnes, an increase but still just about half that consumed in 1973. The basic reason was the sharp decrease in the amount of pig iron produced.

In the years ahead, pig iron production in the United States may not rise above 60 million tonnes. Therefore, the need for coke will be in the area of 30 million tonnes. Capacity is less than that, so it will be necessary either to rebuild idle ovens or build new coke ovens. An alternative will be to import a considerable amount of coke from abroad. In both 1978 and 1979, imports amounted to approximately 5 million tonnes. In the early to mid-1980s, they dwindled to virtually nothing. However, in 1988 and 1989, imports were 2 1/2 million tonnes.

Environmental problems have restricted the use of coke ovens and are a factor limiting building new ones or rebuilding old ones. This condition is prevalent in other industrial countries as well, particularly in Japan and Western Europe where coke ovens are scheduled for replacement. In Japan, 33 percent of the coke ovens have less than fifteen years of life left, which means they will be due for replacement at the end of this century or very early in the next. Nippon Steel, for example, has a total of 435 ovens whose life ends around the turn of the century.

In the decade between 2000 and 2010, some 1,250 coke ovens in Japan will come to the end of their lives. Thus, a very large expenditure will be needed to replace ovens between 1998 and 2010. Assuming that these ovens are not allowed to run out the full length of their lives, a number of them might have to be replaced before these dates. Most of these ovens will be replaced in spite of the fact that the Japanese are working on new processes for producing pig iron without coke.

In order to extend the oven life to the maximum, coke-making practices, such as preheating coal, dry-quenching coke, and briquetting coal, have been put into operation in Japan and elsewhere. Further, the injection of pulverized coal into the blast furnaces has also reduced the demand for coke.

The determined effort on a worldwide basis to reduce, if not eliminate, coke will have limited results in the 1990s. It will remain to the next century to see the full flowering of these processes.

During the next few years, a fairly large number of coke ovens will be rebuilt, along with a few new batteries. The new batteries include one by RuhrKohle, to be erected at Kaiserstuhl. This will be a 1-million-tonne battery with slot ovens 7.5 meters high and 24 inches wide. It is intended to be a modernized replacement for two or possibly three of RuhrKohle's currently operating batteries.

Two other batteries will be built in South Korea at the Kwangyang plant of Pohang Iron and Steel. In India, the new plant at Visakhapatnam will require two more batteries if the plant is to meet expectations. These ovens use a dry quench. China Steel in Taiwan has recently installed a new coke oven battery, and in Brazil, the expansion of Tubarao will require an additional battery of coke ovens. A new battery will also be built in Finland. In the United States, two batteries are planned for LTV's plant in Cleveland.

The number of replacements exceed the new installations by far. There are a number in the United States, including National Steel's at Great Lakes. In Europe, Boel in Belgium will rebuild a battery. In Italy, the Ilva plant at Taranto will have three batteries rebuilt. Sidmar in Brussels will also rebuild a battery, as will Usinor and Hoogovens. In Yugoslavia, there is a desire to build a coke oven battery, import coal from the United States, and export coke back to the United States.

The decline of coke oven capacity can be seen from the number of batteries that were closed in the United States and Canada during the 1980s. Four batteries were closed in Canada, with a total capacity of 550,000 tons, and sixty-one in the United States, with a total capacity of 20.5 million tons. By far, most of these units were operated by steel companies, with the exception of eight, which were merchant coke ovens.

Scrap

Scrap is an essential material in the production of steel, although it is not strictly a raw material since it is derived from previously manufactured products.[4] It constitutes 100 percent of the charge in the electric furnace with few exceptions, as in Venezuela, Mexico, and Arabia. In these countries, DRI is used as the principal portion of the charge, although it is supplemented with scrap.

Scrap is used in the basic-oxygen converter, where it constitutes varying percentages of the charge, depending on the country. In Japan, where there is a large production of pig iron, scrap constitutes 7 to 10 percent of the charge, with the remainder made up of molten iron. In other countries, such as those in Western Europe, as well as the United States and Canada, scrap constitutes as much as 20 to 30 percent of the charge in the basic-oxygen converter.

In the few remaining open hearths in the Western world, as well as the large number in the Soviet Union, it is used in varying amounts. In many instances, it is 40 to 45 percent of the total charge.

Scrap arises from three sources. The first is revert or mill scrap, which is generated as the raw steel moves through the various rolling and forming processes, where there is considerable trimming and cropping. In the years before continuous casting, revert scrap amounted to about 28 percent of raw-steel production. For example, in the United States in 1973, raw steel production was 151 million tons, while shipments amounted to 111 million tons. The difference was mainly scrap that had been trimmed and cropped from the steel as it was processed. Thus, some 26.5 percent of the steel, or 40 million tons, was revert scrap. This amounted to a 73.5 percent yield of finished steel from raw steel.

With the introduction of continuous casting in subsequent years, the amount of revert or mill scrap has decreased considerably. This is the result of casting the entire steel heat, or in some instances, many consecutive heats, into a continuous slab of steel, requiring the front end and the back end to be sheared. The elimination of the slab mill, in which 15 percent of each ingot was cropped off, increased the yield considerably, since formerly every ingot that was converted to a slab was cropped back and front. With the continuous-casting operation, the loss in converting raw steel to a slab is often less than 5 percent since the entire heat is poured into one slab.

In 1989, the percentage of continuous casting in the United States was 64.6 and total yield from raw steel to finished product was 86 percent, as 98 million tons of raw steel were converted into 84.1 million tons of shipments. Only 14 million tons of revert scrap were generated. In 1960, when raw-steel production was also 99 million tons, the equivalent of 1988, shipments were 70 million tons, which represented a yield of 71 percent, with revert scrap amounting to some 29 million tons.

Continuous casting has reduced revert scrap markedly during the last two decades. This is a worldwide phenomenon. In the Common Market, in 1989, continuous casting was 88 percent, in Japan 93.5 percent, and in Latin America 82 percent. Consequently, revert scrap generated in the mill no longer is a large source of good scrap insofar as its chemistry is known and the residuals are at a minimum. In the United States, it will decline further as the percentage of continuous casting grows to 80 to 85 percent in the 1990s.

The second source of scrap, referred to as prompt-industrial, is generated in manufacturing operations by those industries that consume steel. For example, in the recent past in the automotive industry, some 31 percent of total steel shipments to its manufacturing plants became scrap in the course of its manufacturing operations. This figure in the last few years has been reduced to 28 to 29 percent. With improvements in manufacturing, as well as the use of lighter steel, the amount of prompt-industrial scrap declined somewhat in the 1980s and will continue to decline in the 1990s.

The third source of scrap generation is obsolete metal that comes from products made of iron and steel that are discarded year by year. These range from railroad rails and structural steel in buildings that are demolished to iron and steel kitchen utensils that are discarded. Obsolete metal is by far the largest source of steel scrap. It is larger in the United States than in any other country in the world because billions of tons of steel have been used in manufacturing and construction since the turn of the century. In other countries a much smaller amount of steel was employed over most of the twentieth century. Consequently the United States is a main source of obsolete metal scrap for many of the steelmaking countries throughout the world.

Unlike the United States, a surplus scrap area, Japan has had a deficit in this area. This was particularly true in the 1960s and 1970s when prompt-industrial scrap was not a large item because the manufacturing industries of Japan were not built up to the extent that they were in the 1980s. For example, automotive production in 1961 of all vehicles amounted to 814,000 units, as compared with over 13 million units in 1989. Thus, the amount of prompt-industrial scrap from the automobile industry alone reached large proportions, particularly when one considers that the automobile industry purchased 11.6 million tonnes of domestic steel in 1989 as opposed to some 750,000 tonnes in 1961. Further, other uses of iron and steel in Japan over half the century were much smaller than in the United States. Thus, the generation of prompt-industrial scrap and obsolete metal was by no means adequate to support the country's growing steel industry.

In 1961, to produce 28.3 million tonnes of raw steel in Japan, of which 5.9 million came from the electric furnace and 17 million from the open hearth, some 7 million tonnes of scrap were imported, 5.3 million of it from the United States.[5] The development of steel-consuming industries in Japan in the 1970s and 1980s, including the automotive industry, which took over first place in world output, resulted in the generation of more prompt-industrial scrap; thus, the need to import declined.

With a total production of 105 million tonnes, 31 million of it from the electric furnace, Japan in 1988 imported 1.8 million tonnes of scrap, down from 7 million tonnes in 1961. In 1988, U.S. exports of scrap to Japan were 649,000 tonnes, which compares with 5.3 million in 1961, 5.0 million in 1967, and 4.6 million in 1970.[6]

Scrap consumed by the steel industry on a worldwide basis amounted to 332.1 million tonnes in 1987.[7] The United States was by far the largest consumer, with 68.3 million tonnes, followed by the Soviet Union with

55.1 million and Japan with 44.8 million. Other significant consumers were Canada, France, Brazil, Italy, Germany, Spain, Poland, Czechoslovakia, and China, all of which used between 5 million and 10 million tonnes, with the exception of China with 13 million. A very large portion of the Japanese and U.S. consumption was in the electric furnace; these countries produced 31 million and 34 million tonnes of electric furnace steel respectively. Further, the percentage of scrap consumed in the basic-oxygen converter in Japan was relatively small.

In 1987, trade in scrap amounted to some 37.1 million tonnes on a global basis. The United States was the largest exporter with 10.4 million tonnes. Western Germany was in second place with 4.7 million, and the Soviet Union was third with 4.3 million tonnes. Generally, with the exception of the United States, those countries with a relatively small electric furnace production had scrap to export. These included France, United Kingdom, and, to a lesser extent, Australia. Germany produced only 17 percent of its steel in the electric furnace, which amounted to 7 million tonnes in 1988. France produced 26 percent, or 5 million tonnes, and the United Kingdom produced 5 million. Thus, scrap was available for export. The exception was the United States, which was the largest exporter, as well as the largest electric furnace steel producer.

The principal importers in 1987 were Italy, with 5.4 million tonnes, Spain 4.7 million, Turkey 3.1 million, South Korea 3.9 million, Japan 2.6 million, India 1.0 million, and Taiwan 1 million. The United States supplied large tonnages to many of these countries, with the largest amounts going to South Korea (2.6 million tonnes) and Turkey (2.3 million). In 1987, 1.0 million tonnes were sent to Japan.[8]

Unlike the raw materials, such as coal and iron ore, scrap is generated from manufacturing operations, as well as obsolete metal, so every country generates a significant amount depending on its manufacturing industries, as well as the amount of obsolete steel. Usually countries that generate small amounts of scrap from manufacturing produce small amounts of steel, whereas countries that generate large amounts of prompt-industrial scrap do so because their steel output and consumption by local industries are large.

In a number of countries—Italy, Spain, Belgium-Luxembourg, Germany, South Korea, Turkey, Japan, Taiwan, and India—domestic, home-generated scrap is not adequate, and significant tonnages must be imported. These range from 5.4 million tonnes for Italy to 1 million for India and Taiwan. South Korea is becoming a large importer of scrap as its industry grows. In 1983, it imported 2.1 million tonnes of scrap, and by 1989, this figure rose to 4.1 million.

Scrap remains a vital material for steel production, particularly in view of the worldwide growth of electric furnace output. In 1988, this amounted to approximately 200 million tonnes of a total of 780 million. As a country's output in steel, as well as its sale of steel products to its domestic industries, rises, prompt-industrial scrap will be generated in larger tonnages, as will obsolete metal as more products made with steel are discarded. As a consequence, trade in scrap will decline slightly during the 1990s. An outstanding example of this is Japan, which has reduced its scrap imports dramatically. Other newer industries in developing countries, which will continue to grow, will need more scrap for steel output until a point is reached where home scrap increases faster than steel production.

Perhaps the greatest problem faced in the use of scrap is the increasing proportion of this material containing residuals, such as copper, lead, zinc, and other elements. Part of this growth in residual-containing scrap comes from the demand from the customers for steel that contains alloying elements. When this turns up as prompt-industrial scrap or obsolete metal, it is not too desirable as a charge for the electric furnace, particularly when the electric furnace is now called upon to produce products of purer steel, including sheets. Thus, it may be difficult to obtain high-quality scrap in quantities required, so that the electric furnace charge will have to include some virgin metal, such as DRI or pig iron.

One of the principal means of procuring scrap in the form of obsolete metal is the shredder, which has been installed in a number of countries throughout the world to break up automobile bodies and other items into usable scrap size. This has proved an efficient means of preparing scrap. In a matter of minutes, an automobile body is completely broken up into steel scrap pieces about the size of a fist. The material is then run over a magnet that separates the iron and steel from other materials, such as aluminum, plastics, and copper.

This scrap is highly regarded insofar as its price is significantly above that of No. 1 heavy melting. In mid-1989, in the Chicago area in the United States, No. 1 heavy melting scrap sold for $108 a ton, while shredded automobile scrap was $127 to $128 a ton. Table 4–5 gives the number of shredders in selected countries throughout the world along with their total capacity.

In the United States, there have been some problems with shredders in the New England area, where a number have been closed temporarily because the nonferrous material was difficult to dispose of and caused some pollution problems. This has not been a trend, however.

A number of countries have plans to install additional shredders: the United Kingdom with six, West Germany with three, Italy with two, and Japan with three.

The recent demand of the automobile industry for galvanized sheets to be used in exposed parts of automobile bodies in order to reduce corrosion

Table 4–5
Shredder processing Capacity in Selected Countries
(thousands of tonnes)

Country	Total Shredders in Operation	Total Annual Capacity
Belgium-Luxembourg	9	324
Brazil	2	84
Canada	21	1,500
Denmark	5	100
France	34	933
Germany, Federal Republic of	38	1,400
Italy	14	700
Japan	136	3,446
Netherlands	11	450
Spain	11	360 [a]
Turkey	—	—
United Kingdom	54	1,700
United States	200 [a]	2,200 [a,b]

Source: U.S. Bureau of Mines, *Mineral Industry Surveys*, Iron.

[a]Estimated
[b]The numbers for the United States are as of 1984; the others are 1987–1988.

could present a problem. When these automobile bodies are scrapped, the zinc required for galvanizing affects the scrap because it causes pollution when melted. Unfortunately, these galvanized sheets constitute a considerable part of the prompt-industrial scrap that the automobile industry generates.

The amount of high-quality scrap has been diminishing due to a number of factors. First, the revert or mill scrap has been dramatically reduced through the introduction of continuous casting. Yield from raw steel to finished product in the ingot practice was 72 to 75 percent; thus 25 to 28 percent of the raw steel was returned to the furnace in the form of scrap, which was high grade and whose physical and chemical contents were known. The second source of scrap is prompt-industrial. Increased efficiency in manufacturing in many industries has resulted in less scrap being developed. Therefore, this source of high-quality scrap is diminishing and will probably continue to diminish as manufacturers find more effective ways of processing steel or use other materials in the production of their product.

As a consequence, steelmakers, particularly electric furnace steelmakers, must rely more and more on obsolete metal as their primary source of scrap. This material contains considerable tramp elements and must be carefully selected and processed by the scrap dealer if a quality scrap is required, a process that increases the cost.

As this picture continues to deteriorate at a slow rate, more DRI in one form or another will be used if the electric furnace operator is to produce a high-quality product. Further, more of the electric furnace steel customers are requiring better and cleaner steel. This is particularly true if the electric furnace operator makes steel sheets. Steel sheet users, such as the automotive industry, purchase a wide variety of sheets in terms of quality. The highest quality demands clean steel, and this cannot be made from 100 percent scrap because of the tramp elements. More and more DRI will have to be included in the furnace charge in order to dilute the tramp elements so that the final product is acceptable.

There are other products, such as high-quality rods, that require purer steel, and this is furnished, as far as Georgetown Steel is concerned, by the use of 20 to 30 percent DRI in the electric furnace. Raritan River must purchase billets for the high-quality rods. If they could be produced with scrap, there would be no need to do this. This is particularly interesting when one considers that Raritan River has a very sophisticated scrap-purchasing program.

During the 1990s, more DRI will be used as customers demand higher-quality steel products from the electric furnace operators. This will be influenced by the price. Furnace operators will attempt to control costs as much as possible, and the relationship of DRI prices to scrap will be a factor.

In 1980, a survey made of all of the electric furnace plants in the United States asked, "Would DRI be used to upgrade the charge?" Some 90 percent of the electric furnace operators based their possible use on the price in relation to that of scrap. Ten percent of the operators said that they would use DRI even at a higher price in order to upgrade the steel product. In the decade ahead, the price of DRI will be brought into line with that of scrap by many of the producers, and, as a consequence, there will be a considerable increase in the amount used. If the price is right, there could be a market for as much as 6 million to 7 million tons of DRI in the United States in the late 1990s. It will grow where electric furnaces are used, particularly in industrialized countries and in the Third World where scrap is scarce.

Notes

1. The statistics for iron ore production and distribution come from two sources: *Steel Statistical YearBook*, 1988 and 1989, published by the International Iron and Steel Institute, Brussels, and *Iron Statistics, 1988*, published by the Association of Iron Ore Exporting Countries, Geneva.
2. Midrex and HYL Corporations.

3.   Statistics on coal are taken from Gary Doyle, Debra Johnson, and Gerard McCluskey, eds. (London: 1989). Financial Times, *International Coal Reports, 1989.*

4.   Statistics on scrap come from U.S. Department of the Interior, Bureau of Mines, *Iron and Steel Scrap Minerals Yearbook, 1988.*

5.   Japan Iron and Steel Federation, *Statistical Year Book 1972.*

6.   *Monthly Report of the Iron and Steel Statistics* (December 1989).

7.   Raymond Brown, *Iron and Steel Scrap, 1988,* U.S. Department of the Interior, p. 18.

8.   Raymond Brown, *Iron and Steel Scrap, 1988,* U.S. Department of the Interior, pp. 16, 17.

5
International Trade

International trade in steel on a large scale is a development of the post–World War II period that corresponds to the large-scale development of the steel industry during this time. In 1947, global steel output stood at 134 million tonnes. The United States was by far the largest producer, with 76 million tonnes of raw steel, as well as the largest exporter, with 3.8 million tonnes. The steel industry in both Western Europe and Japan was severely damaged by the war; the production in these countries was sorely needed at home, and very little was available for export.

In 1950, world steel shipments were approximately 152 million tonnes, of which 16 million, or 11 percent, were traded internationally. During the late 1950s and through the 1960s, world steel output grew rapidly as the industries in Europe and Japan expanded their capacities. By 1970s, global raw steel production was 595 million tonnes, a threefold growth over 1960, when world raw-steel production was 192 million tonnes. Virtually all of the countries outside the United States increased their capacities with export tonnage in mind. Thus, their production was much greater than domestic needs. This was particularly true of the major European producers and those in Japan.

By 1979, a year of record production up to that time, raw-steel output reached 747 million tonnes. This yielded some 600 million tonnes of finished products, of which 143 million, or 24 percent, were committed to international trade. In 1988, 169 million tonnes, or 26 percent of total steel shipments, were traded internationally.

Steel trade grew tremendously in the 1960s, 1970s, and 1980s, principally because the industrialized countries no longer confined their exports to the Third World countries but rather expanded exports to other steel-producing countries such as the United States.

In the 1960s, the United States became the world leader in imports as many nations with extra capacity targeted the large and lucrative U.S. market. As a consequence, any discussion of world trade in the period starting with 1960 should focus in great part on the United States.

The increase in U.S. steel imports during the 1960s was of such magnitude that at the end of the decade, relief was sought by the steel industry—through either a temporary tariff or a quota system. The transition from net exporter to net importer took place in 1959 as a result of a four-month steel strike, during which consumers were desperate to acquire steel. They sought supplies wherever they were available; in 1959, imports were 4.5 million tons, and exports were reduced to 1.5 million. This was a significant change from 1957 when exports were 5.1 million tons and imports 1.1 million. For the first time in the century, steel imports to the United States surpassed exports.

This change was of little concern since it was based on the lengthy strike of 1959, and it was presumed that exports would soon surpass imports. This did not happen. Since 1959, the United States has been a net importer of steel. Foreign steel was cheaper and met steel consumers' specifications. Thus, in many instances, a decision was made to continue purchasing a certain percentage of imported steel. As a consequence, imports were maintained at a significant level in the early 1960s.

In the mid to late 1960s, there were two strike threats—one in 1965 and the other in 1968. Steel consumers moved to protect their inventory position in both years by increasing the amount of foreign steel they purchased. In 1965, steel imports rose some 4 million tons to 10.3 million, and, in 1968, they rose to an all-time high of 18 million tons, while exports in that year amounted to 2.2 million tons. It was this overwhelming ratio in favor of steel imports that moved the steel industry in the United States to limit imports through temporary tariffs or a quota system.

The quota system was recommended by legislators in Washington as preferable to a temporary tariff. Congressional hearings on the subject caused great concern among the Japanese and Western Europeans. Late in 1968, a combination of Japan and EEC countries led by West Germany proposed that a voluntary limit be placed on their exports in place of mandatory restraints. This was accepted, and the negotiations began. They were concluded in late 1968 with an arrangement through which total world imports to the United States would be limited to 14 million tons, with a 5 percent increase each year for the next two years. Japan would have 41 percent of the total, as would the six EEC countries, with 18 percent for the rest of the world. These were known as voluntary restraint agreements (VRAs).

The VRAs worked well in 1969 and 1970; steel imports fell to 14 million tons in the former year and 13.4 million in the latter. Exporters to the United States shifted to higher-priced products, and the total value of imports remained virtually the same for the 13.4 million tons received in 1970 and the 18 million tons imported in 1968. In 1968, the figure was $1.976 billion; in 1970, it fell slightly to $1.967 billion due to higher prices and higher-priced items. (It should be noted that import restraints had been placed on the Japanese by the EEC countries as far back as 1972, limiting the amounts of exports from Japan to the EEC.)

The VRAs were renewed in 1972, but all restrictions came to an end in 1973 when the worldwide steel market boomed and steel was in short supply. This continued into 1974; however, in 1975, there was a dramatic drop in steel production in the United States, Japan, and the EEC, and measures were taken, particularly in the EEC, to reinstate import restrictions.

In the mid to late 1970s, several companies in a number of countries in Europe as well as in Japan increased their exports to the United States in order to maintain employment. In 1977, imports rose sharply above the previous year; they increased from 14.3 million tons to 19.3 million, a new record. In that year, the United States developed the trigger-price mechanism that was to go into effect in May 1978. The basis for this system was the fact that imports were being sold in the United States considerably below U.S. prices and also below their costs of production, particularly from countries where the government owned or heavily subsidized the steel industry.

To establish an equitable basis for competition, the trigger price was developed based on Japanese costs and a modest profit, since the Japanese were judged to have the lowest costs. This criterion was applied to imports from all other countries. If the price of any import was below that developed in the trigger-price system, this triggered an investigation to ascertain whether that particular batch of steel was being dumped in the United States. The trigger-price mechanism continued for a few years but was rather unsuccessful because it was readily circumvented. As a result, a number of companies in the United States filed extensive antidumping and countervailing duty suits.

In 1984, when steel imports from over thirty countries reached 26.4 million tons, or approximately 26 percent of the U.S. market, a strong appeal was made to President Reagan to limit them. The result was that VRAs were negotiated on a government-to-government basis between the United States and the various other countries that exported steel to the United States. At first, 18.5 percent of the U.S. market was to be given to imports. This was raised to 20–21 percent when semifinished products, such as slabs, were added to the total. The arrangement called for a quarterly forecast of the tonnage required for the steel market, which was allotted on a percentage basis to the various countries that had entered into an agreement with the United States. Japan was conceded 5.8 percent of the U.S. market, the EEC 5.5 percent, South Korea 1.9 percent, and all other countries less than 1 percent each. In all, twenty-seven countries made agreements.

These were completed in July 1985, to run until September 1989. During the first year of the VRAs, exports were not closely controlled and amounted to 24.3 million tons since many of the countries did not enter into an agreement until midyear. In 1986, with the VRAs completed, the import figure dropped sharply to 20.7 million tons. In 1987, it was 20.4

million, in 1988 20.9 million, and in 1989, the figure dropped significantly to some 18 million tons. The objective of the VRAs was attained.

In addition to restricting imports, the five-year period of the VRAs was designed to allow the U.S. steel companies time to modernize their facilities and put them on an equal, competitive footing with the industry throughout the rest of the world. There were certain conditions the U.S. industry had to meet. First, the major U.S. companies had to invest a substantial part of their cash flow to modernize plant and equipment. Second, at least 1 percent of cash flow had to be spent on training programs for employees who lost their jobs as a result of modernization and restructuring. These conditions were met; $5.7 billion was invested in plant and equipment to bring the industry into a competitive position.

In 1988, the steel industry began to develop a case for extending the VRAs for another five-year period. At the congressional hearings, a number of witnesses testified in favor of the five-year extension, although some steel users testified against it. As was to be expected, most of the countries exporting to the United States also opposed the extension.

The VRAs were extended for two and a half years as a compromise in view of the fact that President Bush had committed himself to an extension in his 1988 campaign. In a letter to Senator John Heinz on November 4, 1988, he stated: "One of the key trade policy goals of a Bush Administration will be to achieve an international consensus on eliminating these practices, and, pending that, I can assure you of my intention to continue the voluntary restraint program after September 30, 1989."

On December 12, 1989, President Bush signed into law the VRAs governing steel trade between the United States and seventeen countries. These agreements, which will be in effect until March 31, 1992, are the single most important factor in international steel trade because of the number of countries involved.

When the agreements expire, the International Consensus regulating steel trade worldwide will take their place. The International Consensus is a series of bilateral agreements between the United States and individual trading partners restricting trade-distorting practices. They are intended to be permanent, replacing the VRAs, which are limited.

The International Trade representative, Carla Hills, stated that the agreements for the International Consensus will "include commitments of countries to prohibit subsidies for steel production as well as to keep markets open for steel. They also incorporate a binding arbitration mechanism that will provide quick and effective remedies for countries violating those commitments."[1] These agreements, called Bilateral Consensus Agreements, have been reached with a number of the principal exporting countries to the United States. They include the European Community, taken as a unit, Japan, South

Korea, Brazil, Mexico, Australia, and Trinidad/Tobago. Later, Austria, Finland, Yugoslavia, Poland, East Germany, Venezuela, and Hungary were added.

In addition to the Bilateral Consensus Agreements, VRAs involving quotas for each exporting country were arrived at. The two were negotiated together in order to give more leverage to the U.S. negotiators in arriving at the Bilateral Consensus insofar as they had the quotas to use as a bargaining tool. Presumably, if the Bilateral Consensuses are carried out, they should affect international trade in steel dramatically for the 1990s. A level playing field is envisioned in which most of the steel industries of the world will work under the same rules and regulations insofar as subsidies (or a lack of them) are concerned.

This arrangement envisions the virtual abolition of broad-ranging government supports for steel on a worldwide basis. How much effect this will have on trade remains to be seen. With the United States as the principal recipient of exports, which in the future will not be subsidized, the ability of many companies to compete in the U.S. market will be severely limited since many of them now depend on government subsidies. The subsidies will be discontinued over a period of two years since the Bilateral Consensus does not go into effect until April 1992. Thus, there will be little abrupt change in the steel industry structure in many countries throughout the world.

During the two-and-a-half-year period, those countries that have VRAs are not subject to the trade laws should they choose to dump or subsidize their steel products. The new VRAs make it easier to obtain tonnage over the quota, since the burden of proof for obtaining such relief is on the U.S. producers rather than the consumers.

The current VRAs award a generous segment of the U.S. market to imports. In fact, no other country allows as high a percentage of its market to be taken in comparison with the allotment that the U.S. government has made. As of January 1, 1990, a number of countries had a negotiated percentage of the U.S. market (table 5–1).

Until March 1992, in addition to the signatories, other countries that were not under the VRA agreements signed in 1984 will have access to the U.S. market without any percentage or tonnage limitation. The only safeguard the domestic industry has is to file antidumping and countervailing suits if violations are detected.

An analysis of table 5–1 indicates a significant participation in the U.S. market by Third World countries, as well as others that heretofore were extremely limited. The number of Third World countries with significant participation include Brazil, South Korea, and Mexico. The emerging steel producers not included in the table, such as Taiwan, India, and Indonesia, could constitute a significant percentage if their aggregate tonnage is considered.

Table 5–1
Tonnage Allotted as a Result of Concluded Agreements

Country	Initial Period[a] (%)	Second Period[a] (%)
Australia[b]	0.39	0.49
Austria	.25	.25
Brazil[b]	1.80	2.10
Czechoslovakia	.04	.04
EC[b]	7.00	7.00
Finland	.25	.25
East Germany	.10	.10
Hungary	.05	.05
Japan[b]	5.00	5.30
South Korea[b]	2.45	2.62
Mexico[b]	.95	1.10
PRC	.08	.09
Poland	.13	.13
Rumania	.11	.11
Trinidad and tobago[b]	.12	.13
Venezuela	.33	.33
Yugoslavia	.05	.05
Total	19.10	20.14

Source: U.S. Trade Representation, press release, December 12, 1989.

[a]Numbers are approximate because some VRAs were negotiated for two fifteen-month periods, and others were negotiated for other combinations totaling thirty months. Market shares are based on 1989 apparent consumption.

[b]Includes incentives.

The nonsignatories in the immediate past have accounted for approximately 6 percent of the U.S. market. If this is maintained, imports could rise to as high as 27 percent since signatories will be given an extra percentage point during the next two years that would amount to an aggregate of approximately 1 million tons a year. Thus, the VRAs allow for a higher participation in the U.S. market than was achieved in 1984, when it rose to 26 percent and led to the VRAs in September of that year. The principal country included in the nonsignatories is Canada, which has accounted for approximately 3 percent of the U.S. market in the last two to three years.

The pattern of exports has changed considerably over the last five years. During the past two years, the U.S. market, which was the prime target for exports around the world, has become less lucrative because of the fluctuation in exchange rates, as well as the strength of the steel market in other areas, notably the Far East. Japan has dropped significantly.

Although total Japanese exports have dropped sharply in the past three years—from 30 million tonnes to 20 million—the Japanese are still keenly interested in the U.S. market.

Because of the shift away from the U.S. market, a number of the signatories to the 1984 VRAs did not meet their full allotment. The Japanese, for example, could have shipped in 5.7 million to 5.8 million tons; however, their exports to the United States in 1988 amounted to 4.3 million tons. The Koreans had a quota that would have allowed them to ship in 1.9 million tons; their exports amounted to 1.5 million tons. However, most of the signatories to the 1984 VRAs wished to maintain as high a percentage as possible of the U.S. market from 1989 to 1992, the situation could change during that time, and the U.S. market would again become lucrative and desirable. Further, some Third World countries were interested in increasing their quota since their industry had grown considerably since 1984, and the U.S. market would be an outlet for some of this additional steel.

At least thirty countries export and import in significant tonnages. Some of these countries, particularly the industrialized group represented by Japan, North America, and Western Europe, have been trading steel for decades. Others from the Third World that have recently built steel industries and heretofore were dependent heavily on imports are now exporting steel and cutting back on import tonnage. Consequently, steel trade—both exports and imports—is much more widespread as of 1990. The leading steel exporter is Japan; the leading importer is the United States. Japan, however, has imported significant tonnages in recent years, while the United States stepped up its exports in the late 1980s, although they are still small in relation to imports. Table 5–2 lists the main exporters and importers of steel by rank and tonnage as of 1988.

Table 5–2
Leading Exporters and Importers of Steel, 1988
(millions of tonnes)

Exporting Country	Tonnage Exported	Importing Country	Tonnage Imported
Japan	23.3	United States	19.3
Germany	20.1	Germany	14.1
Belgium-Luxembourg	14.2	Soviet Union	10.5
France	11.4	France	9.5
Brazil	10.9	China	9.0
Soviet Union	9.4	Italy	9.0
Republic of Korea	7.0	Japan	7.0
Italy	6.8	East Germany	5.7
United Kingdom	6.7	Taiwan	5.3
Netherlands	5.6	Belgium-Luxembourg	5.1

Source: International Iron and Steel Institute, *Steel Statistical Yearbook 1989.*

Japan

Japan has been the leading exporter of steel since the mid-1960s. In 1965, it exported 9.9 million tonnes, which increased rapidly to 25.6 million tonnes by 1972. From 1974 until 1986, annual tonnage was in excess of 30 million. In 1988 and 1989, there was a sharp drop to 23.6 million tonnes and 20.2 million, respectively. On the other hand, imports, which were negligible in the 1970s—200,000 to 300,000 tonnes a years—grew significantly, reaching 7 million tonnes in 1989. Thus, the situation in Japan has undergone a substantial change. Nevertheless, Japan remains the leading exporter of steel and is still heavily dependent on the export market. In fact, in the late 1980s, particularly 1988, export prices were increased to a point where revenues from 23.6 million tonnes did not suffer by comparison with those from over 30-million-tonnes.

The philosophy that governed the Japanese exports of steel in the late 1960s led them to install a capacity double that needed to satisfy domestic demand, which provided large tonnages for the growing export market. As the industry progressed into the late 1960s and early 1970s, raising the funds for additional capacity became easier because most of the companies were profitable. In describing the situation in 1973, involving the need for more capacity, a Japanese banker, at the International Iron and Steel Institute meeting, stated:

> Judging from the present world demand and supply situation of iron and steel, while demand is expected to grow steadily both in the advanced and developing countries throughout the 1970s, an increase in the supply capacity of advanced steelmaking countries and an improvement in the capabilities of developing countries to meet their own demand will still take some time to materialize, and so the world demand for Japanese steel exports is expected to remain strong.[2]

Demand did, in fact, remain strong enough so that Japanese exports continued at or above the 30-million-tonne level except for very few years until 1986 (table 5–3).

South Korea, Taiwan, and Brazil provide a major share of recent Japanese steel imports. Brazil accounted for 867,000 tonnes in 1988, while South Korea shipped in excess of 2 million tonnes and Taiwan approximately 1 million tonnes.

In addition to steel products, Japan ships large tonnages of steel in products made of steel, such as automobiles and ships. These are referred to as indirect exports of steel, and in automobiles a considerable amount of steel is involved. In 1987, Japan exported 6.3 million vehicles, or over 50 percent of its production. This would amount to over 6 million tonnes of steel.

Table 5–3
Japanese Exports of Steel 1974–1989
(thousands *of tonnes*)

1974	33,124
1975	29,994
1976	37,035
1977	34,982
1978	31,554
1979	31,496
1980	30,327
1981	29,134
1982	29,474
1983	32,012
1984	32,841
1985	33,342
1986	30,323
1987	25,685
1988	23,652
1989	20,177

Source: Japan Iron and Steel Federation, *Monthly Reports of the Iron and Statistics.*

In the 1990s, the major Japanese integrated steel producers plan to diversify operations so that steel will represent approximately 50 percent of their income. Under these circumstances, the companies will be less dependent on steel and, consequently, less dependent on steel exports. Further, their market will decline because many of the Third World countries, which Japan currently supplies, will continue to increase their own steel production and thus be less dependent on imports. For example, South Korea, which took 2 million tonnes from Japan in 1988, will be adding 6 million to 8 million tonnes of new capacity in the first half of the 1990s and consequently will be less dependent on Japan. China has cut its imports from Japan from a high of 10.9 million tonnes in 1985 to 3.9 million in 1989, and, with the growth of a Chinese industry projected for the 1990s, total imports will decline; those from Japan will most probably not increase much beyond the 1989 level. Thailand, which took growing tonnages between 1986 and 1988 as imports rose from 841,000 tonnes to 1 million, will be installing some steel mill equipment, which will cut into future Japanese imports. Indonesia, which imported as much as 1.5 million tonnes from Japan in 1982, imported 503,000 tonnes in 1989, and this could well decline further with the increased tonnage planned for installation in that country.

Countries in Latin America, such as Brazil and Venezuela, that at one time were significant importers from Japan have cut back. In 1980, for example, Venezuela imported 476,000 tonnes and Brazil 203,000. In 1988,

Venezuela imports dropped to 44,000 tonnes and those of Brazil to a mere 15,000 tonnes. In 1988, Brazil exported 900,000 tonnes of steel to Japan, a complete reversal of the trade picture over a period of eight years.

Although there is a need for a large tonnages of steel in China and India, as well as other countries in the Third World, the purchasing power to import these tonnages is currently lacking and will be for much of the 1990s.

New markets will be difficult for Japan to find because of the increase in capacity in the Third World. Japan will continue to maintain a large tonnage of exports, although they will probably decline below 20 million tonnes. Japan will be forced to export a higher-quality product at prices that will make it worthwhile.

The Japanese are engaging in joint ventures in the United States, Venezuela, and Brazil, and these efforts will probably be expanded, so that income will be derived from participation in companies in these countries.

Japanese Export to the United States

Japanese exports to the United States in 1990 for the first six months amounted to 1.5 million tonnes. At this rate, it will be the lowest figure since 1964 when it was 2.6 million for the year. A number of factors have contributed to this decline, among which is the establishment of joint ventures in steel with a number of American companies that are specifically designed to serve the Japanese automobile transplants. Many of these companies have decided to source 100 percent of their steel from U.S. companies, particularly those that have joint ventures with Japanese. As a consequence, there will be fewer tonnes of steel shipped in from Japan, and this will continue indefinitely with an impact on Japanese exports of steel to the United States.

In the Voluntary Restraint Agreements for 1990 and 1991, Japan is permitted some 5 percent of the American market, which will amount to approximately 5 million tons in 1990. The shipments will be far less if the six-month's figure is maintained for the entire year. This will probably not increase very much in 1991. Thus, Japan will be far under its quota for two years running. The quotas run out in March of 1992, so that calculations for that year have no quota basis. It is conceivable that they will increase in 1992. However, the presence of joint ventures in the United States will exercise a downward bias on the import tonnage from Japan.

EEC

Any analysis of the EEC in terms of steel trade should consider it as a unified market since steel flows freely across the borders of the twelve countries and after 1992 will do so even more. The twelve member countries exchange considerable tonnages of steel. In 1988, the steel trade among these countries amounted to 40.6 million tonnes. In addition, some 29.5 million tonnes were shipped out of the Common Market to other destinations throughout the world. Of the 29.5 million tonnes shipped, 6.8 of them went to other Western European countries, including Sweden, Turkey, Austria, Norway, Switzerland, and Yugoslavia. Some 7 million tonnes were shipped to North America. The United States received the bulk of this—about 6 million tonnes—with all of the remainder going to Canada. Exports of 5.6 million tonnes went to the Soviet Union and the Eastern bloc countries.

West Germany

West Germany is the second largest exporter of steel in the world, with shipments of 20.1 million tonnes in 1988. Much of this went to other EEC members. Interestingly West Germany was the third largest importer of steel, with 14.1 million tonnes, most of it from the EEC. It was a net exporter of 6.0 million tonnes, with shipments outside the EEC, particularly to the United States (1.8 million tonnes) and the Soviet Union (2.5 million). As the second largest exporter and the third largest importer of steel, West Germany was the most active trader in the steel world.

France

France ranks fourth among the world's steel exporters, with 11 million tonnes in 1987 and 11.4 million in 1988. As is the case with West Germany, most of this went to countries within the EEC. Exports to the United States in 1988 amounted to 1.1 million tonnes. In terms of imports, France ranked fifth in the world in 1987 with 8.5 million tonnes and fourth with 9.5 million in 1988.

Belgium and Luxembourg

Belgium and Luxembourg offer an example of unusual heavy activity in steel trade. Because the statistics for the two countries in terms of exports and imports are combined, the two must be discussed as one.

Exports from Belgium-Luxembourg were 12.4 million tonnes in 1987 and 14.2 million tonnes in 1988. This is particularly interesting since raw-steel production in 1987 was 13.1 million tonnes and 14.9 million in 1988. Thus, a very large percentage of the output of both countries is exported. Luxembourg, a very small country, exports well over 90 percent of its output, and Belgium exports virtually the same percentage.

Luxembourg exports to the United States, the Far East, particularly Hong Kong and Singapore, and some Middle Eastern countries.

Imports are listed for Belgium-Luxembourg at 3.8 million tonnes in 1987 and 5.1 million in 1988. A considerable tonnage of semifinished steel is imported into Belgium, turned into finished product, and exported. Much of this goes to the EEC, with some significant amounts sent to other countries. The total sent to the United States in 1988 was 766,000 tonnes.

United Kingdom

The United Kingdom exports from 1982 through 1988 grew considerably from 3.5 million tonnes to 6.7 million. In 1988, almost half of this—some 3.3 million tonnes—was shipped to the Common Market, with large tonnages going to West Germany, Italy, and France. Outside the Common Market, a major recipient was North America with 1.1 million tonnes—772,000 tonnes to the United States and the remaining 368,000 tonnes to Canada. Significant amounts were shipped to Asia, including India, Hong Kong, South Korea, and Taiwan.

In terms of imports, the United Kingdom received 5.2 million tonnes in 1988, over 70 percent of it from the Common Market. Other suppliers included Sweden, with 283,000 tonnes. Japanese exports to the United Kingdom were only 44,000 tonnes.

Italy

In the Common Market, Italy is one of the principal producers and consumers of steel. Production ranged between 22 million and 26 million tonnes of raw steel between 1980 and 1988. In the latter year, Italy ranked seventh among steel producers with 23.7 million tonnes. Shipments of semifinished and finished products were approximately 20.5 million tonnes in 1988. Of this, 6.8 million tonnes were exported, principally to the Common Market.

Imports were 9 million tonnes, most of them from the Common Market, with Belgium-Luxembourg and West Germany the major suppliers.

Netherlands

There is only one integrated mill in the Netherlands—Hoogovens, located near Amsterdam. In addition, there is a small minimill. Steel production has been relatively stable, varying from 4.3 million tonnes to 5.6 million over the fifteen-year period ending with 1988.

Exports of semifinished and finished products during the past fifteen years ranged from 4.0 million tonnes to 5.6 million. At first glance, this seems unusual since exports in some years would be more than production of raw steel. However, in examining the import figures, we see that they range from 3.2 million tonnes to 4.6 million over the same period. Thus, the integrated company imported semifinished steel, which it processed and exported. In 1988, of the 5.6 million tonnes exported, 4.0 million went to the Common Market, with the remainder divided between the United States and other Western European countries.

Spain

Spain recently joined the Common Market and has reduced its steelmaking capacity, particularly the electric furnace segment, by a significant amount. Raw-steel production in 1988 was 11.8 million tonnes, with shipments amounting to approximately 10 million tonnes. Of this, 3.9 million tonnes were exported. Two million tonnes of this went to the Common Market, with France absorbing the largest tonnage. A large tonnage—452,000 tonnes—was shipped to the United States. Other significant recipients outside the Common Market were Canada and Morocco.

In terms of imports—2.7 million tonnes in 1988—the lion's share— over 2.5 million tonnes—came from the Common Market with minimum tonnages from Brazil and Sweden.

It is not surprising that large tonnages of steel are exchanged among the members of the Common Market since its establishment was designed to achieve this objective. Steel producers in one country have had their customers in other EEC countries for a number of years and will continue to supply them. In 1992, with steel consumers exercising more freedom as to location within the EEC, shipping steel across international borders will increase. In a speech given before the British Independent Steel Producers Association in December 1989, Ruprecht Vondran, head of the German Steel Federation, stated that as the industry's customers are becoming more mobile, producers will try to follow their moves. He also stated that the amount of steel sold across country borders is expected to increase. Further, buyers "won't hesitate to use" international joint ventures.[3] Currently, a number of European producers are establishing service center connections in countries other than their own.

The amount of trade among the EEC members will grow to some extent in the 1990s, although it is not expected to increase appreciably since the European steel producers have had access to other markets in the EEC for a number of years. Such items as price intelligence and the creation of more uniform freight rates will be factors in the expansion of trade after 1992.

Currently, there is a move, particularly on the part of Usinor, to increase its ownership in companies outside France. This is particularly true of acquisitions recently made in Italy. Such a maneuver will tend to increase trade. Another possibility would be the Usinor plant at Fos, on the Mediterranean, supplying hot-rolled bands to the Spanish steelworks, Siderurgica del Mediterraneo, which operates a modern cold-reduction mill at Sagunto on the east coast of Spain.

Other Western Europe

The steel-producing countries in Western Europe outside the Common Market are Austria, Finland, Norway, Switzerland, Sweden, Norway, Turkey, and Yugoslavia. The major producer is Turkey with 7.9 million tonnes in 1989, followed by Sweden with 4.7 million, Austria 4.7 million, Yugoslavia 4.5 million, Finland 2.9 million, Switzerland 1.0, and Norway 0.9 million.

Austria

Austria has made a consistent tonnage of steel production in the past decade. During the ten-year period ending in 1989, output ranged from 4 million to 5 million tonnes. In terms of exports, the country recorded 2 million tonnes in 1977 and 3.1 million in 1988. When one considers that raw-steel production was 4.6 million tonnes in 1988, with finished products in a range of 3.8 million to 3.9 million tonnes, virtually three-fourths of the country's steel output was exported. Imports over the 1980s ranged from 800,000 tonnes to 1.3 million. Thus, Austria is predominantly an exporting country. Its principal customers are the Common Market, other European countries, and the Soviet Union. Much of Austria's trade is carried on within Europe, since 2.9 million tonnes of the 3.1 million were shipped there, leaving a small amount to be exported outside Europe. Of this, the United States received 122,000 tonnes.

Sweden

Sweden had a reasonably consistent crude-steel output from 1979 through 1988; volume fluctuated between 4 million and 5 million tonnes. Raw-steel production in 1988 was 4.8 million tonnes, with shipments of approximately 4 million tonnes. Of this amount, 3 million, or about 75 percent, were exported. Most of this—approximately 2.3 million tonnes—went to European countries, principally the Common Market. Some 528,000 tonnes went to the United States. Total imports were 2.1 million tonnes in 1988, of which more than half came from the Common Market.

Third World

The Third World increased its steelmaking capacity from 1974 through 1989, in sharp contrast to the industrialized world, which systematically reduced capacity during the 1980s. In 1974, Third World production, including China and North Korea, amounted to 60 million tonnes. By 1980, this had risen to 100 million tonnes, and in 1988 it reached 164 million. In three of the leading countries—Brazil, South Korea, and Taiwan—exports have increased appreciably since 1975. In Brazil, they were almost negligible in 1975: 149,000 tonnes. In 1988, the figure stood at 10.9 million tonnes, a dramatic increase. South Korean exports rose from 931,000 tonnes to 7.3 million for the same years. Those in Taiwan increased from 249,000 tonnes to 1.7 million. All three countries entered the market seriously within the last decade when the steel industry in the industrialized world was in a period of contraction. Thus, the Third World countries had to break into an existing, relatively stable market rather than participate in an expanding one.

Brazil

Brazil in a sense was an exception in terms of marketing its steel. Almost half of its export tonnage in 1988 was in the form of semifinished products, an expanding market. It has the only large integrated plant, Tubarao, in the Western world designed to produce semifinished steel for sale. The export tonnage of 1988 was widely distributed (table 5–4).

Brazilian imports have dropped sharply in the past decade. In 1977, they were 900,000 tonnes; by 1988, they had fallen to 112,000 tonnes. Clearly Brazil intends to be self-sufficient in terms of steel, and much of the projected increase in its capacity for the 1990s will be shipped into the export market.

In 1988, Brazil ranked fifth among steel-exporting countries of the world; in the 1990s, it could well rank third behind Japan and West Germany. (The recent privatization plans announced by Brazil will have an

Table 5–4
Brazilian Exports of Steel, 1988
(millions of tonnes)

Western Europe	1.4
United States	1.4
Latin America	1.3
Canada	1.0
Japan	.867
Taiwan	.740
China	.602
Thailand	.545
Hong Kong	.487
South Korea	.432
Morocco	.102
Algiers	.097

Source: Instituto Brasileiro de Siderurgia, *A Siderurgia em Numerous 1989*, p. 13.

effect on this country's steel industry in the near future, and some of the expansion plans may not be realized on schedule.)

South Korea

South Korea has made exceptional strides in steel production as well as exports. In 1973, steel production surpassed 1 million tonnes for the first time, reaching 1.2 million. It increased to 21.9 million tonnes in 1989. Exports of steel constituted a very high percentage of product shipments. In 1973, exports were 800,000 tonnes, a very high percentage of total output; imports in the same year were 2.1 million tonnes. Export tonnage has grown steadily, reaching 7.3 million tonnes in 1988. The principal recipients were Japan with 2.9 million tonnes and the United States with 1.4 million. The remainder was distributed in smaller amounts among a number of countries in the Far East.

Imports to South Korea were 3.5 million tonnes in 1987 and 3.4 million in 1988. In 1988 they came principally from Japan (1.9 million tonnes were received) and Brazil (432,000 tonnes). Other countries, such as the United States and those in the EEC, shipped modest amounts to South Korea in 1988. For years, the country has been dependent on Japan for a large part of its imports, which averaged approximately 2 million tonnes a year from 1978 to 1988, with the exception of 1982 when they fell to 1.1 million tonnes.

The construction of the third and fourth phases of the new Kwangyang integrated steel mill will allow South Korea to produce 6 million more tonnes than it did in 1989. Further, its electric furnace companies will produce an aggregate of more than 2 million tonnes over and above the 1989 figure. As its production expands, Japanese and other imports will decline.

In a short time, South Korea has become a major factor in world trade, a status that will continue in the 1990s with increased exports and decreased imports.

Taiwan

Taiwan is another country in the Third World experiencing growth in steel production and exports. Raw steel output was 8.5 million tonnes in 1988, ranking it nineteenth among the world producers. Exports, which were a mere 249,000 in 1975, rose to 1.7 million tonnes in 1988. The country, however, is far from self-sufficient in steel; it imported 5.3 million tonnes in 1988, or three times the tonnage exported. Japan was its dominant supplier, with 2.2 million tonnes.

India

India as a producer of raw steel ranks fourteenth in the world with 14.4 million tonnes in 1989. Exports have been extremely low since 1977, when they amounted to 1.1 million tonnes. In the succeeding ten-year period, they were less than 100,000 tonnes in a number of years. In 1988, they rose to 113,000 tonnes, an appreciable increase above 1985–1987, when they stood at 15,000, 27,000, and 50,000 tonnes respectively.

The country is short of steel; imports in 1988 amounted to 1.9 million tonnes, with Japan supplying 442,000 tonnes. Distribution is on allocation directed by the government.

Although some new capacity is being added, India will continue to import far more than it exports in the 1990s.

China

The steel industry in China has witnessed a spectacular growth in production since 1976 when output stood at 20.5 million tonnes of steel. In 1989, it was over 61 million tonnes, placing China fourth among the nations of the world in raw-steel output.

Because of its vast population and the tremendous need for steel, it was third in imports, with 11.8 million tonnes in 1987, down from a record high of 19.6 million in 1985. In 1988, imports fell somewhat below the 1987 figure to 9 million tonnes. Exports are negligible by comparison, amounting to 150,000 tonnes in both 1987 and 1988. China received most of its steel from Japan, although that has declined precipitously, from 10.9 million tonnes in 1985 to 3.9 million tonnes in 1989. In 1989, Brazil contributed over 600,000 tonnes, and the Soviet Union accounted for 800,000 tonnes in 1987.

China hopes to increase its steelmaking capacity significantly by the year 2000. The target is 100 million tonnes, but that seems unrealistic. If 75 million tonnes are produced by 1995, one could well expect the Chinese to enter the export market on the modest scale.

Other Third World

The remaining steel producers in the Third World with significant exports in 1988 are Mexico with 1.2 million tonnes, Argentina with 1.6 million, Venezuela with 848,000, Indonesia with an estimated 700,000 tonnes, and Qatar with an estimated 480,000. The same countries import relatively minor tonnages with the exception of Argentina, which accounted for 1 million tonnes of imports in 1988.

Brazil, South Korea, and China have plans to increase their capacity appreciably. As this increase in raw-steel output is realized in the 1990s, it will be reflected in larger export tonnages. The cost structure in most of these countries allows for a per-tonne cost below that of most of the industrialized countries and provides an advantage in export trade. Further, the tendency, with the exception of China, has been to export a significant quantity of products made of steel in spite of the need for steel at home because of the necessity to acquire currency in order to pay debts. Consequently the major Third World producers, with the exception of China, will engage in steel trade to the fullest extent that they are able. Their equipment, for the most part, is modern, particularly in Brazil, South Korea, and Taiwan. Consequently, product quality will be comparable to that produced in the industrialized countries.

China is an exception; its steel is desperately needed at home, and the quality for the most part is average. This is particularly true since only some of China's expanded facilities are new. Others are reconditioned mills drawn from every possible quarter of the world. If China's production reaches 75 million tonnes by 1995, and this is quite possible, there will be an attempt to export significant quantities of steel. Between 1995 and 2000, the amount of export tonnage will depend on the growth of steel production. If it should reach as much as 80 million to 85 million tonnes by the end of the century, China will become a factor in the export market. Its costs currently are low, and there is no reason to believe that they will increase dramatically in the 1990s. Consequently, China will be competitive with almost any other country in the world should it choose to enter the export market with large tonnages.

Brazil, because of its current privatization plans, has had to cut back on proposed increases in steel capacity. However, much of what will be realized in the 1990s will be targeted for export, putting Brazil high on the list of exporting steel countries. The Tubarao plant, which produces semifinished steel and exports most of it, has plans to double in size; however, this increase will include a hot-strip mill so that the amount of semifinished for both export and domestic markets will remain relatively stable.

South Korea will be one of the most significant countries in the world steel industry during the 1990s. Indeed, it has already established a firm position. As its output increases to between 28 million and 30 million tonnes in the mid-1990s, it will seek to expand its export market. Further, the joint venture with the United States Steel division of USX, when the VRAs are terminated in March 1992, will allow it to export over a million tonnes of hot-rolled bands to the United States from the Kwangyang works of Pohang Iron and Steel Company. Further, other joint ventures are conceivable, which will result in steady demand for South Korea's output. Export volume could reach 12 million to 14 million tonnes by the end of the century.

Because of land and other limitations, China Steel of Taiwan is seeking to build facilities abroad, possibly in Malaysia, and will bring some steel back to Taiwan in the form of semifinished material. Thus, exports in the future will increase as a result of processing imported semifinished steel. There will be several strip mills in the country by 1995, one of which, now under construction, will have to import large tonnages of slabs—perhaps as much as 1.8 million to 2.0 million tonnes. These will replace coils now imported and should not increase the import tonnage appreciably. The shift will be one of product mix. The decision to erect steel capacity on a joint venture basis outside Taiwan has been finalized; it will be in Malaysia. Taiwan will be a growing export country. However, in regard to imports, the rate of increase will be significant because imports, particularly of semifinished, will be large.

India is planning to increase capacity to as much as 24 million tonnes from the current 17 million tonnes. This may well be realized by the end of the century. However, demand will increase so that very little of the additional capacity will be available for export. India will continue to be a net importer of steel throughout the 1990s.

Other Third World countries, such as Argentina, Venezuela, Mexico, and Egypt and Saudi Arabia in the Middle East, will increase steelmaking capacity; however, the tonnage will be modest, and therefore the increase in exports from these countries will be minimal. In fact, many of them will continue to import at the 1989 level. Some, such as Egypt and Iran, which have had large imports in the past, will cut back because of new capacity coming on stream.

Steel trade for the Third World will continue to represent large tonnages of imports and exports. In 1988, total imports amounted to 37.3 million tonnes, and exports amounted to 26.9 million tonnes.

Australia

Australia and Brazil are the two main suppliers of iron ore for the world steel industry. Unlike Brazil, steel output in Australia has been relatively stable but has declined slightly in the last few years. In 1977, it was 7.3 million tonnes, and in 1989 it was 6.7 million.

In terms of exports, some 2.5 million tonnes were shipped in 1977. This has declined and remained considerably below that figure during the past five years. In 1987, it was 1.1 million tonnes. Most of the exports are to Asian countries, including the Philippines, Thailand, the Malay states, and China; over 10 percent (155,000 tonnes) went to the United States.

Imports, which were over a million tonnes for several years in the 1970s, declined significantly in the mid-1980s to as low as 600,000 tonnes in 1986. In 1987 and 1988, they recovered to approximately 900,000 tonnes. A significant portion of the 1987 and 1988 tonnage came from Brazil.

The Australian industry is planning an expansion of approximately 1.0 million to 1.2 million tonnes through improvements at Port Kembla, Newcastle and Whyalla as well as the construction of a minimill. This additional amount of steel could result in an increase in exports; however, it will be minimal. As of 1988, exports were 790,000 tonnes. They could vary between this figure and 1 million tonnes, or possibly 1.1 million, in the next decade.

Canada

Canada's steel output grew substantially after World War II from approximately 2 million tonnes in the late 1940s to a peak of 16 million tonnes in 1979, after which it declined slightly to 15.5 million tonnes in 1989.

Exports increased gradually from 2.1 million tonnes in 1977 to 4.2 million in 1987 and then fell to 3.6 million in 1988. The majority of these go to the United States, since Canada's trade with the United States is very active. Over the five-year period 1984–1988, an average of somewhat less than 3 million tonnes of steel products were exported annually to the United States.

Imports grew gradually from 1.5 million tonnes in 1977 to 4.0 million tonnes in 1988. Brazil provided more than 1 million tons, with the EEC contributing 1.5 million. The U.S. share was relatively small at 450,000 tons.

Canada relies on the United States as its principal export market, and this will continue during the 1990s. The trade treaty between the two nations will make it more attractive for the Canadian steel industry to ship to the United States and will also help U.S. exports to Canada. The tonnages of steel shipped into the United States from Canada will remain approximately as they have been in the past few years with the possibility of a 500,000-tonne increase; exports from the United States to Canada should more than double during the 1990s.

South Africa

South Africa's steel production since 1977 has fluctuated between 7.0 million and 9.6 million tonnes annually. Much of it is consumed domestically, but exports have been averaging approximately 2 million tonnes over the last ten years. The principal consumers are the EEC and other Western European countries, other countries in Africa, and Asia outside Japan.

Imports have been negligible, reaching 200,000 tonnes only once in the past 10 years.

The South African steel industry will remain quite static in terms of raw-steel production, and this will tend to keep exports at about the same level as they were during the 1980s.

The Soviet Union and Eastern Europe

In the final months of 1989, dramatic political changes took place in Eastern Europe. There was also a significant economic change in the Soviet Union put in motion when President Mikhail Gorbachev introduced *perestroika*. The changes in the Eastern European countries, including Czechoslovakia, East Germany, Hungary, Poland, Bulgaria, and Rumania, will affect not only their political structures but also their economies.

The steel industry has a place of considerable significance in all of these countries, and it will be seriously affected. In 1988, the last full year in which the Eastern bloc operated under Soviet influence, some 26 million tonnes of steel were exported, 9.4 million tonnes of them from the Soviet Union. Much of this steel was exchanged among the Eastern bloc countries, with relatively small amounts shipped to the rest of the world. For example, the Soviet Union shipped 3.4 million tonnes to East Germany, 800,000 to Hungary, and 600,000 to Bulgaria. Relatively small amounts were exported to other Western European countries with the exception of Yugoslavia, which received 600,000 tonnes. Very little tonnage was shipped to the United States.

In terms of imports, in 1988, the Soviet Union and the Eastern European countries received 23.2 million tonnes, 10.5 million of them by the Soviet Union. The Eastern European countries imported relatively little steel, with the exception of Eastern Germany and Bulgaria. The former accounted for 5.7 million tonnes and the latter for 2.6 million. The pattern for imports and exports could well change in the 1990s.

The Eastern European bloc, particularly Czechoslovakia, the second largest producer, has a great deal of antiquated steel equipment. Furthermore, the amount of steel continuously cast is a woeful 9 percent. If these countries are to market steel outside their own sphere, a great deal of investment will be required to modernize their facilities. In order to supply their internal needs, they will import steel provided they have the currency to pay for it; however, a period of time will be required before they are in a position to compete in the world market.

It is anticipated that the changes will result in dislocations in the first few years of the 1990s, since not only technology but management will undergo considerable change. It is entirely possible that exports may drop, and imports, particularly from Western Europe, may increase. There will probably be a trend to greater cooperation with Western Europe, and in the latter part of the 1990s, this should result in a more modern industry in Eastern Europe, which should also be profitable and be in a position to export steel.

As far as the Soviet Union is concerned, it will probably remain the largest steel producer in the world for a number of years into the 1990s. However, if *perestroika* leads to privatization, it is quite probable that a number of plants may be closed. Nevertheless, the steel industry is so fundamental to the economy of the country that it is doubtful that it will undergo privatization in the 1990s. For the economy to operate more efficiently and profitably, a number of plants will be scaled down and some closed. The Soviet Union may be exporting fewer tonnes because it will not have a captive market in Eastern Europe.

In terms of imports, the requirements of the Soviet economy are such that they should continue at about the level that has persisted for the past five years: approximately 10 million tonnes.

Indirect Exports and Imports

In addition to the products shipped from the steel mills into international trade, a large volume of steel is traded in the form of products made of steel, such as automobiles and machinery.[4] The total tonnage involved is somewhat difficult to ascertain, although for certain products, it is reasonably calculable. For example, the vehicles traded among nations contain significant amounts of steel, which can be measured. In some other products, the task is more difficult, particularly with such complex items as machinery and appliances that cover a large variety of products. Nevertheless, estimates have been made that present a reasonably good analysis of the steel content.

The total amount of steel traded throughout the world in indirect steel imports and exports runs into millions of tons. For example, it is estimated that in 1987, the United States imported 8.4 million tons of steel in automobiles, 5.3 million in machinery, and 3.5 million tons in other products, for a total of 17.2 million tons. Exports of steel-containing products from the United States were: automobiles and parts, 2.8 million tons; machinery, 4 million tons; and other products, 1.8 million tons, making a total of 8.6 million tons and leaving a net negative balance of steel in imported products over exports of 8.6 million tons.

Studies in indirect steel trade reveal that in 1986 some 57.6 million tonnes of steel were traded in products made of steel. This represents the exports of some sixteen countries and consequently does not give a total for the world. The world total is estimated at somewhat over 63 million tonnes. Presumably the export tonnage was imported on a world basis. The sixteen countries—Belgium-Luxembourg, France, West Germany, Italy, Netherlands, United Kingdom, Denmark, Spain, Austria, Sweden, Switzerland, United States, Canada, Japan, and South Korea—are the major exporters and account for more than 90 percent of the Western world's indirect steel exports.

Another study concentrating on U.S. indirect imports and exports covers most of the countries that trade products containing steel with the United States. Figures are available for 1985 and 1986 for the study embracing the sixteen countries and for 1987 in the U.S. study. Estimates are made of the steel contained in the products covered, which represent all those containing steel. (Because this is a complex and complicated process, the total figures are not absolutely accurate.) The sixteen-country study presents the exports of steel-containing products from each of these countries to the rest of the world.

The leading export nation of steel contained in products is Japan with 15.6 million tonnes in 1985 and 14.7 million in 1986. The largest segment was in vehicles—passenger cars, trucks, and parts—amounting to 8.5 million tonnes. Japan's exports of products containing steel were sent to most of the other countries throughout the world. However, there was a heavy concentration to the United States. Of the 14.7-million-tonne total, the United States received 6.5 million. No other country received as much as a million tonnes of steel contained in products. The second largest amount was 749,000 tonnes to the People's Republic of China. The third largest was Canada with 581,000, and the fourth was West Germany with 537,000 tonnes. All other countries were well under the 500,000-tonne mark. The majority of them were less than 100,000 tonnes. Imports to Japan in 1986 of products containing steel had less than 400,000 tonnes.

The second largest exporter of steel-containing products was West Germany with 11.4 million tonnes in 1986. Of this amount, items with 8.6 million tonnes were sold in Western Europe, 1.2 million in the United States, and smaller amounts throughout the rest of the world. Most of the remaining countries imported less than 100,000 tonnes. Only China and Japan took approximately 100,000 tonnes.

For the most part, exports from countries in the European Community were concentrated in Western Europe; however, France, Italy, and the United Kingdom shipped substantial tonnages outside Europe. Most of these were exported to the United States: 493,000 tonnes from the United Kingdom, 411,000 from Italy, and 337,000 from France.

Indirect steel exports from the United States, which in 1987 amounted to 8.6 million tons, went to Canada, Latin America, and the EEC. Canada was by far the largest recipient, taking 45 percent, or 3.7 million tons.

Twenty Latin American countries took 15 percent, or 1.3 million tons, and the EEC took approximately the same amount.

Indirect steel imports have a decided impact on the steel industry of steel-producing countries. This is particularly true of the United States with special reference to automobiles. The 8.4 million tons of steel that came in the form of automobiles represented a large tonnage, which would have been produced by the steel industry in the United States if all or a portion of these automobiles were made in the United States, as was the case in the 1950s and 1960s. The same can be said for the industry in some of the EEC countries, where large tonnages of indirect steel imports have been imported. The reason often given for these imports is a matter of quality and price—the people in a particular country or a group of countries feel that the imported item is either a better value or cheaper than that produced domestically.

Indirect steel imports and exports, which amounted to 63 million tonnes in 1986, represent a major contribution to the worldwide trade in steel.

The future of indirect imports and exports will depend on the trade in the products involved. For example, exports of automobiles came principally from Japan, which in 1988 sent more than 50 percent of its motor vehicle output overseas. The amount sent to the United States, its largest customer, will diminish in the early to mid-1990s, since Japanese automobile companies have built a number of plants in the United States. These facilities will be fed principally by steel from U.S. companies, some of them in joint ventures with Japanese steel producers. Thus, exports to the United States will be reduced in proportion to the output from Japanese-owned automobile plants located in the United States, and indirect steel imports will decline.

After 1992, there will be a much-increased flow of goods across borders in the EEC. Many of these will contain considerable amounts of steel, so that indirect imports and exports within the community should show a significant increase. Further, the political and economic changes in Eastern Europe should contribute to more trade between these countries, particularly those in the Common Market. In this respect, indirect imports and exports of steel should increase.

Notes

1. Office of the U.S. Trade Representative, press release, December 12, 1989.
2. *IISI proceedings 1973*, p. 1151/E/766/7.
3. *Metal Bulletin*, December 14, 1989, p. 25.
4. Material on indirect imports and exports have been taken from two studies: American Iron and Steel Institute, *United States Indirect Steel Trade 1987*, and International Iron and Steel Institute, *Indirect Trade in Steel, 1985 and 1986*.

6
Markets

On a worldwide basis, the market for steel is determined by the performance of individual economies, both in general terms and within their various sectors, particularly those that are steel intensive or require large amounts of steel. While many factors govern economic performance (business cycles, energy prices, inflation rates, interest rates, exchange rates, and the volume and patterns of international trade), the steel requirements of individual economies also depend on their demographic characteristics, degree of economic development, and related structural considerations that determine the size of their steel-consuming industries. In the final analysis, steel demand is, for the most part, derived, or dependent on the demand for manufactured goods containing steel and the extent of construction and other steel-consuming industries.

Trends in End-Use Sectors

Generally worldwide expenditures for the types of products manufactured by the major steel-consuming industries have been expanding but at a rate somewhat slower than economic activity as a whole. Meanwhile, mixed secular trends in the steel requirements of the various end-use sectors have resulted in an overall negative impact on the steel industry during most of the last decade. However, an improvement in the situation in the last years of the 1980s, as well as growth in steel demand in the Third World, presents a reasonably optimistic picture for world steel demand in the 1990s.

The steel consumed by each end-use sector is determined by its level of output and intensity of steel usage, that is, the quantity of steel it requires per manufactured unit produced. For example, although the automobile industry remains one of the most important steel markets, reductions in the steel content of the average vehicle, particularly in the United States, have resulted in a downtrend in the industry's total steel requirement. This is due in the United States to downsizing and the use of other materials, such as aluminum and plastics. Other major auto-producing countries have not had the same experience since their cars were small to begin with; in fact, Japan is sizing up its cars.

The growth or decline of other end-use sectors can be traced to a variety of economic, technical, and sociological influences. The computerization of railroad operations, for example, has reduced the steel market for railroad equipment by improving the efficiency of freight car use, so that fewer cars are needed to move a given volume of freight. The declining use of steel beverage cans can be traced to the introduction of alternative packaging materials such as aluminum. The use of substitute materials has also eroded the market for steel barrels, drums, and pails. Further, a slowing of the growth in electricity demand has reduced the steel used in power-generating equipment. On the other hand, the need to replace infrastructure in the industrialized world and install it in the Third World will create a large demand for steel.

While there are varied reasons for the shifting importance of individual end-use sectors, nearly all steel consumers have been affected, directly or indirectly, by foreign trade influences, which change over time, together with the relative competitiveness of manufacturers in international markets and fluctuations in the exchange values of their respective currencies.

Economic Development and Steel Use

Steel use also varies in terms of product and quantity depending on the grade of development of the country in question. In terms of the entire world, countries can be classified as industrialized, developing, and extremely underdeveloped. The Third world is by no means a monolith. It encompasses countries with a very low level of per capita income such as some of the African countries and other countries that have considerable industrial development, such as South Korea, Brazil, and Taiwan.

In general, extremely underdeveloped countries with very low levels of per capita gross national product (GNP) consume only small quantities of steel, both on an absolute and per capita basis. Examples are Chad, Mozambique, and Bangladesh, each with a GNP per capita at about $150 in 1989.[1] In these countries, fundamental necessities receive priority.

Initially, the building of a basic infrastructure (roads, shelter, schools, hospitals, etc.) generates a growing steel requirement focused on a limited range of products, including concrete reinforcing bar, structural shapes, corrugated sheets, and other construction-related steels. Since little if any manufacturing activity is conducted locally, the need for power-generating and transportation equipment and other steel-containing items must be satisfied through imports, and until industrialization occurs, the end uses for steel products remain limited to little beyond the construction markets.

As industrialization progresses from the start-up stage and begins to accelerate, steel demand encompasses a greater range of end-use activities and product requirements. Increasing rates of plant and equipment investment to support manufacturing operations give rise to more varied forms of construction activity to provide the necessary industrial and commercial infrastructure. Often at least part of the requirement for construction steels is met by installing relatively simple, small-scale steel mills, which serve as an initial manufacturing nucleus. Examples of this occurrence can be found in Peru, Tunisia, Malaysia, Singapore, and Thailand, whose annual production of steel in 1974 was minimal, ranging from 131,000 tons to 597,000 tons.[2]

At the outset, light manufacturing dominates, much of it labor intensive and generating more employment than steel demand. Over time, as the sophistication of a country's steel and other industries starts to increase, its end-use profile as a steel consumer becomes increasingly complex. An outstanding example is South Korea, whose economy has developed to a point where steel production increased from 1.2 million tons in 1973 to 21.9 million tons in 1989. Further, the number and size of steel-consuming industries has grown extensively. The country now produces over a million motor vehicles, as well as large tonnages of ships.

The industrialized countries have reduced their capacity and production since 1974, and despite a resurgence in demand, production in Western Europe, Japan, and the United States fell far short in 1989 of the 1974 record. Thus, demand has declined in terms of raw-steel production. However, the installation of large tonnages of continuous casting since 1974, when it represented 13 percent of steel industry production in the EEC now represents 88 percent and in Japan 93 percent of steel production. This provided more products with less raw steel. Further, the development of lighter steels has reduced the need for tonnage in the industrialized world, so that a measurement only in terms of raw steel tonnage no longer presents a completely valid comparison of steel needs.

The relationship of steel consumption to the growth in GNP similarly is no longer as valid as it was up to the 1970s. Consequently, estimated steel demand in the 1990s will depend on an analysis of the principal steel-consuming industries, since steel demand is derived from its consumers.

Automotive

One of the principal steel consumers in the industrialized world is the automobile industry, since production of sizable quantities of motor vehicles, with two exceptions, is confined to the industrialized world. The two exceptions are South Korea, which in 1989 produced 1.1 million vehicles, and Brazil, which also produced 1.0 million vehicles in the same year. The Soviet Union, which can be considered an industrialized country although it is not part of the Western world, produced 2.1 million vehicles in 1989.

Total world production in 1989 was 48.9 million vehicles; Japan was the leading producer with 13.0 million, the United States was in second place with 10.9 million, and Germany was a distant third, with 4.9 million. This total figure for the world is an all-time high, having surpassed the previous record of 48.3 million vehicles established in 1988.

In the five-year period 1985–1989, total world production, and consequently consumption, was 233 million vehicles; of this total, 167 million were passenger cars, which resulted in a significant degree of market saturation in a number of countries, so that future demand in those areas will be more for replacement rather than significant growth. The increase in saturation between 1973 and 1988 in countries such as Japan has been noteworthy. A number of other countries have increased their automobile population, including Spain, the Soviet Union, and South Korea, and consequently their advance in saturation ratios of the number of people per passenger car reduces their potential growth and increases their replacement markets.

In terms of growth, a large potential exists in the Third World, with a much smaller one in the industrialized countries. Table 6–1 gives the number of persons per passenger car for the years 1973 and 1987 for selected countries. This period represents significant growth in automobile output; the number of vehicles produced annually increased substantially

Table 6–1
Persons per Passenger Car, 1973 and 1988

	1973	1988
Japan	7.5	4.0
United States	2.1	1.8
West Germany	3.6	2.1
France	3.6	2.5
Italy	4.1	2.4
spain	9.1	3.7
United Kingdom	4.1	2.7
Canada	2.8	2.1
Brazil	26.0	13.0
South Korea	475.0	40.0
Soviet Union	138.0	18.0
China	26,756.0	1,188.0
India	738.0	482.0
Nigeria	822.0	149.0
Austria	4.8	2.7
Czechoslovakia	12.0	5.2
Bulgaria	44.0	7.9
Turkey	228.0	42.0

Source: *Motor Vehicle Facts & Figures* '75, pp.26, 27; *Motor Vehicles Facts & Figures* '89, p. 36.

from 39 million in 1973 to 48.3 million in 1988 and then to 48.9 million in 1989. For nine years of the sixteen-year period, world production was over 40 million vehicles.[3]

The growth potential in the Third World must be evaluated not only in terms of population but also by the income available to purchase an automobile. In countries such as China and India where saturation is at a minimum, per capita income for the vast majority, although improving, is significantly below that necessary for a person to move into the automobile market. The number of people per car in China dropped dramatically from almost 27,000 to somewhat over 1,000 due to the increase in the number of passenger cars registered—from 29,900 in 1973 to 900,000 in 1988. More significant was the advance in the number of trucks registered during the same period; they increased from 649,100 to 3,425,000. In India, there has been a significant increase in the registration of automobiles, which now stands at 3.3 million (1.7 million passenger cars and 1.6 million trucks). Recent analyses of the income in that country indicate that approximately 15 percent of the population has the income necessary to purchase an automobile.

Countries where the number of persons per passenger car has declined, such as Brazil where it fell from 26 to 13, still represent a potential for growth. The same is true of South Korea, which has prospered as a nation in the last ten years, so that the number of vehicles had grown to 2.0 million in 1988, of which 1.1 million were passenger cars. At 40 people per car, this country has a distinct potential for growth.

The demand for steel for the automotive industry will be heavily concentrated in those countries producing a million or more vehicles (table 6–2). The others, with one or two exceptions, turn out fewer than 500,000 vehicles and, consequently, represent a limited market for steel.

Table 6–2
Countries Producing over 1 Million Vehicles in 1989
(millions)

Japan	13.0
United States	10.9
West Germany	4.9
France	3.9
Soviet Union	2.1
Italy	2.2
Canada	1.9
Spain	2.0
United Kingdom	1.6
South Korea	1.1
Brazil	1.0

Source: *Motor Vehicle Facts & Figures '89*, p. 30.

Although the increase in the rate of saturation over a fifteen-year period gives rise to concern about the possibility for growth in the automobile industry and, consequently, the amount of steel to be used, there is a very large replacement market. In the United States, 11.2 million vehicles were discarded in 1988. The 9 million passenger cars and the 2.2 million trucks and buses presumably were replaced. In Japan, the number of vehicles discarded annually is in the area of 4 million. This offers a substantial market. In Western Europe, the discard rate is in the area of 7 to 8 percent of total vehicles.

Total world registrations have increased more than sevenfold since 1950, when they represented 70 million vehicles. In 1988, the figure was 540 million vehicles. If one calculates a percentage rate of scrappage at 7 to 8 percent, the total number of vehicles scrapped and presumably replaced would range from 37 million to 43 million vehicles, a very large market in terms of replacement.

Steel consumption in all of the major automotive-producing countries, with the exception of the United States, has remained proportionate to the production of vehicles. In the United States, there has been a decided decline in the amount of steel used by the automotive producers. In 1973, the automotive industry purchased 23.2 million tons from the domestic steel producers for the production of 12.7 million vehicles. In 1988, although production was down to 11.2 million vehicles—a drop of almost 12 percent—shipments from domestic steel producers fell to 12.5 million, or 46 percent.[4] This was a result of downsizing automobiles, as well as replacing steel with substitute materials, such as aluminum and plastics, and sourcing automobile parts from abroad. Thus, the automobile industry in the United States drastically reduced its steel requirements.

In the future, with pressure being brought to bear from substitute products, such as aluminum and plastics, the steel industry will do well to maintain its position, for it appears that the automotive industry in the United States will not be a significant growth market for steel. In view of the degree of saturation, production in the United States will be principally for replacement. There will, however, be some limited growth.

During the years from 1984 to 1989, production was relatively stable, as was steel consumption. U.S. automobile output averaged approximately 11.2 million units, and steel consumption averaged 12.4 million tons.

The Japanese automotive industry has had phenomenal growth in the postwar period, increasing from 482,000 vehicles in 1960 (308,000 of them trucks) to 13.0 million in 1989. Since 1980, the Japanese industry has held first place in world automotive production and consequently has become a large consumer of steel. In 1978, when production was 9.3 million vehicles, the Japanese steel industry shipped 7.3 million tonnes to its automotive customers. In 1989, when production rose to 13.0 million vehicles, the Japanese domestic steel industry shipped a record 11.6 million tonnes to the automobile producers.[5] Unlike the U.S. industry, the Japanese built small cars from the outset and thus had no reason to downsize them. Consequently, as automobile production increased, steel consumption increased proportionately.

As for the future, the amount of growth in Japanese automotive production will be somewhat limited. Since 1980, when the industry produced 11 million vehicles, it increased its output to 13 million vehicles by 1989. This is a significant growth but by no means comparable with the nine years prior to 1980, when annual production advanced from 5.8 million vehicles in 1971 to 11 million in 1980.

The Japanese market absorbs about half of its automotive production. Exports in 1988 were 6.1 million vehicles out of a total production of 12.7, or more than 48 percent.[6] Thus, the growth of the Japanese industry will depend in great part on its ability to export.

The establishment of Japanese automobile-producing plants in other countries, such as the United States and Western Europe, will place some limitation on the units produced at home. Consequently the steel to be shipped to the Japanese automobile producers by their own steel industry will probably not grow very much in the years ahead.

In the 1980s, the Japanese home market became more saturated. In 1973, there were 7.5 people per passenger car, and, by 1988, the number had declined to 4.0. Further, traffic congestion in Japan is an inhibiting factor. Although there is room for growth in the domestic market, dependence on exports will continue to be heavy.

A recent development, which may in the future be called a trend, is the production of larger cars; however, their number is limited and for the next year or two will not affect the total amount of steel consumed to any great extent. The government of Japan has reduced the luxury tax from 20 percent to 6 percent, thus making it more attractive to buy the larger cars.

Steel demand by the principal producers of automobiles in Western Europe should remain reasonably stable throughout the 1990s. Here again, the saturation point indicates that the market will be basically a replacement market, although there will be some growth. The production of motor vehicles in West Germany, France, and the United Kingdom has been increasing slowly over the past five years. Italy and Spain have grown somewhat more rapidly; their production increased significantly on a percentage basis during that time—Italy by 38 percent and Spain by 54 percent. However, the number of vehicles involved was relatively few. Table 6–3 gives automotive production, in millions of vehicles, from 1984 through 1989 for the principal automotive producers in Western Europe.

Table 6–3
Western European Automotive Production, 1984–1989
(millions of units)

Country	1984	1985	1986	1987	1988	1989
France	3.2	3.1	3.2	3.5	3.7	3.9
West Germany	4.0	4.4	4.6	4.6	4.6	4.9
United Kingdom	1.1	1.3	1.2	1.4	1.5	1.6
Italy	1.6	1.6	1.8	1.9	2.1	2.2
Spain	1.3	1.4	1.5	1.7	1.9	2.0

Source: *Motor Vehicle Facts & Figures '89.*

In the future, the growth of the Western European automotive industry will be relatively small, as will its demand for steel. The mills in the EEC ship steel across national borders and supply the automotive industry in almost all of the EEC countries. Thus, a clear-cut analysis of steel shipments on a country basis is not as possible as it is in the United States and Japan. However, the figures are available for the shipments of the German steel industry and Arbed to the automotive industry. In 1989, they were approximately 2.2 million tonnes.

The Canadian automotive industry is intimately tied to that of the United States, particularly since 1965 when a virtual common market was arranged between the two countries in terms of automobile imports and exports. Access to the U.S. market increased Canadian automotive production. In 1988, it was 2 million units, of which 1.6 million were exported to the United States. Shipments of steel from the Canadian domestic producers to the automotive industry in 1988 were 2.2 million tons. This should remain steady without much of an increase during the next decade, since the production of Canadian cars probably will not increase significantly.

During the past five years, production of vehicles in Brazil has averaged slightly fewer than 1 million units. Peak production in 1988 was 1.1 million vehicles. This could increase significantly during the next decade, particularly in view of the fact that exports have been on the rise. In 1987, they were 346,000 vehicles, a substantial increase over the previous high of 213,000. As a result, Brazil will ship more steel to its automotive industry in the coming decade. In 1988, it was in excess of 1 million tons, and in the mid- to late 1990s, with automotive production projected to increase to 1.4 million to 1.5 million vehicles, annual steel shipments should be approximately 1.5 million tons.

South Korea has increased its automobile output since 1984 at a more rapid pace than any other producer. In 1984, total output was 265,000 vehicles. By 1988, it had grown to 1.1 million vehicles, and with the capacity installed in recent years, it is expected that, by 1992, automotive production will increase to 2 million vehicles. Thus, the amount of steel required, most of which will be produced domestically, will be in the area of 2 million tons.

In the 1990s, South Korea will depend heavily on exports. In 1987, with a production of 1 million vehicles, exports amounted to 546,000 units, 474,000 of them to North America. The largest producer, Hyundai, accounted for over 600,000 of the country's total output. However, since this company has established a manufacturing plant in Canada, its production in South Korea could be somewhat curtailed.

Production in the Soviet Union in the last five years has been virtually static at 2.2 million vehicles. New policies in the Soviet Union with respect to the economy could lead to an increase in automotive production, although this is not expected for several years. Consequently, the amount of steel consumed will remain stable.

The amount of steel that will be required for automotive production during the 1990s on a world basis should increase moderately, but there is a constant threat from other materials, such as aluminum and, particularly, plastics. Much has been said about the inroads that plastics have made and will continue to make in the production of the automotive body. However, the steel industry is exerting great efforts to ward off the challenge by improving the quality of its product, particularly sheets, since it is this product that plastics hope to replace. Thus far, plastic's success has been quite limited, and an estimate of the total amount of steel required for automotive production will depend, to a significant extent, on the ability of the steel industry to maintain its position against competition from other materials.

To accomplish this, the steel industry has increased its capacity to produce galvanized sheets, which the automotive industry is now demanding as a corrosion-resistant material. Six new lines were installed in the late 1980s, and 12 more are under construction or active consideration. In addition, much has been done to improve the quality of the steel sheet through the introduction of side shifting and roll bending, as well as hydraulic screwdown on the finishing stands of the hot-strip mill. These improvements have reduced the crown in the center of the sheet dramatically. Further, on the cold-strip mill, the introduction of the six-high mill at Inland and United States Steel has resulted in what has been generally considered an excellent product. More of these mills will be installed throughout the industry in the United States in the decade to come. Several of them are already in operation in Japan and South Korea.

Construction

In addition to the automotive industry, one of the largest consumers of steel is construction. This covers a multitude of projects, ranging from public works, such as highways, bridges, and tunnels, to residential construction of single-family homes. The major use of steel is obviously in the heavier projects, which in addition to public works also include multistory buildings for residential and commercial use. Perhaps the principal group of projects consuming steel in construction comes under the heading of infrastructure. Usually these are massive items, such as bridges, tunnels, and communications and transportation systems, requiring large tonnages of steel.

The term *infrastructure* has been variously defined; however, all of the definitions stress some of the same fundamental ideas. It was defined in a paper presented to the IISI meeting in 1985: "Simply put, infrastructure includes the basic structures and facilities (capital assets) owned by governments of all types to provide basic public services to constituents. Large facilities (at times referred to as public works) are necessary for health, welfare, safety and economic growth of any community."[7]

Fundamentally, infrastructure is provided in most countries throughout the world by public funds, since the projects are used by the public and in many instances are too large and expensive for private industry to undertake.

In several instances, particularly in the United States, some segments of infrastructure are provided by the private sector: energy facilities (electric, gas, nuclear), hospitals, railroads, and communications. In most other countries throughout the world, these are provided by government. The list of items under infrastructure indicates the broad nature of this segment of the economy:[8]

Airports
Bridges
Communications
Dams/reservoirs
Drainage, flood control
Drinking water
Educational facilities
Energy (electric, gas, nuclear) facilities
Government offices
Highways/roads
Hospitals
Housing (multifamily and low income)
Locks

Mass transit
Parks and recreational facilities
Ports
Post offices
Prisons
Railroads
Resource recovery
Sewage treatment
Solid waste disposal
Wastewater treatment
Waterways

As is evident from the list, infrastructure is put in place and maintained, for the most part, by public funds because of the projects it embraces. In the industrialized countries of the United States, Japan, and Western Europe, infrastructure expenditures are primarily directed at replacing and improving existing facilities. By contrast, emphasis in the Third World is on building new infrastructure, as well as some replacement, since countries such as India, China, Korea, and many in Africa and South America require the construction of fundamental infrastructure encompassing such facilities as roads, bridges, tunnels, irrigation systems, sewage treatment plants, and transportation systems.

In both the industrialized and developing countries, much remains to be done in improving and installing infrastructure, which implies ongoing steel requirements of substantial proportions. In recent years, public funds expended on infrastructure have declined significantly. This is true of virtually all the industrialized countries, where public funds have been allotted on the basis of priority to social programs and thus have been withdrawn from capital investment, creating a significant backlog of delayed infrastructure projects.

In the industrialized world, unfortunately, it often takes a crisis to bring about replacement. In the United States, several bridges have collapsed, drawing attention to the glaring need for maintenance and replacement which has long been neglected. The total number of bridges in the United States is in the area of 550,000, and relatively conservative estimates indicate that almost half of these require replacement or improvement. These range from small highway bridges over streams and gullies to large spans over rivers and harbors.

Other areas where much needs to be done, and fortunately there are plans to do a great deal, are water systems, sewage-treatment systems, airports, highways, hospitals, and detention facilities. In the large cities during the late 1980s, significant improvement has been made in the installation of sewage treatment systems. Further, airports, particularly terminals, have been expanded to handle the growing amount of passenger traffic. This is particularly noticeable in Chicago and Atlanta.

In terms of investments in new and replacement projects, the industrialized countries have made some significant contributions. However, as long as the old or original facility is operable, there is a marked tendency to put off replacing it even though it appears to be necessary. However, in the late 1980s a significant improvement has taken place. In Japan, for example, a program is currently underway, and long overdue, for the construction of much-needed highways to relieve traffic congestion, virtually omnipresent in many of its urban centers. The solution to the highway problem has recently been put in operation, and an investment has been made, completing some 3,600 kilometers out of a planned 7,600 kilometers.

A major bridge project has been initiated that will continue through most of the 1990s: the construction of nineteen bridges linking the islands of Honshu and Shikoku in Japan's inland sea. Nine of the structures are among the world's longest suspension bridges. Several of these have been completed, but more remain to be built. One bridge, the Akasi Kaikyo bridge, was started in 1988 and will not be completed until 1998. The entire project, which will be completed at the end of the century, will use an estimated 2 million tonnes of steel.[9]

In Japan, much attention is being given to the construction of housing in metropolitan areas such as Tokyo and Osaka. The population density demands high-rise construction in order to provide decent living standards. One program underway will result in the construction of thousands of units of apartments in Tokyo and other large cities in the next ten years. The exodus from the central city has motivated this program. The large apartment houses will be constructed of steel to a great extent instead of reinforced concrete.[10] Another project in Japan is the Kansai International Airport, under construction near Osaka.

In 1987, the Japanese government published a list of infrastructure ventures in the planning stage. This was intended to improve the infrastructure but also to provide a home market for Japanese steel and other materials and lessen the dependence on exports. Several trillion yen were set apart for various public expenditures:

1. 700 billion yen for public housing.
2. 3.7 trillion yen for other projects, including 800 billion yen for local government projects, 450 billion for disaster relief work, and 350 billion yen for government building maintenance.
3. 2.2 trillion yen for infrastructure projects.[11]

Infrastructure allocations are as follows:

232.4 billion yen for reforestation and flood control.

374.1 billion yen for highway maintenance.

94.1 billion yen for airports, harbors, and fishing ports.

48.9 billion yen for housing loan interest subsidies.

244.3 billion yen for sewerage and other public hygiene programs.

169.5 billion yen for agricultural infrastructure maintenance.

27 billion yen for rural roads and industrial waste treatment.

1.4 billion yen for an adjustment fund.[12]

The steel required to support Japan's future infrastructure program can be estimated from the quantities consumed in the late 1980s, when many infrastructure projects were initiated. The category, Construction and Repairing, indicates a very large tonnage. In 1989, it amounted to 17 million tonnes of a variety of steel products, which compares to 11.6 million tonnes for the automotive industry. These two categories, representing over 28.7 million tonnes, accounted for some 43 percent of total domestic steel consumption in Japan.

A recent issue of *Steel Today and Tomorrow* reviews the large-scale infrastructure projects under consideration and provides estimates of steel requirements in some instances:

1. The world's largest undersea tunnel: Seikan tunnel. This will require an estimated 168,000 tonnes of steel.
2. Unique urban development: Tsukoba Academic Research Community.
3. Offshore airport: Kansai International Airport near Osaka.
4. Long-span bridge construction: Honshu-Shikoku Bridge project.
5. Oil storage: Kamigotoh Oil Storage Base. This is a giant offshore oil storage base in the Gotoh Islands of Nagasaki Prefecture. It is the island's first offshore storage base utilizing floating storage vessels.
6. Road: Trans-Tokyo Bay Bridge. A 15-kilometer tunnel. Estimated steel consumption is 400,000 to 500,000 tonnes.
7. Man-made island: Rokko Island. This will accommodate a population of 30,000 people with 8,000 housing units.
8. Railway: Chuo Linear Express. This will be an alternative trunk line for the Tokyo-Osaka Super Express, which will cut travel time from 3 hours to 2 hours.[13]

Infrastructure in Western Europe has been built up to a high degree in the postwar period. Attention has been given particularly to highways. In the 1990s, a great deal of investment will be made in tunnels, bridges, and railways, particularly high-speed railways. The tunnel between England and France should be built by 1992 or 1993 and will cost some $14 billion. It will contain a railroad, which will be connected on the English side with a high-speed line from London and on the French side with high-speed lines to Paris and elsewhere. The tunnel will be used exclusively for rail transportation. Cars, trucks, and buses will be loaded onto flat cars and sped through the tunnel.

Other rail lines will span France and Spain, in addition to lines that will be built in Italy, Germany, Austria, Belgium, Holland, and Denmark. Called the Pan-European Network, it will employ a number of high-speed trains that will require new track construction, as well as the upgrading of more than 10,000 miles of rails. One of the projects will encompass five major European cities: London, Paris, Amsterdam, Frankfurt, and Brussels.

A bridge will connect the two sections of Denmark, and possibly another will connect Denmark and Sweden. This latter link could be a 10-mile bridge and tunnel carrying a railroad, which will start at Copenhagen and run to the Swedish port of Malmö. All of these projects will involve the use of large tonnages of steel in the form of rails and structural members, as well as the material required for the high-speed trains.[14]

High-Speed Trains

Development of the high-speed train took place in Japan a number of years ago when the high-speed line between Tokyo and Osaka was installed. Known as bullet trains, they traveled at approximately 125 miles an hour on a right-of-way built especially for them.

In France, a high-speed system, traveling at more than 150 miles an hour, connects Paris and Lyons. In the United States, there are several such projects under consideration. The number has been placed at ten or eleven, located in a number of different states. One that seems to be becoming a reality is in Florida, where a line about 320 miles long would connect Miami, Orlando, and Tampa. It is estimated that speeds of 180 miles an hour could be achieved. Total investment is in the area of $2 billion. There are other large projects planned, ranging from a 17-mile stretch between Orlando airport and Disneyworld, to others: Houston-to-Dallas, Pittsburgh-to-Philadelphia, and Chicago-to-Detroit lines. The installation of a high-speed train would require a new roadbed with new rails and would give impetus to the rail producers in the United States.[15]

In the United States, activity in the purchase of railcars handling freight has begun to revive. This dropped, incredibly, from a figure of 95,000 cars in 1979 to 5,800 cars in 1983. A number of manufacturers dropped out of business, so now the capacity to produce railcars is in the area of 50,000 a year. Railcar output revived from the low point of 5,800 in 1983 to 22,500 in 1988, with the assurance of an even higher figure in the 1990s.

The railroads were the largest consumer of steel in the nineteenth century and for the first ten years of the twentieth century. In the 1980s, they fell sharply as a market for steel. Rail production in the United States in the late 1970s was approximately 1.1 million tons. In Japan, it was some 650,000 tonnes. In the 1980s, production in the United States fell off drastically to a low point of 350,000 tons in 1987. In Japan, production also fell to less than 400,000 tonnes in both 1987 and 1988.

For the most part, rails have been a replacement item, since very few new railroads have been constructed. However, with the recent interest in building entirely new rail lines for high-speed trains, the 1990s could well see a revival in the demand for rails and railroad accessories. Thus, the future of the rail market may be somewhat brighter than its recent past.

Oil and Gas

The oil and gas industry has been a large consumer of steel but on a fluctuating basis. In 1981, with the price of oil over $30 a barrel, many wells were drilled. In the United States in December of that year, 4,530 rigs were in operation. In other countries, the number was many fewer, since 71 percent of the drilling of new wells took place in the United States, with a consequent large demand for oil country tubular goods. The average number of rigs in operation in the United States for the entire year 1981 was 3,969, while the world's total for the year was 5,635. By 1988, the percentage for the United States had dropped to 43 percent of a much lower total figure. In the United States, the rigs in operation in 1988 amounted to 936, while for the world, including the United States, they were 2,154. Clearly the dominant market for oil country tubular goods is in the United States.

In terms of operating rigs, the second largest number is found in Canada. In 1981, compared to the 3,969 rigs of the United States, Canada had a mere 263. In 1988, with the United States at 966, Canada was at 196. The only other countries with more than 100 rigs in operation were Mexico, with 155, and India, with 127.

Statistics are not available for Soviet Union. The countries in the Middle East, which have by far the greatest oil reserves, had a total of 144 rigs operating in 1988. This was spread over thirteen countries, including

Table 6–4
Total U.S. Shipments to the Oil and Gas Industry
and Shipments of Oil Country Tubular Goods,
1980–1989
(millions of net tons)

	Total Shipments	Shipments of Oil Country Tubular Goods
1980	5.4	3.6
1981	6.2	4.2
1982	2.7	1.8
1983	1.3	.7
1984	2.0	1.4
1985	2.0	1.3
1986	1.0	.5
1987	1.5	.9
1988	1.5	1.1
1989	1.2	.9

Source: American Iron and Steel Institute, *Annual Statistical Reports*, 1980–1989.

Saudi Arabia with 4, Iraq with 23, Egypt with 21, and Iran with 18. In 1981, during the oil boom, the same thirteen Middle East countries had 170 rigs in operation as compared with the 3,969 in the United States. Another large oil producer is Venezuela, which in 1981 had 63 rigs operating; in 1988, only 25 were in operation.

In 1981, shipments of U.S. producers to the oil and gas industry were 6.2 million tons, of which 4.2 million were oil country tubular goods. As drilling dropped precipitously in subsequent years, steel shipments to the oil and gas industry in the United States fell accordingly. Table 6–4 indicates the volatility of steel shipments from 1980 to 1988. Oil country tubular goods followed the same trend as total steel shipments to the oil and gas industry.

Future demand for steel by the oil and gas industry will depend on the rate of drilling which, in turn, will depend on the price of crude oil, which is expected to increase in the 1990s. Before the Middle East crisis of August 1990, it was predicted by some that the price of oil would rise to $25 a barrel in the early 1990s from its 1989 level of $18. Such an increase on a permanent basis would bring on an increased drilling program and more steel would be required. The crisis of 1990 has driven the price of oil beyond $30 a barrel. However, this is looked upon as a temporary condition and will not inspire drilling, unless it continues for a long period of time which is doubtful.

In addition to oil country tubular goods, a considerable amount of line pipe is used by the oil and gas industry. The pipeline currently under construction in Canada will carry natural gas from Alaska and the Northwest Territories to the western and central United States. It is expected to be completed by the year 2000. Consequently, the demand for large-diameter pipe will be considerable during the 1990s. The total length of pipe to be laid will be in the area of 4,500 miles and could consume well over a million tons of line pipe.

Shipbuilding

Shipbuilding has at times been a major consumer of steel on a world basis. However, like oil and gas, it has been a cyclical industry, although in the postwar period, the size of large-bulk cargo carriers increased tremendously. In the early 1950s, ships of 50,000 deadweight tonnes (DWT) were constructed and considered large. In the 1960s and 1970s, size grew rapidly to reach more than 300,000 DWT, with one as large as 500,000 DWT.

Beginning in the mid-1970s, ship construction began to decline, and with it the amounts of steel required. Prior to that time, the Japanese had secured a leading position in the industry, producing in some years half of the world's tonnage. In 1970, for the first time, the Japanese steel industry shipped over 4 million tonnes of steel to shipbuilders. This increased rapidly to a high of 7.3 million tonnes in 1974; it became the second largest consumer of steel in Japan, surpassed only by construction and repairing. Since 1974, the steel shipped to shipbuilders has declined precipitously, hovering in the 3-million-tonne range until 1985 and hitting a low point of 1.8 million tonnes in 1987. There was a recovery in 1988 to almost 2 million tonnes as shipbuilding in Japan began to pick up. In spite of the overall decline, however, the Japanese accounted for approximately 50 percent of the ship tonnage between 1980 and 1987 but dropped to about 40 percent in 1988.

For the ten-year period 1979–1988, the Japanese produced 70.6 million DWT out of 153 million worldwide, or 46 percent. The second largest producer was Korea, which expanded from 495,000 DWT in 1979 to 3.4 million in 1988, accounting for 18.1 million DWT over the ten-year period, or 12 percent.[16]

There is a considerable consensus that the world shipbuilding industry after fifteen years of depression will recover in the early 1990s. This is based on an aging international maritime fleet, with an average age of ships being sold for demolition of twenty-five years (it was seventeen years in the mid-1980s).

The industry in the United States has been a minor factor in shipbuilding, with steel shipments of less than a half-million tons annually from 1982 to 1988. Tax problems have been a factor in this poor performance.

With the upsurge in shipbuilding projected for the early 1990s, it should become a significant market, regaining at least part of its previous tonnage. It seems from the records of the past ten years that it will be concentrated in Japan and Korea, with significant activity in Taiwan and West Germany.

Machinery

Machinery covers a vast multitude of items, ranging from heavy earth-moving equipment to computers. Some type of machinery is used in every manufacturing industry and in most service industries. Some of the subclassifications include lathes; grinding machinery; honing, broaching, drilling, and milling machinery; earth-moving equipment; materials-handling equipment; paper machinery; and presswork equipment. Also under the category electrical equipment are a number of subdivisions, which include massive equipment such as turbines and generators down to small motors and computers. The steel market includes carbon steel; electrical steels, such as grain-oriented sheets; and tool steels.

Steel shipments to these industries follow the business cycle to a great extent. In the United States, during the ten-year period 1979–1988, shipments for use in machinery, industrial equipment, tools, and electrical equipment fluctuated from 8.8 million tons in 1979 to 4.0 million tons in 1985. Since that time, there has been a minor revival; figures were almost 5.0 million tons in 1989. In Japan, shipments recorded for the same categories—machinery and electrical machinery—reached 4.5 million tonnes in 1973. In 1980, the figure rose to 5.0 million tonnes, declining to a low point of 3.6 million tonnes in 1986, with a revival to 4.6 million tonnes in 1988. Shipments to the West German machinery industry by West German steel producers and Arbed was 700,000 tons in 1989.

Projections for the future in the various fields will closely parallel the rate of capital investment. There will be considerable activity in steel mill equipment as some of the larger and more basic units, such as strip mills and other rolling facilities, are replaced and updated. Heavy earthmoving equipment will depend to a great extent on basic construction, often involving infrastructure. Office equipment, principally computers, has grown rapidly in the past decade, however, the amount of steel used is relatively small compared with other types of machines. Electrical machinery, particularly for massive generating facilities, has had a long period of growth, which in some of the industrialized countries slowed in the last few years of the 1980s.

In terms of the future, the growth of this industry in all of its segments will depend heavily on projected capital expenditures. Six of the largest steel companies in the United States have projected a $10 billion investment figure up to 1993 or 1994. Utilities will have to replace equipment, and this can mean considerable activity in electrical machinery. The normal wear and tear on and exhaustion of manufacturing facilities will require a rate of replacement that will increase in the next five years over the previous five, when activity in capital goods had slowed.

One of the largest markets in the next five years should be Eastern Europe and the Soviet Union, where much has to be done in the way of improving plant facilities in virtually every industry. For a number of years, modernization has not taken place, and this will have to be compensated for in the period immediately ahead. Third World countries, such as China, Korea, and Taiwan, are expanding their production activity, which will require investment in capital equipment, including various types of machinery.

Thus, although it is difficult to place a figure on steel to be consumed by this segment of the economy, it should improve over the amounts consumed in the latter half of the 1980s.

During the 1990s, the market for steel will remain relatively stable in the industrialized world, with some cyclical fluctuations. The Third World will show a growth trend as these nations attain greater industrialization, which will engender greater demand for steel.

Service Centers

In the United States, Japan, and several EEC countries, service centers are large customers of their steel industries. Service centers are distributors of steel to consumers. They can be considered the retail arm of the steel industry and have a wide variety of customers. Usually they supply tonnages that are smaller than the mills like to handle. In the United States, service centers took 20.8 million tons in 1989, as compared to 11.5 million tons for construction and contractors' products and 11.8 million tons for the automotive industry. In Japan, the service centers took 22.3 million tonnes in 1989, compared to 17.0 million for construction and repairing and 11.6 million for the automotive industry. In West Germany in 1989, shipments to service centers were 3.4 million tonnes as compared to 2.2 million tonnes to automotive.

There is every reason to believe they will continue to be the largest customers of the steel industry, since they have grown considerably since 1988. In that year, service centers in the United States accounted for 16.2 million tons of steel industry shipments; and in Japan, the figure was 15.1 million tonnes.

A service center performs a middleman function insofar as it takes steel from the mills in large tonnages and sells it in much smaller amount to its many customers. It also performs a processing function, which varies from slitting and cutting to burning shapes. It handles tonnages that are too small for the mills, and it performs processing functions that are very often too large for its customers.

In addition to these consuming industries, a number of others are significant in terms of their steel consumption. These include containers and packaging; this industry in the United States consumed 4.4 million tons of steel in 1988, of which 3.3 million, or 75 percent, was tin-mill products. The remainder was made up of sheets and strip, both hot and cold rolled. In Japan, containers accounted for 2.1 million tonnes in 1988.

There has been considerable competition in the past decade from aluminum. This is particularly true in the United States where the beer can market, the largest segment of the can market, is now almost completely served by aluminum. In 1979, the container industry in the United States took 6.8 million tons, of which 5.2 million were tin-mill products. In 1988, of the 4.4 million tons shipped to the container industry, 3.3 million were tin-mill products. This is considered by some a permanent loss; however, the steel industry is striving to regain some of the lost tonnage. In Japan and the EEC, aluminum has not made nearly the inroads in can production that it has in the United States. In the 1990s, tin-mill products in the United States will not vary much from the 1988 figure.

Among other consumers, appliances account for a considerable tonnage, principally flat-rolled products. In 1988 in the United States, total shipments to this industry were 1.6 million tons, of which 1.5 million were flat-rolled product, including sheets and strip. Domestic and commercial equipment accounted for 1.2 million tons, 1.1 million of which were flat-rolled products, both sheet and strip. Other consuming industries include mining and agriculture, each of which consumed approximately 500,000 tons in the United States.

In terms of global markets, the Third World will require steel for infrastructure, and depending on the countries' development, machinery, automotive, and railroads will require considerable tonnages. The industrialized world is overwhelmingly a replacement market as contrasted to the growth market of the Third World. Consumption of steel in the industrialized countries should average close to the 1988–1989 tonnages, while Third World tonnage will increase somewhat, although countries such as India will be slower to increase consumption than others, including South Korea and the Latin American countries.

Notes

1. World Bank, *World Development Report 1989* (New York: Oxford University Press, 1989), p. 164.

2. International Iron and Steel Institute, *Steel Statistical Year Book 1983*, pp. 2, 3.

3. Most of the statistics on automobile production, as well as registrations, have been taken from *MVMA Motor Vehicle Facts Figures '89* (Detroit: Motor Vehicle Manufacturers Association of the United States).

4. American Iron and Steel Institute, *Annual Statistical Reports for 1973 and 1978*.

5. Japan Iron and Steel Federation, *Monthly Report of Iron and Steel Statistics* (May 1990): 10.

6. Japan Automobile Manufacturers Association, Inc., *Motor Vehicles Statistics of Japan, 1988*, p. 19.

7. *Report of Proceedings*, IISI Annual Meeting and Conference, London, October 1985, p. 63.

8. Ibid., p. 64.

9. *Steel Today and Tomorrow* (July–September 1989): 11–12.

10. "Steel in High-rise Housing—Japanese Techniques," panel discussion speeches, IISI 23, Berlin, pp. E2314/1-4.

11. Plans announced May 19, 1987, as part of the Emergency Economic Package and Supplemental Budget for the fiscal year 1987 adopted July 24, 1987, by the Diet.

12. Ibid.

13. *Steel Today and Tomorrow, 1990 Special Edition—Large Scale Projects*. Japan Iron and Steel Exporters Association, Tokyo, Japan.

14. *Fortune*, November 10, 1989, pp. 131–136.

15. Ibid.

16. Conversation with shipping industry executives.

7

Technology

Over a period of forty-five years since the end of World War II, there have been a number of technological advances affecting virtually every phase of steel industry operations. These developments have been applied worldwide in steel plants in the industrialized countries, as well as in many of those that have sprung up recently in the Third World. Most steel-producing companies have taken advantage of the new technologies, many of which have brought radical changes to steelmaking.

As in recent applications of technology, those in the future will emphasize improvements that increase productivity, reduce costs, and improve quality. The technological advances currently being installed, as well as those planned during the 1990s, are built on earlier developments. These improvements in technology can be classified under two headings: those that involve basic, fundamental changes in some phase of steelmaking and those that are more numerous but less significant, each of which makes a contribution to advancing the state of the steelmaking art. This chapter will discuss the basic fundamental advances in technology in the successive stages of steel production.

Coke Ovens

Coke ovens which convert coal to coke, are essential to the production of pig iron, which is processed into steel and the products of steel. They provide material for the blast furnace operation, which reduces the iron ore to pig iron. Although essential to the integrated mills, they constitute the steel industry's greatest pollution problem. (Much work has been done to solve this problem.)

Two significant attempts have been made to change the process, one with a considerable degree of success and the other with so little success that there is limited interest in it. The more successful attempt has been the dry-quench process. It eliminates the cooling tower in which water is poured on the red-hot coke as it comes from the oven. A huge white cloud, containing steam as well as pollutants, emerges from the top of the cooling tower when the hot coke is quenched by water. The dry quench eliminates this since it uses nitrogen rather than water to cool the coke; as a result, the steam that normally passes into the air is captured and used to generate energy. The elimination of the white cloud also eliminates the pollutants it carries. This process is popular in Japan but has not been installed to any great extent in Western steelmaking countries.

The second innovation, which seemed to hold considerable promise but has lost much of its appeal, is the production of formed coke. In this process, nonmetallurgical coal can be used in a closed system, the final product of which is a bonded briquette of relatively uniform size. The Food Machinery and Chemicals Corporation (FMC) built a plant that produced a relatively small amount of formed coke, which was used in a small blast furnace with reasonable success. This inspired Inland Steel in the United States to consider building a facility in the late 1970s. However, because of a lack of adequate funding, the plan was abandoned. The Japanese have been working on form coke for a number of years, although they have no production plant in operation.

Developments that have become part of coke technology in recent years consist of much higher slot ovens, reaching 7 meters. In addition, ovens have recently been constructed with a width of 24 inches as opposed to the traditional 18 inches.

One significant development planned for the 1990s is an attempt to reduce the amount of coke required for blast furnace operations. The reduction could take place through the substitution of pulverized coal injected at the blast furnace tuyeres. This has been done in Europe and Japan. In Europe, amounts are injected at rates up to 350 pounds per tonne of iron produced; the Japanese injections are more modest, ranging up to 120 pounds per tonne of iron produced. Given a coke rate of 900–1,000 pounds per tonne of iron, this approach could significantly reduce the amount of coke required. The basic reason for this is to avoid the replacement of aged coke ovens, which involve significant expenses as well as pollution problems. In the United States, Armco has been using this process at its Ashland, Kentucky, furnaces for a number of years, and United States Steel has contracted to install the process on all blast furnaces at its Gary works. Further, most other steel companies are considering it.

Other developments aimed at eliminating coke include reducing iron ore to iron with the use of coal and gas rather than coke. There is a particularly active project in Japan where the integrated steel companies are combining their efforts to develop an ironmaking process, called the Dios process, that will bypass the blast furnace and eliminate the need for coke ovens. The process was inspired in part by a survey of the coke ovens in Japan. There are thirty plants producing coke, eleven of which are operated directly by steel companies, with five more by steel companies and related chemical companies.

Since most of the Japanese coke ovens will be thirty to thirty-five years old by the end of the century, they will need replacement. This is an expensive investment and brings with it pollution problems. Given their expected life, most coke ovens will come to the end of their useful, productive lives between 1999 and 2004. By that time, it is hoped that the new processes producing iron without coke will be in operation.

Nippon Steel and NKK have assumed the task of research and development on the commercial viability of a basic-oxygen furnace for the smelting and reducing process. This is the core of the technology study. It has been reported that Nippon Steel will invest some $9 million in research and development over the first three years of the 1990s, with NKK investing $4.8 million. Kawasaki Steel is attempting to establish technology for a blast furnace–type reduction facility, earmarking $5 million for the research. Kobe Steel has assumed the task of studying the coal gasification process at a cost of some $2.3 million, and Sumitomo Industries will study the peripheral technology.

The Japanese Iron and Steel Federation will undertake the design of the overall system to coordinate the cooperative effort. Research and development to establish a commercially viable technology is to continue for a period of seven years at a total investment estimated in excess of $100 million. This is considered too large an outlay and too risky for a single company, explaining the joint effort. Eight integrated steel producers have pledged their cooperation. In addition to the five mentioned, the others are Nisshin Steel, Nakayama Steel, and Godo Steel.

Under current plans, a test or pilot plant with a daily capacity of 300 to 500 tons will be built at a designated Nippon Steel works between 1991 and 1994. The Ministry of Trade and Industry (MITI) has granted this joint effort national project status and allocated $4.6 million for fiscal 1988 to help finance the initial year. It is estimated that the research program will involve $23 million in investment between 1989 and 1992, the initial phase of the seven-year cooperative effort.[1] Much of this will be subsidized by the government. Advantages stated for the Dios process are low capital cost, high flexibility, direct using of coarse and fine ore like sinter feed, and direct using of noncoking coal.[2]

Other attempts to produce iron ore without coke and the blast furnace are being made in Europe, particularly by Klockner of Germany. All of this activity carries the hope of eventually eliminating the blast furnace and coke oven, which will reduce not only pollution problems but also the large investment required to replace a blast furnace–coke oven complex.

In spite of these efforts, little in the way of large production is expected by the year 2000. It seems virtually certain that at the turn of the century, the preponderance of iron will be produced through the traditional blast furnace–coke oven operation. It is possible that as much as 15 percent may be produced by the new processes.

Other iron-producing methods outside the blast furnace and coke oven combination have been in operation for a number of years. Several of these are referred to as the direct reduction of iron (DRI). One such method is the Midrex process, now owned by Kobe Steel of Japan. Another is the HYL process, owned by HYL of Mexico; and a third is the Fior process, developed by Exxon and now in operation in Venezuela. Units of the first two processes have been installed in many parts of the world, particularly in areas where abundant cheap gas is available, since all three depend on gas as a reducing agent. Facilities have been operating for several decades in Mexico, Venezuela, Saudi Arabia, and Indonesia, as well as a limited number in the United States and Canada. The Fior process, in operation in a plant in Venezuela, produces a briquette through the use of gas on a fluid bed. The millions of tons of DRI produced by these processes are used predominantly in electric furnaces to upgrade the charge by diluting residuals in scrap.

The Midrex process is a shaft furnace fed for the most part by iron-bearing pellets with about 60 percent iron content. The oxygen in the pellets is reduced by the passage of gas so the resultant product contains a very high percentage of iron, ranging from 88 to 90 percent. The HYL process was at first a batch process but is now a continuous operation in a shaft furnace combining iron pellets fed at the top with gases from the bottom passing through to remove the oxygen.

In the 1990s, there will be more DRI produced since Venezuela and other countries are building additional units to provide feed material for electric furnaces throughout the world. Many of these furnace operations aimed at the production of high-quality steel must improve their charge, for they can no longer operate on 100 percent scrap to produce high-quality steel because of the residuals it contains.

There is considerable interest throughout the world in other iron-producing processes that have been developed or are in the developmental stage. These use coal or gas, thus bypassing the blast furnace and coke oven. One process with a production unit in operation at Iscor Ltd. in South Africa is the Corex process. This is described as "an ironmaking technology for the production of hot metal, bypassing the coking stage where coke can be replaced by a wide range of coals. The replacement of coke is the primary goal."[3] Construction of a pilot plant was completed in Kehl-Rhein in West Germany in 1981. This plant produced a considerable tonnage of molten iron from a variety of lump ores and pellets using a number of different coals, ranging from high-volatile bituminous to anthracite. In 1985, Iscor decided to install a 300,000-tonne unit. It began operations in 1988 with the usual break-in problems, which have been solved.

Corex technology claims to fill two gaps: (1) a partial feed for minimills to allow them to enter the flat-rolled products market and (2) additional minor tonnages for integrated plants where an added blast furnace would be too large and too expensive. An attempt made to install a unit of the Corex process at Weirton Steel in the United States in the late 1980s was abandoned for a variety of reasons.

Another process, known as the iron carbide process, which uses iron ore and coal, is being developed in Australia. It produces a substance with 93 percent iron and 7 percent carbon, which can be used in both integrated mills and electric furnaces. The iron carbide is produced from preheated iron ore fines mixed with gas. Thus far, it is in the experimental stage, with a pilot plant operating in Australia. Recent announcements indicate that by mid-1991 a production plant will be functioning in the United States with a capacity of 350,000 tons per year. The location could be on the Gulf Coast. The company installing the unit has optimistic plans to install a second and third plant shortly after the first becomes operative.

There is also a plan to install a plant somewhere in the Far East. The investment cost for a 350,000-ton plant is calculated to be between $80 million and $85 million. Currently small amounts of the finished product are being sent to Japan, Europe, New Zealand, and the United States from the pilot plant in Australia.

The steel industry in the United States is engaged in a cooperative project referred to as continuous steelmaking. The American Iron and Steel Institute is spearheading the work, which means that all of the members are involved. One member, the HYL division of HYLSA, located in Mexico, has a special function in the project. HYL is to produce prereduced iron ore that will be fed into the smelter, which will be developed by the American Iron and Steel Institute: "The process is essentially direct smelting of preheated, prereduced iron ore with coal and oxygen to form a liquid iron bath. . . . Iron ore and coal are added to the bath of liquid iron, whilst oxygen is blown from the top and bottom of the vessel. Heat given off during the reaction preheats the raw materials and ensures the formation of liquid steel at the reduced temperature."[4] The project has been funded in part by the Department of Energy with additional funds provided by the American Iron and Steel Institute. Currently it is in the pilot plant stage; however, there is a possibility that there will be production by the mid-1990s .

Blast Furnace

The era of blast furnace construction has passed in the industrialized countries. There will be very few new furnaces constructed in Japan, the United States, and Western Europe. One is scheduled for Germany to replace three other furnaces, but the construction of new furnaces in the 1990s will be almost entirely confined to Third World countries, where steel expansion is underway. New furnaces will be built in South Korea,

Brazil, India, China, and at a new plant to be built by China Steel, probably in Malaysia.

In the industrialized world, investment in the blast furnace segment of the steel industry is directed to improving operations and the quality of the iron. In this respect, much has been done to upgrade the furnace burden. As of the late 1980s, most of the ore charged into the furnaces was beneficiated and consisted of sinter and pellets rather than raw, direct shipping ore. In the United States, for example, natural, direct-shipped ore in 1987 and 1988 constituted 3.0 million and 5.7 million tons, respectively, of the blast furnace burden while pellets, with a 65 percent iron content made principally from taconite, were 54.6 million and 67.3 million tons, respectively. Sinter represented 15.4 million and 17.1 million tons, respectively. Blast furnace operators in the United States favor and will continue to favor pellets over sinter; in Japan, the opposite is true.

Pellets will continue to provide the major portion of the blast furnace burden in the decade ahead in the United States, particularly since sinter plants involve a pollution problem. In Japan, efforts have been made to reduce pollution with the installation of 600-foot-high stacks at the facilities in most plants. The preference for sinter in Japan is evident from the fact that, in 1987, 86 million tonnes were charged into the blast furnaces, as opposed to 2.6 million tonnes of pellets. The dominant use of sinter in Japan and Western Europe will continue through the 1990s.

The most basic change in the blast furnace in the postwar period has been the increase in its size. The output of iron per day has increased from 2,500 or 3,000 tonnes to 10,000 tonnes. The huge blast furnace capable of this production was pioneered in Japan, since the Japanese ambition to produce large quantities of steel for the world market, as well as for their domestic consumption, was hampered by a lack of scrap. Consequently, their large blast furnaces provided much higher percentages of iron to be charged into oxygen converters.

Among the other significant developments in the blast furnace has been the increase in temperature, which has had a definite effect on the reduction of the coke rate. For those furnaces applying 1,400°F temperature, the increase to 1,900°F reduced coke rate by 15 pounds per ton for every 100°F of increased temperature. Many blast furnaces throughout the world are still operating at what is considered a low blast temperature of 1,400–1,500°F. In the years ahead, these temperatures will be increased, resulting in a better coke rate and improved production.

Another development is improved refractories for the blast furnace linings. The higher blast temperatures have required new and upgraded stoves incorporating more advanced refractories of silica, high-alumina, and fireclay, all manufactured to more exact mechanical and physical standards. Further, improved cooling methods, together with new gunning systems, have facilitated intermediate refractory repair. The result has been to push the life of the blast furnace stack to the ten-year level, with the hearth reaching twenty years or more.

Since very few new furnaces will be built in the 1990s in the industrialized countries, there will be increased activity at upgrading those now in existence.

Steelmaking

Steel in the world in 1989 was produced principally by the basic oxygen converter, which turned out over 60 percent of the total; the electric furnace produced more than 30 percent and the open hearth less than 10 percent. By the end of the century, it is a virtual certainty that the open-hearth furnace, if not eliminated, will be reduced to a very small fraction of steel production. Emphasis will be placed on improving the BOF through the injection of oxygen, both at the top and bottom, and also the use of other gases. No radical change in the process is foreseen as it will continue to dominate steel production in the years ahead. This is particularly true since the Soviet Union, now producing almost half of its steel by the open hearth, has scheduled substantial replacement by the basic-oxygen converter during the next five years.

The electric furnace will account for more than 35 percent of the world's output as it will replace a portion of the abandoned open-hearth furnaces. Much has been done to improve its output, including higher transformer ratings, the application of oxygen, the installation of sidewall cooling panels, and roof cooling. Furnaces have increased in size so that many produce more than 100 tons per heat, and some are in the 300-ton-per-heat class.

For the most part, the electric furnaces use alternating current (AC). However, in recent years, the direct current (DC) furnace has achieved a degree of acceptability it lacked previously. There are two DC units operating in the United States, with two more planned; in Japan, several units have been installed and others announced. Most DC furnaces operate with one electrode as opposed to three in the AC counterpart. As a consequence, there is a significant saving in electrode consumption, particularly in units where it has been relatively high (7–8 pounds per ton). One Japanese company places the savings on electrodes at over 50 percent. It also claims a reduction in power costs of 5 to 10 percent and about the same reduction in refractory costs.

On the negative side, the installation cost is higher since a rectifier must be installed to change AC current to DC current. It is believed that the increased cost of installation will be recouped in a relatively short time by the resultant savings in operating costs. The American companies using the furnaces are somewhat more conservative in their assessment of the savings that result from its operation. There is general agreement on the electrode saving at a fairly high rate of 35 to 40 percent.

It is likely that the installation of a number of DC furnaces will take place in Japan, since the units in the electric furnace segment of the industry in that country are aging and must be replaced. One of Japan's announced DC furnaces is being installed by NKK and MAN-GHH of West Germany and another by a group consisting of Nippon, Daido, and Usinor of France. The second group's furnace departs from most other DC furnaces in that it has three electrodes and claims to derive its advantage from a reduction in melting time. Given activity such as this, the 1990s will undoubtedly see more DC furnaces in operation around the world.

One of the recent developments affecting the electric furnace is the continuous steelmaking process known as Consteel. This has received some acceptance and could well become widespread in the 1990s. Basically, it is a continuous scrap-charging process during which the scrap is preheated by off-gases and charged into the furnace. Preheating the scrap reduces the time required for the production of a heat, as well as the kilowatt-hours. Relatively few of these process arrangements are in operation. In the United States, one is in operation at Nucor's Darlington, South Carolina, plant, and another will be installed at the North Carolina plant of Florida Steel. Tap-to-tap time is between 45 and 55 minutes, with an energy consumption somewhat less than the conventional electric arc furnace. According to some calculations, it saves 25 to 30 percent on power in the actual furnace operation. Since the scrap is fed continuously, the process is a continuous one, and its advocates believe that it will make the melting and refining of steel a controlled process with a more stable environment than with a batch (top-charged) operation. The process virtually requires computerization since it is difficult to control otherwise.

A steelmaking process recently developed by the Korf group is known as the EOF, or energy-optimizing furnace. It uses coal and oxygen in place of electric power and is in operation in Brazil. Further installations are under consideration in India and the United States. This could have potential for smaller steelmakers in the 1990s.

Continuous steelmaking, in the experimental stage in the United States, has already been described.

Ladle Metallurgy

Ladle metallurgy is a relatively new process, particularly in the United States. It is employed to improve the steel as it leaves the oxygen converter or electric furnace. The ladle used in this process has a cover and an electrode. It serves several functions, including maintaining the temperature of the steel or, if necessary, increasing it so that, should there be a delay at the continuous caster, the casting temperature can be maintained and the steel need not be put back in the furnace, as is required with the ordinary ladle when the temperature falls below that required for casting.

The ladle is also used to refine the steel and thus increases the capacity of the electric furnace, since the furnace is used to melt the scrap while the refining can be done in the ladle. Thus, much less time is required per heat in the electric furnace itself. The facility also reduces sulfur content in the steel and either eliminates or reduces undesirable elements such as inclusions.

The future expansion of this facility in the 1990s is assured. In 1985, there were only five such units in operation in the United States; in 1989, there were thirty in operation or under construction. The improvement in quality and the reduction in costs of production provided by this facility will raise it to the level of standard equipment in virtually every steelmaking shop by the turn of the century.

Continuous Casting

Continuous casting of semifinished steel has expanded rapidly since its inception in the late 1950s and 1960s. In 1989 the largest producer in the industrialized world, Japan, cast 93 percent of its steel output; a number of countries in the EEC also continuously cast very high percentages of their steel production. France and Italy cast 94 percent, Western Germany 90 percent, and the entire European Community 88 percent. The vast majority of countries in the Western world cast over 60 percent of their output.

The widespread use of continuous casting, involving over 1,400 casters with more than 4,000 strands on a global basis, has lowered the investment cost, so that the technology is within the reach of most steel producers.

New developments in continuous casting have progressed rapidly to a point where steelmakers have been offered alternatives to the conventional caster in the form of a thin slab caster. There are three versions of the thin slab caster in operation or under development. The first of these, developed by SMS Concast, is in operation at the Nucor plant in Crawfordsville, Indiana. Thus far, this is the only production unit functioning in the world, and the steel industry worldwide has a keen interest in its progress.

The facility involves a caster that produces slabs 2 inches thick. It is fed by electric furnaces that, as of 1990, are dependent on 100 percent scrap charge. When the 2-inch slab emerges from the caster, it passes through a tunnel furnace to maintain its temperature, after which it proceeds directly into a four-high, four-stand hot-strip mill. The operation is continuous from the time scrap is charged into the electric furnace, through the caster, the tunnel furnace, and the rolling mill, ending with the hot strip in coil form.

The second version of the thin-slab caster, now in the pilot stage, is being developed in Germany by Thyssen Steel, Usinor, and SMS. This functions by casting a 2-inch slab and, within the casting machine after the top and bottom of the slab are solidified to the extent of 1/2 inch each, it is squeezed together to form a 1-inch thick slab. This is done by rolls that are incorporated within the casting machine. When the slab emerges 1 inch thick, it is thought that it will be possible to reduce it to sheet gauge in one four-high finishing stand. This is not completely determined; a second stand may be needed.

The third version of the thin slab caster, developed by Demag and Mannesmann, is being installed at the Arvedi plant in Cremona, Italy. The facility resembles both the SMS Concast unit at Nucor and the facility under construction at Thyssen's plant. Like the Thyssen facility, after it casts a slab 60 millimeters thick (approximately 2 1/2 inches), it is squeezed down with rolls contained within the caster to 35 millimeters (1 1/2 inches). As the slab emerges from the caster, it immediately passes through three four-high, rolling-mill stands, which reduce it to 15 millimeters (somewhat more than 1/2 inch). It is then sheared and moved on to a Cremona furnace before it enters the four-high, four-stand, hot-strip mill. Thus, like the Thyssen version, the slab is squeezed before completely solidifying, and like the SMS facility at Nucor, it passes directly through rolling mills. However, in the case of Arvedi, there are seven stands in place of four. The mill is designed to produce 500,000 tons of strip, 300,000 tons of it carbon steel and 200,000 stainless steel. The Arvedi Group expects the plant to go into operation by 1991 at a cost of about $200 million.

In addition to the slab casters, perhaps the most ambitious attempt in the area of continuous casting is that directed to casting strip and, thus, bypassing the hot-strip mill completely. Allegheny-Ludlum in the United States has been working on this project for a number of years and has recently entered into a joint venture with Voest-Alpine, which, it is hoped, will produce a facility capable of directly casting strip. Thus, it is intended to free the operation entirely from the hot-strip mill on which thin-slab casters still depend for a finished product. The objective of this joint venture is to produce the ultimate in a continuous-casting facility. The process has limitations insofar as in the experimental state it has been confined to producing specialty steel, particularly stainless, although the proponents speak optimistically about the possibility of casting carbon strip. Further, the strip has been relatively narrow, usually less than 30 inches in width.

The chief proponent of strip casting, Richard Simmons, chairman and chief executive officer of Allegheny-Ludlum, says of the thin-slab caster, "It should be clearly recognized that this does not eliminate the need for a hot-strip mill, although it does reduce total capital investment required for the continuous caster and the number of hot-strip mill stands, nor does this process [the thin-slab caster] change the fundamental technology of the metal being produced."[5] On an experimental basis, the strip-casting facility has produced strip from the molten stainless steel ranging from 1/8 inch down to 1/32 inch in thickness. It is hoped that an experimental unit will be in production in the early 1990s.

Inland Steel, in conjunction with several other steel companies, is also working on a strip-casting facility, which differs somewhat in its operation from the Allegheny-Ludlum/Voest-Alpine version. It is projected that in addition to eliminating the hot-strip mill, the resultant strip will reduce the amount of cold rolling and annealing necessary for the finished product. Although the new process may not necessarily produce a superior product, it will significantly reduce the capital investment required.

The thin-slab casters have decided advantages insofar as the amount of capital required is significantly lower—perhaps 50 percent less than that required for the conventional slab caster and rolling mill. Fewer finishing stands are needed in the hot-strip mill, and in place of reheating furnaces, usually the walking-beam type, the tunnel furnace is installed. Further, the roughing section of the hot mill is eliminated—whether a reversing stand or several continuous stands. The number of finishing stands in conjunction with the thin-slab caster has been reduced to four from the standard six or seven. In addition, the thin slab cools more rapidly than the conventional slab, which could be as much as 10 inches thick. Quicker cooling provides smaller grain structure and thus results, some say, in a superior product as compared to the grain structure obtained with the thicker slab, which cools much slower. The surface of the thicker slab has a small-grain structure. However, as one moves more deeply into the interior, the longer amount of cooling time required produces a larger grain structure. The thin slab of only 2 inches has a much smaller grain structure throughout, which allows a greater reduction to be taken by the finishing stands of the hot-strip mill.

In a period of ten years, it is quite conceivable that the development of the thin-slab caster could reach significant tonnage proportions on a worldwide basis. However, the growth will be slow in the first few years of the 1990s, but could pick up in the last half of the decade. One of the drawbacks to the expansion of the thin-slab caster is the fact that in most instances it operates with an electric furnace. Thus, in many instances, it is dependent on a 100 percent scrap charge. Unless this is supplemented by DRI, there will be contaminants in the steel that will prevent its use for a number of critical applications. Consequently, the steel will have to be used for applications that do not require stringent specifications.

Continuous Annealing

Continuous annealing has been in operation in the steel industry for many years, although it was confined to steel for tinplate and hot-dipped galvanizing until recently. In the last decade, a number of units have been installed throughout the world to process cold-rolled sheets for many other applications. Previously these have been batch annealed in bell-like furnaces, which combined with other operations, including pickling, cleaning, and temper rolling, could require a period of eight to ten days. The continuous-annealing operation, when placed in line with the other operations, can process steel in less than an hour, increasing productivity tremendously and reducing operating costs. A continuous-annealing line, although expensive, is another step to replace a batch process with a continuous process.

In the new plants, particularly the Inland-Nippon joint venture for cold-rolling sheets, as well as the United States Steel–Posco operation, continuous annealing, as well as other functions, such as pickling, temper rolling, and electrolytic cleaning, have been combined. The improvement in labor productivity is enormous; days are cut from the operation. Further, since the material travels through the annealing furnace in an uncoiled stage for reheating, soaking, and cooling, its quality is much more uniform than the coil placed as such in an annealing furnace.

Despite the cost of continuous-annealing lines, many of them will be installed in the 1990s in sheet mills throughout the world since the advantages over batch annealing are great.

Rolling Mills

In the rolling mill category, the continuous hot-strip mill is the most important finishing facility in the steel industry, since some 55 percent of finished steel products pass through it on the way to further processing. They include hot- and cold-rolled sheets, as well as coated sheets, narrow strip, and skelp for manufacturing welded pipe and tubing.

Much was done to improve this facility in the 1980s and more is underway. A recent trend is to replace the train of roughing stands with a single reversing rougher. This is being installed on a number of units that are being rebuilt. The reversing rougher permits heavier slabs to be rolled, although it does cut down to some extent on production tonnage because of the extra time needed for the reversing passes.

Another development that will be much more widespread in the coming decade is the coil box, whereby the bar, before it passes into the finishing stands, is coiled to retain its heat. This also makes it possible to shorten the length of the hot-strip mill.

The mill's finishing stands have been improved through the installation of roll bending, side shifting, hydraulic screw-downs, and more accurate computer control. These changes make it possible to roll strip with much more uniform gauge from side to side, as well as with better surface and shape. A number of newly constructed strip mills have utilized virtually all of these improvements and consequently produce an excellent sheet. In order to remain competitive, companies with somewhat older mills will need to improve them through the addition of these devices. Examples are the strip mill at Weirton Steel, as well as that at the Sparrows Point plant of Bethlehem Steel, both in the United States.

Cold-reduction mills used to reduce the steel band from the hot-strip mill have improved significantly, particularly with the development of the six-high mill, which has four backup rolls supporting two work rolls in place of the traditional four-high mill with two backup rolls supporting two work rolls. There are not many of these in operation throughout the world. However, the number has grown, and during the 1990s, they will replace a substantial segment of the four-high, cold-reduction mills.

Developed in Japan in the 1970s, there were but a few installed in that decade. It was not until the early to mid-1980s that their installation received wider acceptance. The mills provide a number of advantages over the traditional four-high tandem mill. The motivation for the development of the mill was the need for an improved quality sheet with more uniform shape and improved flatness, as well as a consistency in gauge. The six-high mill has significantly reduced the crown in the strip. The work rolls are relatively small and permit heavier reductions without adversely affecting the shape. The product of the mill presents economic advantages insofar as the cost of production is reduced and the productivity increased. Because of heavier reductions, the number of mill stands required is reduced. In many instances, the five-stand, four-high mill can be replaced by a four-stand, six-high mill.

A number of these facilities have been installed in Japan, South Korea, and Taiwan. In the United States, there are two. One went into operation in 1989 as a joint venture in Pittsburg, California, between United States Steel and Pohang Iron and Steel Company of South Korea. Another, at New Carlisle, Indiana, is a joint venture between Nippon Steel and Inland Steel, which began operations in 1990. The product of these mills has been described as excellent; most believe it is superior to that produced by the four-high mill. The gauge is relatively perfect, and the surface and flatness of the strip are considerably improved, so that it can be used to improve the finished product into which it is incorporated, such as appliances and parts of automobiles.

In the 1990s, it is quite probable that this superior product will force sheet producers throughout the world to install this type of facility in order to remain competitive. One can envision major sheet producers with at least one six-high cold-reduction mill in operation in each company. The mills employ roll bending and side shifting, as well as a high degree of computerization.

Other rolling mills that produce bars, tubes, rods, and structural steel underwent significant improvements in the late 1980s. Advances have been made in rolling-mill technology for wire rods. One of the principal developments has been an increase in the speed of the mill: speeds of 20,000 feet per minute have been achieved. The record, 22,000 feet per minute, was achieved at a new rod mill purchased by Pohang Iron and Steel Company for its Pohang works. Advances have also been made in controlling temperature for this rolling process. It is questionable as to how many of these high-speed mills will be installed throughout the world, although undoubtedly there will be some in response to the demand for rods.

Structural mills, particularly those producing wide-flange beams, have been significantly improved in both the rolling and finishing processes. One of the outstanding developments has been achieved by Arbed, the Luxembourg steel producer, which for years has specialized in structural steel. By a special heating and cooling process, a beam has been developed that is lighter than the normal wide-flange beam and used for the same purposes. It has high-yield strength, a toughness at low temperature, and excellent weldability. The development is brought about through improvements in the finishing end rather than the rolling process.

Other advances have been made in rolling technology in Japan and are now employed in the Nucor-Yamato joint venture producing wide-flange beams in the United States.

Coated Products

In the late 1980s, a number of galvanizing lines were installed or announced—a result of the demand of the automotive industry for material that would resist corrosion. In North America, some six lines were installed in the late 1980s, five of them representing joint ventures. By 1989, twelve more had been announced, many of them also joint ventures. In the Common Market, fourteen lines were announced by late 1989 and eight in Japan.

The recently announced lines are reasonably well divided between the hot-dipped process, in which a strip of steel is passed through a molten bath of zinc, and the electrolytic coating process, which plates zinc on steel strip so that the amount deposited is closely controlled. Further, with the electrolytic process, zinc can be plated on one side. In the first surge of these mills, most were electrolytic. In the second wave, a number of them are hot-dipped lines.

The recent installation of many galvanizing lines throughout the world brings to attention the variations that have been developed in the galvanizing process. Two of these for which superior corrosion resistance is claimed are the Galvalume and Galfan processes.

Galvalume is a process whereby the steel is coated with a combination of aluminum and zinc, which is reputed to have excellent corrosion resistance and heat reflectability, a characteristic of aluminum-coated sheets, as well as formability and protection, which are characteristic of the zinc-coated sheet. The contents of the coating are 55 percent aluminum, 43.5 percent zinc, and 1.57 percent silicon. The process was developed by Bethlehem Steel in the mid-1960s and began commercial production in 1972. A number of steel companies throughout the world have licenses to produce this product.

Galfan is another variation of galvanized steel that uses zinc and 5 percent al–misch metal alloy with small amounts (less than 2 percent) of antimony, magnesium, tin, and copper. Much of this development was undertaken by Inland Steel.

Other Developments

In addition to these technological developments, which are basic and in some instances involve fundamental change in steelmaking technology, there are numerous other developments, each of which makes a significant contribution to the steel industry's operations. In the 1990s, with heightened concern for the environment, a number of technologies under development will likely be employed to handle steel-plant wastes. One of these is the Tetronics process, which allows the recovery of metal such as zinc, lead, and cadmium from electric furnace flue dust. They are reduced to metal vapors and passed through a condenser. The zinc is precipitated out and recovered as prime metal.

In addition, there are a number of other processes for handling electric furnace flue dust, including the Super Detox process, the Dereco Briquetting process, the Davy Hi-Plas process, the Elkem Multi Purpose process, the ZIA Inclined Rotary Reduction process, and the HRD Flame Reactor process.

In terms of processing steel plant wastes in general, other examples of technology include the Pelletech and Inmetco processes, which employ various configurations using rotary kilns and rotary hearth furnaces to agglomerate and process the waste and recover useful by-products.

Among technologies likely to evolve in the 1990s are the casting of stainless steel strip, a rolling and heat-treating process for structural steel, developments in continuous annealing for steel sheets, developments in the production of silicon steel for application in the electrical industry, improvements in the charging and tapping processes at the blast furnace, application of plasma-form irradiation allowing the reduction of core losses in transformers by improving grain-oriented steel, and improvements in refractories to increase their durability. These are just a few of a very long list.

During the 1990s, most of the technological advances made in the 1980s will be improved. There will be constant efforts to improve technology in order to increase quality and reduce the costs that will be evident in every phase of the steelmaking process.

Notes

1. *Japan Steel Journal*, June 30, 1988, pp. 3, 4.
2. Tsutomu Fukushima, *"Smelting Reduction in Japan,"* in *Future Ironmaking Proceedings*, Hamilton, Ontario, June 1990, p. 6-4.
3. Hanns Feichtner, "Hot Metal Cost Comparison—Corex versus Blast Furnace Route" (paper presented at Steel Survival Strategies, June 1989).
4. *Steel Times International* (January 1990): 34.
5. Speech before the Steel Service Center Institute Meeting, Washington, D.C., May 15, 1990.

8
Joint Ventures

I n the early post–World War II period, a few companies in the steel industry entered into joint ventures, both domestic and international. In the 1980s, this activity was considerably accelerated, extending to various stages of steel operations. The early arrangements dealt with raw materials, principally iron ore. In North America, a number of consortia were formed to develop and mine iron ore reserves. Two outstanding examples were the Iron Ore Company of Canada and Wabush Mines, both formed in the 1950s to develop iron ore deposits in the Labrador-Quebec area.

A number of companies participated in each operation on a percentage basis, involving a take-or-pay contract to the extent of their percentage participation. The Iron Ore Company of Canada included the following companies with their percentage participation:

Hanna Mining Company, 27.24 percent.

Bethlehem Steel Corporation, 19.41 percent.

National Steel Corporation, 18.20 percent.

Armco Steel Corporation, 6.06 percent.

Jones & Laughlin Steel Corporation, 6.06 percent.

Republic Steel Corporation, 6.06 percent.

Wheeling-Pittsburgh Steel Corporation, 4.86 percent.

Hollinger Mines Ltd., 8.27 percent.

Labrador Mining & Exploration Co. Ltd. Wabush Mines, 3.84 percent.

The second venture, also formed in the 1950s, was composed of the following steel companies in the United States, Canada, and Europe, each with a take or pay contract:

Steel Company of Canada, 25.6 percent.

Dominion Foundries & Steel Ltd., 16. 4 percent.

Youngstown Sheet and Tube Company, 15.6 percent.

Inland Steel Company, 10.2 percent.

Wheeling-Pittsburgh Steel Corporation, 10.2 percent.

Interlake, Inc., 10.2 percent.

Finsider, 6.6 percent.

Picands Mather & Company, 5.1 percent.[1]

A third venture, Fire Lake, established in 1976, involved Sidbec-Dosco with 50.1 percent, British Steel Corporation with 41.67 percent, and United States Steel with 8.23 percent.

In the iron ore regions of Lake Superior , a number of ore projects with joint participation were organized in the 1950s, 1960s, and 1970s. That of the Empire Mining Company contained five partners, four of them steel companies and one an ore company. Other joint ventures in mining and pelletizing plants included the Reserve Mining Company, composed of Armco and Republic as equal partners. The Hibbing Taconite Company was international in scope; the partners were Bethlehem, Stelco, and Picands Mather.

In the 1970s and early 1980s, the political climate in the United States was hostile to joint ventures other than for raw materials. There was great concern that competition would be lessened, and as a result, much discussion about joint ventures was held, but there was very little action.

The attitude of the Justice Department changed in 1984 when there was considerable criticism of the department's decision to turn down the mergers between Republic and Jones & Laughlin, as well as between United States Steel and National Steel. Many felt that these mergers would improve the competitive position of the American steel industry.

The merger between Jones & Laughlin and Republic was subsequently allowed. That between United States Steel and National was not. However, within a matter of months after this denial, National Steel sold half of its steel operation to NKK of Japan, thus establishing the first venture in the form of joint ownership between a large U.S. integrated steel company and a foreign company.

In 1984, shortly after the denial of the USS-National merger, the Justice Department became a proponent of joint ventures in the steel industry and encouraged companies to form them. Within the next two years, a number were formed involving various aspects of steel operations. These included international arrangements between integrated steel companies such as United States Steel and Pohang Iron and Steel Company of South Korea, Nippon Steel and Inland Steel, Armco Steel and Kawasaki, United States

Steel and Kobe, Wheeling-Pittsburgh and Nisshin, LTV Steel and Sumitomo, and National Steel and NKK. All of the companies with the exception of Pohang were Japanese. Up to 1990, there were no major ventures between U.S. and European companies. One was proposed in 1985 (but never realized) between British Steel and United States Steel to provide slabs for the Fairless Works, which would then eliminate its blast furnace and steelmaking facilities.

The USS division of USX and Pohang of South Korea entered into a union that was particularly advantageous. United States Steel had a finishing mill in California producing cold-rolled sheets and tinplate that had become outdated and obsolete for the production of some high-quality products. It was determined that it should be replaced with a modern facility, at a cost of $400 million. Further, the supply of steel for this West Coast facility came from a plant at Geneva, Utah, that had been built during World War II and in terms of producing a quality sheet product was somewhat obsolete. It would have required an investment of $800 million to $1 billion to modernize the Geneva facility. Thus, the total investment for the two locations would have been between $1.2 billion and $1.4 billion.

Pohang was constructing the first phase of a new fully integrated steel mill at Kwangyang in South Korea and was looking for markets. This plant had the most modern, efficient equipment available and would ultimately have a capacity for 11.4 million tons of raw steel. The arrangement between United States Steel and Pohang called for a California-based cold-reduction mill that was to be newly built and modern in every respect. It would be fed by hot-rolled coils from the Pohang mill, which, with its ultra-modern hot-strip mill, made an excellent product. These coils when processed by the new cold-reduction mill at Pittsburg, California, would result in a sheet superior to most other produced in the world and the equivalent of any. Pohang invested half of the cost of the Pittsburg mill, which amounted to $200 million. United States Steel was relieved of the need to modernize the Geneva mill. Therefore, in place of a total investment of $1.2 billion to 1.4 billion, it achieved the same purpose with an investment of $200 million. In many respects the joint venture was a perfect fit.

U.S.-Japanese Joint Ventures

The U.S. and Japanese steel industry's joint ventures offer considerable advantages to both parties. The arrangement between Nippon Steel and Inland Steel made possible the construction of a cold-reduction facility and two galvanizing lines. The two ventures involved an investment of more than $900 million. Without Japanese participation at the start of the first venture (the cold mill), the plant never would have been built. Inland did not feel it could finance the cost (over $400 million) the funds from Nippon—$60 million—added to Inland's $90 million, plus the $250 million from the three Japanese trading companies, made the facility possible. Here, the joint venture was not only helpful but necessary for the mill to be built. Inland owned 60 percent and Nippon 40 percent of the cold mill. Nippon has the right to buy 20 percent of the output of the cold-reduction mill and dispose of it as it sees fit. Most likely this will be through the three trading companies.

The cold mill began operations in early 1990, and the galvanizing lines, which cost more than $450 million extra, will be in operation by late 1991 or early 1992. The financing for this fifty-fifty ownership project includes $60 million each from Nippon and Inland; the remainder, which would be well over $300 million, will be provided by the Industrial Bank of Japan. Here again, financing was possible by virtue of the fact that it was a joint venture. As a consequence, Inland and Nippon will be able to provide excellent quality cold-rolled sheets, as well as some 900,000 tons of galvanized sheets, which will be marketed by Inland Steel.

Nippon Steel in 1989 became the largest stockholder in Inland Steel through the purchase of 185,000 shares of preferred stock at $1,000 a share, or a total of $185 million. This preferred stock carries a 9.48 percent interest. Inland has agreed to redeem this stock at the same price in two stages: 85,000 shares after seven years and 100,000 after ten years. With the consent of Inland, the stock can be converted. The ownership of the 185,000 shares gives Nippon the right to vote 13 percent of the company's ownership. Further, as a gesture of goodwill, Nippon previously bought 1 percent of Inland's stock, and Inland bought 1 percent of Nippon. Consequently, Nippon has 14 percent of the vote. As part of the transaction, Nippon has agreed not to acquire additional Inland shares prior to the final redemption of the preferred stock or to transfer the preferred stock without Inland's approval.[2] Nippon benefits insofar as it will participate in the U.S. steel market without any concern about quotas. It also has entrée to the Japanese automobile transplants constructed in the United States.

Another particularly timely joint venture was between Armco and Kawasaki. As a result of investing some $375 million, Kawasaki became a 40 percent owner of Armco's carbon steel business. There is a possibility that further investment will be made, to bring ownership close to 50 percent.

The infusion of a considerable amount of cash was especially welcome in view of Armco's investment plan for the five-year period through 1994, which called for an additional continuous caster and galvanizing lines among other items, with a total investment estimated at well over $1 billion.

As part of their joint venture, Armco and Kawasaki plan to build an electrolytic galvanizing line at the Middletown works, which will be owned 50 percent by each company and have a 290,000-ton capacity. The unit will cost $116 million and will go into operation in 1991. It complements the existing line, which was installed in 1986.

The $375-million investment by Kawasaki was of significant help and will allow Armco to finish the program in less time than was originally contemplated. Armco's carbon steel facilities consist of plants at Middletown, Ohio; Ashland, Kentucky; and Hamilton, Ohio. Kawasaki will benefit also; it participates in the ownership of a plant that will supply sheet products to the Japanese automobile transplants. This guarantees them participation free of any quotas that might be placed on imports from Japan to the United States.

Another example of an international joint venture of mutual benefit to both parties is the arrangement between the United States Steel division of USX and Kobe Steel. Kobe Steel was desirous of penetrating the U.S. market to sell bar products to the Japanese automobile transplants. Further, the transplants were anxious to get Kobe's product since they valued it highly. Kobe contemplated building a facility in the United States that it would own completely and would be free of import quotas. However, upon considering the possibilities, they decided a joint venture would be preferable to the construction of a steel facility. It could be achieved in less time and would not pose Kobe as a new entrant into the steel business with a plant in the United States where additional capacity was not needed.

As a consequence, the company decided to form a joint venture with a U.S. producer. After considerable discussion and negotiations with the United States Steel (USS) division of USX, it was decided that the Lorain, Ohio, plant would be set aside and be established as a joint company in which there would be a fifty-fifty participation between Kobe and USS. Kobe's investment, over $300 million, will permit modernization and improvement at the plant. It will also bring Kobe's technology and know-how to bear on the production operations. Output will be concentrated on bar products, and the joint venture will market these products. The tubular products, which are still to be produced at Lorain, will be marketed by the USS sales division. Here again, there is mutual benefit: USS will participate in the sale of high-quality bars to the Japanese automobile transplants, and Kobe will have access to the U.S. market without concern about import quotas. The plant will be improved by installing, among other things, an additional continuous caster for the production of bar products and completely rebuilding a blast furnace. Kobe achieved its objective without a need to construct a new plant in the United States.

A second joint venture involving equal partnership between Kobe and United States Steel has been announced. It is a hot-dipped galvanizing line with an annual capacity of 650,000 tons. The new venture will be called Aztec Coating Company, to be located at Leipsic, Ohio, and will involve an investment of some $200 million. The intention is to serve the Japanese automobile plants built in the United States. The plant will be supplied with cold-rolled sheets from USS's plants at Gary, Fairfield, and Irvin Works.

The National Steel–NKK joint venture came as a result of the Justice Department's refusal in 1984 to allow the merger of National and the USS division of USX, which was turned down after protracted negotiations. The Justice Department wanted the proposed combination to divest itself of both the Fairless Works and the Granite City plant, which would constitute 6 million tons of steel making capacity—about the same amount that USS would gain from the merger. This was not acceptable to the companies, and the matter was dropped.

National was anxious to form a relationship that would reduce its ownership in steel. The *Annual Report* of 1979 stated:

> The overall strategy of our company has included, as a major thrust, diversification into other lines of business which either (a) complements or supports our business or (b) affords us the opportunity to grow in totally unrelated lines where prospects for profitability are promising. We propose to continue to emphasize that effort.[3]

This philosophy was responsible for spinning off the Weirton division. Thus, when the USS merger fell through, National was anxious to acquire a partner that would own a portion of its steelmaking operation. NKK had been negotiating with the steel division of Ford Motor Company to acquire 75 percent, if not all, of the operation. The negotiations were not successful, however, and when the opportunity to acquire part of National arose, it was quickly seized. Like the other joint ventures involving Japanese steel companies, NKK benefited by establishing a position in the U.S. market that would allow it to serve the Japanese auto transplants and free it from possible import quotas.

In 1986, Sumitomo Metals Industries and LTV Corporation entered into an agreement to construct an electrolytic galvanizing line. The ownership was 40 percent for Sumitomo and 60 percent for LTV. This worked out so well that an agreement was made for a second line to be set up as a joint venture on a fifty-fifty basis. Known as L-S II Electro-Galvanizing Company, it is to be based in Columbus, Ohio, rather than Cleveland, where the first line is located. The installation cost is estimated to be $200 million, and capacity will be 360,000 tons a year. The first venture involving a 400,000-ton line is operating at capacity. The decision to install the second line was made at the urging of Japanese automakers with plants in the United States.

Nisshin Steel and Wheeling-Pittsburgh made an agreement in 1984, supplemented in 1988, to produce a coating line that would involve not only galvanizing but aluminum. The line is owned two-thirds by Nisshin and one-third by Wheeling-Pittsburgh. Further, Nisshin has taken 10 percent ownership in the Wheeling-Pittsburgh Company.

A joint venture that does not involve integrated steel companies but is of considerable size has been entered into between Nucor and Yamato, which has resulted in a large structural mill capable of producing 650,000 tons of wide-flange beams up to 24 inches. The plant, located in Arkansas on the Mississippi River, has been in operation since 1989 and represents a $190 million investment.

A joint venture in the United States not involving an American company is California Steel. This company is jointly owned by Kawasaki Steel and CVRD, the Brazilian ore company. The plant was formerly the Kaiser Steel Company's facility and was sold originally to a combination of three: Kawasaki, CVRD, and the Wilkenson Group. Subsequently, Wilkenson sold its share so that the ownership is now on a fifty-fifty basis between Kawasaki and CVRD. The plant purchases slabs and produces sheets as a finished product. Some 600,000 tons of these slabs come from the Tubarao plant in Brazil, and the remainder are gathered from various sources in the United States and abroad. The plant included a plate mill, which subsequently has been purchased by Oregon Steel, although it will be operated at the California Steel location.

European Joint Ventures

A major joint venture, involving an investment of some $3 billion, was the plant constructed in Brazil at Tubarao for the production of semifinished steel. Studies began on this venture as early as 1973, when Italsider of Italy, Kawasaki, and Siderbras of Brazil weighed the possibility of establishing such a plant. The initial cost was judged to be about $800 million. Subsequently, it rose to approximately $3 billion, the final figure.

The plant, which consists of coke ovens, a blast furnace, an oxygen-steelmaking operation, and a slabbing mill, was finished and went into operation in November 1985. The ownership was divided among the three, Italsider and Kawasaki each having 24.5 percent and Siderbras 51 percent. The percentages of the partners changed in the late 1980s; now the Italians have 5.5 percent, Kawasaki 5.5 percent, and Siderbras 89 percent.

Each of the participants was to take one-third of the output. The plant's total production has been sold for several years, since it represents the only facility in the world dedicated to the production of semifinished for sale. Other tonnages of semifinished are usually sold from surplus capacity of integrated steel plants. A plan under consideration is to double the size of the plant from 3 million tons to 6 million and add a continuous caster and a hot-strip mill, so that the output will consist of 3 million tons of slabs for sale and 3 million tons of hot-rolled strip, also for sale.

A major joint venture, developed in the early 1970s, involved the construction of an integrated steel mill with 3.5 million tonnes of capacity at Fos, on deep water near Marseilles. The mill, called Solmer, had three partners: Usinor with 47.5 percent, Sacilor with 47.5 percent, and Thyssen with 5 percent. Thyssen subsequently dropped out, and Usinor and Sacilor were merged, so that now the plant is under one management.

In Germany, a joint venture for the production of electrical sheets was entered into between Thyssen Grillo Funke and Stahlwerke Bochum on a fifty-fifty basis. The new name is EBG Gesellshaft fur elektromagnetische Werkstoffe.

Thyssen of Germany and Francisco Ross Casaras, a service center in Spain, have formed a joint venture unrelated to the production of steel but involved in its distribution. A new service center will be built in Valencia, equipped with modern facilities to handle flat-rolled products. This project is an indication of the use of joint ventures in other than basic steel production and will be repeated often in the future, particularly since a number of steel companies in the EEC wish to acquire outlets in other than their own country.

Voest-Alpine of Austria has arranged a joint venture related to steel with Uralmasch, a Soviet heavy-machinery producer. The company will be owned on a fifty-fifty basis and will be located in Linz. Its purpose is to develop continuous-slab casters for the Soviet mills, as well as for other countries. Uralmasch has constructed continuous-casting machines in Pakistan, India, and Algeria.

Usinor-Sacilor of France purchased 50 percent of Georgetown Industries of the United States in 1990 and will supply technology for the production of rods.

Other Joint Ventures

United States Steel has established a joint venture with Worthington Industries to operate a steel-processing facility in Jackson, Michigan. The plant will be operated by Worthington with steel supplied by United States Steel. The function of the joint venture is to process steel coils into slit coils and sheared, first-operation blanks. The industry to be served principally is automotive; however, the appliance, furniture, and metal-door industries will be served as well.

In making the arrangement, the comment of an executive of United States Steel in terms of future developments in joint ventures is interesting: "This business arrangement will enable United States Steel to further improve quality and service . . . and thereby increase its capability to be even more competitive."[4] He further stated that the success of this facility will lead to the establishment of others in the future.

Bethlehem Steel Corporation and Usinor-Sacilor entered into a joint venture of a relatively minor nature for the production of steel mill rolls.

In Japan, Mitsubishi and Nippon Steel have agreed on a venture at Muroran to produce over 400,000 tonnes of specialty steel by 1994. This will help to save the town of Hollaido, which could be severely hurt by the closure of some of Nippon's steel facilities at Muroran. The blast furnace at that location is due to be closed down in 1990.

The Japanese have also been active in the Far East with joint ventures in Thailand. A project directed at expanding the tin-plate production of the Siam Tinplate Company will begin operations in 1991. It involves the construction of an electrolytic-tinplate line, as well as a tin-free steel line. As now organized, the company is owned 40 percent by Unicord, a Thailand canning operation, and 40 percent by the Japanese, of which Sumitomo holds 14.25 percent, Mitsubishi 12 percent, and Nippon 13.75 percent. The remaining 20 percent is owned by the Asian Development Bank and the World Bank's International Finance Corporation. The total cost of the project is 12 billion yen.[5]

The black plate, to be tinned as well as turned into tin-free steel, will be supplied from Japan by both Nippon and NKK; most of it, however, will come from Nippon. Without Japanese participation, it is doubtful that this plant would have come into existence.

Those That Failed

Several other attempts at joint ventures did not materialize. Two of these were in Australia where a site was chosen for the erection of an integrated plant to produce semifinished steel based on local deposits of rich iron ore. The participants were two U.S. companies, Armco and Kaiser. The project was abandoned shortly after it was conceived, since it was not possible to fill the Australian government's requirement that an Australian partner be found to take a 50 percent interest.

Another venture attempted in Australia involved thirteen partners in a plant producing 10 million tonnes of semifinished steel. Europeans,

Japanese, and Americans were among those interested; however, the project proved to be unwieldy and came to naught.

In the early to mid-1970s, a joint venture was conceived between the Japanese and the Brazilians for a plant to be built in northern Brazil. It was never undertaken.

In 1973, Iscor of South Africa inaugurated a joint venture to build a steel mill at Saldanha Bay that would produce 3 million tonnes of semifinished steel. Iscor was to hold 51 percent of the shares, with Voest-Alpine of Austria as a principal partner with 26 percent. The scheme was an ambitious one, which was ultimately to be a 12-million-tonne plant. The steel depression of 1975, which affected much of the world steel industry, gave the prospective partners second thoughts, and in 1976, the plan was quietly shelved.

Joint Ventures on Galvanizing

In the last half of the 1980s, there was considerable activity in the installation of lines to produce galvanized steel sheets. Many of these facilities have been joint ventures. The activity came in two waves. One began in the mid-1980s when the automobile industry signified its intention of using galvanized steel in vehicle bodies to resist corrosion and demanded electrolytic galvanized sheets rather than hot dipped. As a consequence, lines were installed in the United States, Japan, and Western Europe, many as joint ventures, both domestic and international.

One of the first lines built was that by Inland Steel, Bethlehem Steel, and PreFinish Steel. The integrated companies each own 25 percent, and PreFinish has 50 percent. The output, however, was taken 50 percent by Inland and 50 percent by Bethlehem. Inland has an agreement with Bethlehem by which, when its joint venture with Nippon on the galvanized lines is complete, it will sell Bethlehem half of its 25 percent interest in their joint venture galvanizing line. Thus, Bethlehem will have 37 1/2 percent and Inland will have 12 1/2 percent. As part of the agreement, Inland will take one-fourth of the 400,000-ton output.

LTV and Sumitomo built an electrolytic galvanizing line and are now in the process of building a second one on a joint venture basis. United States Steel and Rouge built a 700,000-ton electrolytic line on a fifty-fifty ownership basis. The line at National was a joint venture; NKK owned 50 percent of the company, and Nisshin and Wheeling-Pittsburgh have a line of which Nisshin has a two-thirds ownership.

The second wave of galvanized sheet installations came in the late 1980s and will continue through the early 1990s. As of early 1990, there were sixteen lines scheduled for the EEC, twelve for the United States and Canada, and at least eight for Japan. Other countries installing lines include Poland, South Africa, Brazil, and the Soviet Union.

The large number of lines projected for the EEC are spread among most of the member countries. British Steel has scheduled two, one of them a replacement. Spain announced three and Thyssen of Germany two, one of them replacement and the other a joint venture with Hoogovens. Sidmar in Belgium has announced two, one of them a joint venture with Klockner. Usinor-Sacilor will install one at Sollac, and Italy has announced three.

In North America, at least twelve new lines were projected as of January 1990. A number of these are joint ventures and have already been mentioned. In addition, Bethlehem has announced three lines—one at Sparrows Point, one at Burns Harbor, and one in southwestern United States, which could be a joint venture. National Steel and Dofasco have announced a joint venture, although the location has not yet been determined. California Steel has also announced a line, as have Ultimate Technology and Nextech.

In Japan, a number of new lines have been announced by most of the major integrated steel producers. Sumitomo will add a new hot-dipped line at its Kashima plant. Kawasaki will add two lines—one hot dipped and one electrolytic. Nippon plans to add two hot-dipped lines—one at Nagoya and one at Kimitsu. NKK will add one hot-dipped line, and another is under consideration, and Kobe has a hot-dipped line under construction.

In Eastern Europe, Poland has announced the installation of a line at its Lenin works in Krakow. It will be an electrolytic line, financed through a barter arrangement with Impianti of Italy. Poland will repay the investment with finished steel products.

By 1991, when the current surge of galvanizing lines is in place, there will be about 200 operating lines throughout the world, at least forty of which are now under construction or being actively considered. Total capacity, including both hot dipped and electrolytic lines, will be in the area of 51 million tonnes.

The concern expressed in a number of quarters about the possibility of overcapacity in galvanized steel is valid; however, a number of companies installing galvanized equipment feel that the future lies with coated sheets. This is particularly true with the automotive industry in its battle against corrosion.

The market in the United States for all sheet products is in the area of 40 million tons. In 1989, a good year, cold-rolled sheet shipments were 13.9 million tons, while galvanized, both hot dipped and electrolytic, amounted to 10.7 million tons. Hot-rolled sheet shipments were 12.9 million tons, while other items, including electrical as well as other coated sheets and strip, amounted to approximately 4 million tons, for a total in excess of 40 million tons. Many feel that sheet products will be coated in the years ahead; thus, the category of cold and hot rolled may be reduced, while that of galvanized may be increased. This is in keeping with the sentiments voiced by a number of consumers in addition to the automotive industry that they would prefer galvanized sheets.

The same reasoning has been applied in Japan and Western Europe, where galvanized capacity will be greatly increased in the next few years. Thus, in addition to the automotive industry, it is expected that a significant tonnage of galvanized sheets will be used in the manufacture of appliances and in construction. The main problem here is price; galvanized steel is much more costly than hot- or cold-rolled sheets.

Currently, the automotive industry absorbs 40 percent of the galvanized sheet production in the United States and 25 percent of that in Japan. Consequently, in view of the increase in galvanized capacity, there is a need to develop other markets.

Future of Joint Ventures

The joint venture, both between companies within a country and those contracted on an international basis, became widespread in the late 1980s. In the 1990s, more of them will be arranged, particularly those of an international nature. Many of the joint ventures entered into in the 1980s involved major participation by one integrated company in the ownership of another; witness the purchase of 40 or 50 percent of several U.S. companies by Japanese firms such as NKK and National and Kawasaki and Armco, with smaller percentages in the cases of Inland and Nippon and Wheeling-Pittsburgh and Nisshin. Other ventures have been confined to specific facilities such as galvanizing lines, as those between United States Steel and Kobe and LTV and Sumitomo.

Future joint ventures will involve a broad variety of steel operations but must have advantages for both parties. There are few possibilities remaining in the United States involving the purchase of a large portion of integrated companies, since virtually all of the major integrated companies, with the exception of Bethlehem and LTV, already have such arrangements.

The major joint ventures entered into in the United States involve the Japanese and Koreans; there are very few between European and U.S. companies. The advantages brought to the joint ventures by the Japanese in almost every instance consist of technology—for sheet products, particularly coated sheets, as well as structurals and bars—and cash, in many instances over $300 million. This was welcomed by companies that had gone through a severe depression in the 1980s and were planning large capital investments to modernize their plant and equipment. In some cases, this permitted time needed to complete the work to be reduced since more cash was readily available.

The Europeans have joint ventures among themselves; however, they have not been of a major nature involving company ownership but rather confined to specific facilities such as coating lines. In the future, one can look for more activity in Europe in regard to joint ventures, not only within the Common Market but also of a broader international scope.

In terms of major joint ventures between European and U.S. companies, there are some possibilities but these have been reduced considerably by Japanese activity. Of the six major companies, National Steel, Armco, and Inland are owned partly by Japanese companies. Thus, it is not likely that they would enter into a major joint venture with a European company. The other three, USX, Bethlehem, and LTV present possible opportunities. United States Steel, a subsidiary of USX, has two joint ventures, one with POSCO and the other with Kobe. However, these involve individual plants, and it is conceivable that further partnerships could be worked out with European companies involving other plants.

Among Europeans, there is definite interest on the part of British Steel and Thyssen. Bethlehem has a minor venture with Usinor, and since it has no others is in a position to make a major arrangement in terms of significant plants or the entire company. LTV has been in contact with Usinor-Sacilor. However, the pension liability has been a hurdle. This apparently must be solved before any further negotiations of a serious nature can take place. In addition, there are other integrated companies which could be attractive for Europeans. These include Rouge, Weirton, and possibly Warren.

The Europeans are not particularly interested in joint ventures with the Japanese as of 1990; they regard the technology in Europe as equal to that of the Japanese, and therefore one of the incentives that inspired the Japanese–U.S. ventures is lacking. However, the number of Japanese automobile company transplants in Europe has been increasing, with three in the United Kingdom and two on the Continent, one of them a joint venture. This development inspired most of the joint ventures in steel in the United States.

There is a strong possibility that joint ventures will be developed between companies in the industrialized nations and those in the Third World. There have already been some examples of this, including the Tubarao semifinished plant and the Japanese interest in Usiminas, one of the integrated plants in Brazil.

The industry will undergo a major change in great part because of environmental pressures and the increased cost of replacing major facilities. When it becomes necessary to replace such costly equipment as coke ovens and blast furnaces, companies in the industrialized countries will look for alternatives. This is not only cost-driven but also based on increasing pressures to improve the environment.

The major problem in the steel industry has been coke ovens. Despite all that has been done to remedy this situation, it still remains. Other aspects of the industry, including blast furnaces, steelmaking, and finishing facilities, present very little in the way of insuperable environmental problems. However, the blast furnace and coke ovens are intimately linked, and the problem with the coke ovens, if a solution is not found, would limit the operation of the blast furnace and result in the reduction of its numbers. This will drive the steel companies of the industrialized countries to look to the Third World, from which many of them draw their raw materials. There will be a definite movement to encourage through joint ventures the establishment of more raw steel production in the Third World. This will be welcomed by the Third World countries and the industrialized countries alike.

It is envisioned that large tonnages of steel will be imported in semifinished form. Most of the integrated producers in the industrialized world will maintain a large percentage of their steel production at home, but more and more will be imported from abroad. The joint venture is necessary for such an operation to function, since the companies in the industrialized world will have to depend on continual receipts of semifinished steel, and this can be guaranteed best through partial ownership. Contractual arrangements, although good in many respects, have limitations. Thus, the joint venture will be pursued much more than the contractual arrangement.

Many steel producers in Japan and Europe feel that they are now receiving most, and in the case of Japan virtually all, of their raw materials from abroad so they are dependent on those countries as a source of supply. A number have felt that in place of raw materials, at least part of their semifinished steel could come from abroad, thus avoiding large expenses to replace all their blast furnaces and coke ovens.

One of the principal advantages of joint ventures, particularly when they have been developed in such numbers, is the containment of capacity, which otherwise could be excessive. In the United States, for example, in the 1980s when six galvanizing lines were installed, five were joint ventures. If they had not been, there would have been several more than six, since every integrated steel company producing sheets for the automotive industry had to offer galvanized material. Thus, capacity was restrained, and all the lines operated full out.

It developed that this was not enough capacity, and more is being installed, much of it also on a joint venture basis. Thus, there is less of a chance that there will be an overcapacity to produce galvanized than there would have been if these joint ventures were not in effect and double the number of lines were installed.

The joint venture also reduces the capital investment required of each partner to half or less. This makes it possible in a number of instances to install a facility when the individual companies lack the funds to install a facility or are not equipped to borrow enough for that purpose.

The operation at full capacity also reduces operating costs. If there were two lines in place of one and each of the two operated at less than full capacity, which is possible, operating costs would be higher. Thus, the saving is twofold: operating costs and capital costs.

Joint ventures have also been formed to develop new technology, witness the arrangement between Thyssen, Usinor, and SMS to develop a thin slab caster, as well as that among eight Japanese integrated steel companies to develop a new process for making iron.

Mergers

Mergers between two large companies have taken place in the past twenty years. Significant among these was the merger of Fuji and Yawata of Japan to form Nippon Steel in 1969. Another large merger was between Republic Steel and Jones & Laughlin in 1984 to form LTV Steel. In Europe, there was a merger in 1972 between Hoogovens of the Netherlands and Hoersch of Germany, although it later dissolved. Another example is Usinor and Sacilor in France in 1988.

There were several other mergers that would more properly be called acquisitions. An example was the acquisition of Youngstown Sheet and Tube Company by Jones & Laughlin in 1978.

It is doubtful that there will be many major mergers in the 1990s. This is due to the number of joint ventures, which in many respects are preferable to mergers. When two major companies merge, plants are sometimes closed, but the most significant difficulty arises with the top management. There just are not enough jobs at the top to go around, since there are two people for every major position. Often rivalries spring up, and an otherwise efficient operation is in jeopardy; it may take a number of years before the problems are resolved.

In contrast, in joint ventures, the partners still maintain most of their own identity, as in the case of Armco and Kawasaki. There is some exchange of personnel; however, rarely is there a major difficulty.

It is possible in the 1990s that there may be some acquisitions of smaller companies by larger ones. This is possible in Europe in preparation for the ultimate step in the Common Market in 1992 or shortly after.

Another possibility is the acquisition of part of a company by another company, such as resulted from the discussions between Klockner and British Steel.

There is little opportunity for major mergers in Europe since, with the exception of Germany, one major company dominates a country, such as Usinor-Sacilor in France, British Steel in the United Kingdom, Hoogovens in the Netherlands, Ilva in Italy, Cockerill in Belgium, and Arbed in Luxembourg. One can envision a number of joint ventures among these companies, but the possibility of a merger is remote.

Testimony to the value of international joint ventures was given by Hiroshi Saito, president of Nippon Steel, in commenting on the Inland-Nippon arrangement when he stated, "With the growth of global manufacturing enterprises, strong international relationships are increasingly important to assure our steel customers' needs in North America. We look forward to a long, mutually productive relationship."[6]

Notes

1. William T. Hogan, *World Steel in the 1980s* (Lexington, Mass.: Lexington Books, 1983), p. 140.
2. Inland Steel Industries, News release, December 18, 1989.
3. National Steel Company, *1979 Annual Report*, p. 4.
4. United States Steel Corporation, Press release, January 6, 1986.
5. *Metal Bulletin*, October 19, 1989, p. 29.
6. Inland Steel Industries, News release, December 18, 1990.

9
Summary and Conclusions

B ased on a worldwide survey made between 1988 and 1990, it is clear that there will be major developments and changes in a number of areas in the steel industry. These will include adjustments in growth, technology, international trade, markets, joint ventures, raw materials, and employment.

The steel industry on a global basis will expand moderately during the 1990s, with virtually all of the growth in the Third World. The industrialized countries will maintain their capacity at about the 1990 level. Whatever growth there will be in the industrialized countries will not come from the integrated mills but from minimills that will be upgraded or built. This is particularly so in the United States, where there will be a possible increase in capacity of 4 million to 5 million tonnes as a result of minimill activity.

A substantial investment of many billions of dollars will be made across the world steel industry during the coming decade. In the industrialized countries, this will be directed almost exclusively to a continual modernization of equipment to reduce costs, increase productivity, and improve quality. In the Third World, the investment in a number of countries, including China, South Korea, India and, to a lesser extent, in the Middle and Far East, will be directed toward increasing capacity.

Brazil currently has a financial problem and is privatizing the government-owned segment of the steel industry, which constitutes all of the flat-rolled producers. There were elaborate plans for increasing capacity, but these have been put on hold until privatization is completed, when they may be carried out to some extent.

Raw materials for steel production, particularly iron ore, coal, and scrap, will vary in their availability. Iron ore, the most significant of these since it contains the element, iron, from which steel is made, is virtually limitless in supply; it constitutes 4 to 5 percent of the earth's crust. Estimated reserves worldwide are in excess of 250 billion tonnes, although these are not equally distributed among steel producers. Japan, South Korea, and Taiwan in the Far East must import all of their requirement, and Western Europe is tending in that direction. Abundant resources exist in a number of areas, with Brazil and Australia predominant. Consequently, trade in iron ore will continue at 400 million to 450 million tonnes annually.

Coal, particularly metallurgical coal, is somewhat limited. However, there is a large supply in selected spots throughout the world, including the United States, the Soviet Union, and Australia. Here again, trade is a necessity; since this material must be moved in large tonnages from its source to where it is needed.

There is a decided movement in most of the steel-producing countries, particularly the industrialized countries, to develop processes for the production of iron outside the blast furnace to reduce the need for metallurgical coal and coke.

Coke ovens, which in many countries are due for replacement toward the end of the 1990s, are expensive and to date pose a pollution problem. Serious and sizable efforts will be made during the coming decade to reduce the number of coke ovens and, with them, blast furnaces. However, the current state of this technological development will not permit the replacement of many coke ovens and blast furnaces in this decade. By the year 2000, most of the iron production will come from blast furnaces involving coke. It is possible, however, that as much as 20 percent of the world's iron will be produced outside the blast furnaces by the end of the century.

Scrap is abundant in general; however, high-quality scrap is somewhat limited, and as the demands of the customer require better and cleaner steel, there will be a need to supplement scrap in the electric furnace with DRI. In this decade, significant expansion in the production of DRI will take place. Capacity and production could be doubled by the mid- to late 1990s.

Technological advances will take place in virtually every segment of steel production. One of the most notable of these in addition to the development to produce iron outside the blast furnace will be the application on a somewhat expanded scale of the thin-slab caster. This facility is currently in operation on a production basis in just one plant in the world, Nucor in the United States. Although predictions have been made that it will expand rapidly, there are limitations.

The thin-slab caster was conceived for applications where relatively small tonnages of steel sheets are produced. Further, it has been tied to an electric furnace and a small hot-strip mill. Thus, in many instances, the caster will require the construction of an entire plant. It certainly will require the construction of a strip mill to reduce the thin slab to sheet gauge.

Part of the advantage claimed for the facility is the fact that the strip mill is much smaller and less expensive than the conventional mill. Nevertheless, a large investment will be required, limiting the number of minimills installing the facility. Further, in the industrialized world, there is very little need for additional sheet capacity. Most countries have excess capacity to produce this product.

The thin-slab caster with the accompanying rolling facilities will find a place in the Third World since it will be far less expensive—perhaps half the cost of a conventional caster and strip mill.

The quality of steel sheets as produced from the thin-slab caster can be improved if the scrap charge in the electric furnace is supplemented by a generous percentage of DRI. By the end of the century, a limited number of thin-slab casters and truncated rolling mills will be installed throughout both the industrialized and Third World countries.

The market for steel products during the 1990s will remain relatively stable dominated by automotive and construction, especially where infrastructure will be replaced and improved.

The main threat to steel will come from substitute materials, such as concrete, ceramics, other metals, and plastics. Inroads have already been made by some of these materials. Perhaps the most serious challenge will come from plastics, since the producers of this material are aiming at the automobile sheet business. The steel industry has responded to this challenge in a number of ways, including cooperating with the automobile industry in many of the phases of production and design and improving the quality of the sheets by investing heavily in hot- and cold-strip mills. This challenge will remain through the decade.

International trade will be closely tied to international joint ventures, particularly between industrialized and Third World countries. There are a number of these in existence, and more will be developed as the decade progresses. Western Europe and the Far East rely heavily on imported raw materials, particularly iron ore and coal. The ore comes from a number of sources in the Third World, and must be processed in blast furnaces fed by coke ovens with the accompanying pollution problems. Consequently, industrialized countries are seriously considering the possibility of joint ventures with Third World countries to obtain part of their steel requirement in semifinished form, thus reducing ore imports as well as coke oven and blast furnace operations. Through such joint ventures, trade in semifinished steel will grow during the 1990s, while trade in finished products will remain active, although the increased steel production in the Third World will reduce the tonnage it receives from the industrialized countries.

In the 1970s and 1980s, the steel industry was a declining source of employment. In the United States in 1973, over 500,000 people were employed in the steel industry; now only 170,000 are so employed. In Europe, the same situation applies. In 1974, the year of peak production, almost 900,000 people were employed in steel in the EEC. By 1989, this had shrunk to slightly less than 400,000, a reduction of more than 50 percent. In Japan, a sharp reduction has taken place from 450,000 employed in 1974 to 300,000 in 1989, and according to plans, this number will shrink further by the mid-1990s.[1]

In contrast, some Third World countries have seen employment in steel rise significantly; India's rose from 200,000 people in 1974 to 300,000 in 1989. Many of the integrated steel plants in the Third World, particularly those owned by the government, are much more heavily manned than their counterparts in the industrialized world. In a sense, a government-owned steel plant has been a source of jobs, and because of the political situation, it is very difficult to reduce staff, although some efforts will be made in this respect in the coming decade. For the industry in general, and particularly in the industrialized countries, there will be some decline in employment during the 1990s; however, it will by no means be as drastic as it has been in the previous fifteen years.

The reduction in employment during the late 1970s and 1980s brought with it a substantial increase in productivity measured in man-hours-per-ton of steel shipped. In the late 1970s and early 1980s, this amounted to an average of ten man-hours-per-ton in the United States and somewhat less in Japan and Western Europe. By 1989, the figure had been drastically reduced in the United States from ten man-hours to an average of five while some plants registered less than four man-hours-per-ton shipped. The same improvement has taken place in Western Europe and Japan. In particular plants in Japan, the United States, and Western Europe, man-hours-per-ton shipped are down to less than four and approaching three.

The basic reasons for this increase in productivity are the elimination of obsolete and high-cost plants in all three industrialized areas, so that the most efficient plants are in operation with modern equipment which is continually replacing the older machinery. Further, a number of plants have been reduced in terms of capacity as well as the number of people employed.

The increase in productivity has reduced costs in some cases by more than $100 a ton, and along with the installation of modern, efficient equipment, the industry in most of its plants will continue to improve productivity, thus reducing costs to a point where the competition with substitutes for steel will be vigorously carried on.

In the Third World, a number of new plants, particularly those in South Korea, have maintained their work force at the necessary level, and consequently with the most modern, efficient equipment, man-hours-per-ton-shipped are in the area of four to five, and in a few cases, a bit less. With a lower wage, Third World plants still have an advantage over those companies in the industrialized world. However, the wide gap on labor costs per ton has been significantly narrowed in the last decade.

A recent trend that is assuming worldwide proportions, the privatization of government-owned steel facilities, will continue into the 1990s. In many instances, governments have operated steel plants at a loss in order to preserve and, in some instances, increase employment. However, this seems to have come to an end in a number of countries where, in the late 1980s and 1990s, announcements to privatize the industry have been made. The most significant was British Steel in the United Kingdom, which was privatized in 1989. A number of other countries have announced either partial or complete privatization of government-owned facilities including Brazil, Mexico, Turkey, Italy, and Belgium.

The recent political changes in Eastern Europe will have an impact on its steel industry, as well as that in Western Europe. It will take some time, perhaps two to three years, before this can be fully measured. The steel plants of Eastern Europe, which are relatively obsolete, must be upgraded. Further, the management philosophy that has dominated this area for almost half a century will have to be altered. Eastern Europe will be moving into a competitive market economy where steel is no longer simply allocated but must be sold on the basis of quality, service, and price. The companies in this region will be considerably helped by joint ventures, as many companies in Western Europe, particularly Western Germany, are anxious to form alliances. The Japanese have also expressed an interest.

Steel has provided the world's economies with a basic and necessary product for well over a century and will continue to do so in the years ahead. However, the industry will be significantly different in the year 2000 from that of 1990. There will be changes in technology, trade, markets, and corporate organization. The application of new and developing technologies will be worldwide, enhancing the operation of steel companies in the industrialized countries and the Third World. The continual effort being made to reduce costs and improve quality should keep steel competitive with substitute materials on a price basis.

In terms of size, the industry will not be much larger in 2000 than it is in 1990. There will be an addition of 50 million to 55 million tonnes in capacity, most of which will come from the Third World whose contribution will continue to increase. By the year 2000, 25 percent to 27 percent of the world's steel production will come from the Third World, much of which will be exported. International joint ventures, particularly between companies in the industrialized countries and those in the Third World, will permit a more judicious use of raw materials and will allow a much more productive application of capital which will continue to be scarce.

Note

1. IISI World Steel In Figures 1990, p. 18. Brussels.

Bibliography

American Iron and Steel Institute. *Annual Statistical Reports.* Washington, D.C.: AISI, various years.

———. *Directory of Iron and Steel Works of the United States and Canada.* Washington, D.C.: AISI, various years.

———. *United States Indirect Steel Trade, 1987.* Washington, D.C.: AISI, June, 1989.

American Metal Market. New York: Capital Cities/ABC Inc. Diversified Publishing Group, various daily issues.

American Metal Market Co. *Metal Statistics: The Purchasing Guide of the Metal Industries.* New York: AMM, various years.

ARBED, S.A. *A Portrait of the Group.* Luxembourg: ARBED, 1979.

———. *Press Release.* Luxembourg: ARBED, September, 1989.

Bird, Tony. *Steel—Planning for Growth.* London, England: Financial Times Business Information, 1986.

British Steel Corporation. *Press Release.* London, England: BSC June, 1990.

———. *Ten Year Development Strategy.* London, England: Her Majesty's Stationary Office, 1973.

British Steel Corporation, Statistical Services. *International Steel Statistics: World Tables.* Croydon, England: BSC, various years.

Broken Hill Proprietary Co. Ltd., Public Affairs Department. *BHP Pocketbook.* Melbourne, Australia: BHP, various years.

Calarco, Vincent J., Jr. *World Coal Outlook, A Reassessment.* New York: The Chase Manhattan Bank, N.A., 1985.

Comtroller General of the United States. *Report to the Congress of the United States: New Strategy Required for Aiding Distressed Steel Industry.* Washington, D.C.: General Accounting Office, 1981.

Concast AG. *World Survey of Continuous Casting Machines for Steel.* Zurich, Switzerland: Concast Documentation Center, various annual editions.

Doyle, Guy; Johnson, Debra; and McCloskey, Gerard, eds. *International Coal Reports's Coal Year 1989.* London, England: Financial Times Business Information.

Etienne, Gilbert; Astier, Jacques; Bhushan, Hari; and Zhong, Dai. *Asian Crucible: The Steel Industry in China and India.* Geneva, Switzerland: Modern Asia Research Center, 1990.

European Coal and Steel Community, Commission of. *Investment in the Community Coalmining and Iron and Steel Industries.* Luxembourg: ECSC, January, 1988.

———. *Restructuring of the Italian Public Steel Industry.* Brussels, Belgium: ECSC, October 25, 1988.

Gillerio, Giovanni. "International Steelmakers' Strategies for the 90s." *Steel Survival Strategies V.* New York: American Metal Market and PaineWebber, World Steel Dynamics, July 26–27, 1990.

Hogan, William T. *Economic History of the Iron and Steel Industry in the United States*, five volumes. Lexington, Massachusetts: Lexington Books, 1971.

————. "Future Steel Plans in the Third World" *Iron and Steel Engineer* 54 (November, 1977): 25–37.

————. *Minimills and Integrated Mills: A Comparison of Steelmaking in the United States*. Lexington, Massachusetts: Lexington Books, 1987.

————. *Siderurgia Mundial: Perspectives para la Decada del '80*. Buenos Aires, Argentina: Centro Internacional de Informacion Empresaria, 1981.

————. *The 1970s's: Critical Years for Steel*. Lexington, Massachusetts: Lexington Books, 1972.

————. *World Steel in the 1980s: A Case of Survival*. Lexington, Massachusetts: Lexington Books, 1983.

Hogan, William T., and Koelble, Frank T. *Analysis of the U.S. Metallurgical Coke Industry*. Washington, D.C.: U.S. Department of Commerce, 1979.

————. *Direct Reduction as an Ironmaking Alternative in the United States*. Washington, D.C.: U.S. Department of Commerce, 1981.

Holschuh, Lenhard J. "Report of the Secretary General." *Report of Proceedings, Twenty-third Annual IISI Meetings and Conference* Berlin, West Germany. October 1–4, 1989. Brussels, Belgium, International Iron and Steel Institute, 1990.

Instituto Brasileiro de Siderurgica. *IBS Yearbook, Anuario Estatistico da Industria Siderurgica Brasilerira*. Brazil: IBS, various years.

International Bank for Reconstruction and Development, The World Bank. *World Development Report*. New York: Oxford University Press, various annual issues.

International Iron and Steel Institute Committee on Economic Studies. *Indirect Trade in Steel 1985 and 1986*. Brussels, Belgium: IISI, 1989.

————. *Infrastructure: Problems and Prospects for Steel*. Brussels, Belgium: IISI, 1985.

————. *Investment Appraisal in the Steel Industry*. Brussels, Belgium: IISI, 1983.

————. *Steel and the Automotive Sector*. Brussels, Belgium: IISI, 1983.

International Iron and Steel Institute, Committee on Raw Materials. *Scrap and the Steel Industry*. Brussels, Belgium: IISI, 1983.

————. *The Seaborne Transport of Iron and Steelmaking Raw Materials*. Brussels, Belgium: IISI, 1986.

————. *Western World Cokemaking Capacity*. Brussels, Belgium: IISI, 1985.

International Iron and Steel Institute, Committees on Raw Materials and Technology. *Western World Cokemaking*. Brussels, Belgium: IISI, 1983.

International Iron and Steel Institute, Committee on Statistics. *Statistics on Energy in the Steel Industry (1990 update)*. Brussels, Belgium: IISI, 1990.

————. *Steel Statistical Yearbook* Brussels, Belgium: IISI, various years.

————. *Steel Statistics of Developing Countries*. Brussels, Belgium: IISI, various editions.

International Iron and Steel Institute, Committee on Technology. *Energy and the Steel Industry*. Brussels, Belgium: IISI, 1982.

————. *The Electric Arc Furnace*. Brussels, Belgium: IISI, 1983.

International Iron and Steel Institute. *Report of Proceedings, Fourth Annual Conference, Paris, France, October 12–16, 1970*. Brussels, Belgium: IISI, 1971.

Iron Age. New York: Fairchild Publications, various issues.
Iron and Steel Engineer. Pittsburgh, Pennsylvania: Association of Iron and Steel Engineers, various issues.
Japan Economic Journal. Tokyo, Japan: Nikon Keizai Shimbun, Inc., various weekly issues.
Japan Steel Journal. Tokyo, Japan: Japan Steel Structure Journal Co., Ltd., various issues.
Japanese Automobile Manufacturers Association. *Motor Vehicle Statistics of Japan.* Tokyo, Japan: JAMA, various years.
Japan Iron & Steel Federation. *Monthly Report of Iron and Steel Statistics.* Tokyo, Japan: JISF, various monthly issues.
———. *Statistical Yearbook.* Tokyo, Japan: JISF, various years.
———. *The Steel Industry in Japan.* Tokyo, Japan: JISF, various years.
Kawata, Sukeyuki, ed. *Japan's Iron and Steel Industry.* Tokyo, Japan: Kawata Publicity, Inc., various years.
Kim, Edward H., ed. *Twenty Years of Posco: A Miracle on Yongil Bay.* Seoul, South Korea: Pohang Iron & Steel Co., Ltd., 1988.
King, James F. *World Capacity and Production Report, Primary Iron and Steel, Annual Plant-by-Plant Information for Liquid Steel.* Newcastle, England: James F. King, April 1990.
Koelble, Frank T. "Strategies for Restructuring the U.S. Steel Industry." *33 Metal Producing.* Vol. 24, No. 12 (December 1986): 28–33.
Labee, C.J. and Samways, N.L. "Developments in the Iron and Steel Industry, U.S. and Canada." *Iron and Steel Engineer.* February issues for various years.
Marcus, Peter F., and Kirsis, Karlis M. *Global Steelmaking Capacity Track.* New York: PaineWebber, World Steel Dynamics, January, 1988.
Marcus, Peter F.; Kirsis, Karlis M.; and Kakela, Peter G. *The Threatened North American Iron Ore Industry.* New York: PaineWebber, World Steel Dynamics, April, 1987.
Metal Bulletin. London, England: Metal Bulletin Journals Ltd., various issues.
Metal Bulletin Monthly. London, England: Metal Bulletin Journals, Ltd., various issues.
Midrex Corporation. *Direct from Midrex.* Charlotte, North Carolina: Midrex, various quarterly issues.
Motor Vehicle Manufacturers Association. *Motor Vehicle Facts and Figures.* Detroit, Michigan: MVMA, various years.
———. *World Motor Vehicle Data.* Detroit, Michigan: MVMA, various years.
National Steel Corporation. *Annual Report for 1979.* Pittsburgh, Pennsylvania: National Steel: 1980.
Organization for Economic Cooperation and Development. *The Iron and Steel Industry.* Paris, France: OECD, various years.
Park, Tae-Joon. *The "Separated" Families and Other Essays.* Seoul, South Korea: Su Jung Dang Printing Co., 1988.
Ruhrkohle Aktiengesellschaft. *Figures, Data, Facts.* Essen, West Germany: Ruhrkohle, various years.
Salvatore, Dominick. *International Economics*, Second Edition. New York: Macmillan Publishing Company, 1987.

Serjeantson, Richard; Cordero, Raymond; and Cooke, Henry, eds. *Iron and Steel Works of the World*, 9th edition. Surrey, England: Metal Bulletin Books Ltd., 1988.

Siderbras. *Study on the Restructuring of the Brazilian Steel Industry.* Rio de Janeiro: Siderbras, 1989.

Steel Times International. Surrey, England: FMJ International Publications, Ltd., various monthly issues.

Sullivan, Edward J. "Internationalization of the North American Automotive Industry." *Metal Bulletin/Beddows World Conference.* Atlanta, Georgia: February 27, 1990.

33 Metal Producing. U.S. Steel Industry Data Handbook, 1989. Cleveland, Ohio: Penton Publishing, May, 1989.

Tully, Shawn. "Full Throttle Towards a New Era." *Fortune.* November 20, 1989, pp. 131–136.

U. K. Iron and Steel Statistics Bureau. *International Steel Statistics.* Croyden, England, various countries and years.

Union de Empresas Siderurgicas. *La Industria Siderurgica Espanola.* Madrid, Spain: UNESID, various years.

———. *The Spanish Iron and Steel Industry, the Steel Process.* 2nd Edition. Madrid, Spain, UNESID, 1987.

United Nations, Economic Commission for Europe. *Quarterly Bulletin of Steel Statistics for Europe.* New York: United Nations, various years.

———. *Statistics of World Trade in Steel.* New York: United Nations, various years.

———. *The Steel Market.* New York: United Nations, various years.

United Nations, Industrial Development Organization. *Proceedings of the Second General Conference.* Lima, Peru: UNIDO, 1975.

United States Department of the Interior, Bureau of Mines. "Iron and Steel Scrap, Monthly." *Mineral Industry Surveys.* Washington, D.C.: U.S. Government Printing Office, various monthly issues.

———. *Minerals Yearbook.* Washington, D.C.: U.S. Government Printing Office, various years.

United States International Trade Commission. *Annual Survey Concerning Competitive Conditions in the Steel Industry and Industry Efforts to Adjust and Modernize.* Washington, D.C.: USITC Publication 2226, October, 1989.

———. *Monthly Report on the Status of the Steel Industry.* Washington, D.C.: USITC, various monthly publications.

———. *U.S. Global Competitiveness: Steel Sheet and Strip Industry.* Washington, D.C.: USITC Publication 2050, January, 1988.

United States Trade Representative, Office of. *Press Release*, December 12, 1989.

Index

About the Author

Rev. William T. Hogan, S.J. received his Ph.D. in economics from Fordham University in 1948. He has conducted economic studies of the steel industry and other basic, heavy industries for the past thirty-five years. During this time he has authored a number of books, including *Productivity in the Blast-Furnace and Open-Hearth Segments of the Steel Industry*, the first detailed study of steel productivity; *The Development of American Heavy Industry in the Twentieth Century*; and *Depreciation Policies and Resultant Problems* (1967). His five-volume work, *Economic History of the Iron and Steel Industry in the United States* (Lexington Books, 1971) covers industry developments from 1860 to 1971. Additional books authored by Father Hogan on the steel industry are *The 1970s: Critical Years for Steel* (1972), *World Steel in the 1980s: A Case of Survival* (1983), *Steel in the United States: Restructuring to Compete* (1984) and *Minimills and Integrated Mills: A Comparison of Steelmaking in the United States* (1987).

In 1950, Father Hogan inaugurated Fordham University's Industrial Economics Research Institute, which has produced numerous studies dealing with economic problems of an industrial nature. He has appeared before legislative committees of both the U.S. Senate and the House of Representatives and has testified several times before the House Ways and Means Committee on legislation affecting depreciation charges and capital investment. He has also appeared before the Senate Finance Committee to testify on tax incentives for capital spending. He was a member of the Presidential Task Force on Business Taxation and a consultant to the Council of Economic Advisers to the President and the U.S. Department of Commerce.

During the past twenty years, Father Hogan has visited most of the steel-producing facilities in the world and has delivered papers at steel conferences in France, United Kingdom, Switzerland, Sweden, Czechoslovakia, Russia, Venezuela, Brazil, South Africa, India, the Philippines, South Korea, and Japan. He is the author of numerous articles on various aspects of steel industry economics.

In 1985, Father Hogan was awarded the Gary Memorial Medal, which is the highest honor the steel industry can bestow. In 1987, he was granted a distinguished life membership in the American Society of Metals International, and in 1990, the Association of Iron and Steel Engineers established the William T. Hogan, S.J. annual lecture series.